Trying to Think with Emily Dickinson

Illustrations

Acknowledgments

IN THE ANALYTICAL WAY she had of thinking about emotions, Emily Dickinson once distinguished between a gratitude so profound that it lies beyond "the Plumb of Speech" and another, more superficial, where one at least emerges from awe long enough to express thanks for tenderness received (Fr1120). Written acknowledgments always fall into the latter category, but I hope these will reflect my ongoing experience of the former.

Much of this book was written in 2006/7 at the Academia Sinica in Taiwan. I am grateful to Lee Yu-cheng and the Institute for European and American Studies for supporting me there—with boundless generosity and collegiality—as a visiting researcher. A generous grant from National Sun Yat-Sen University enabled me to try out several arguments, as did a travel grant to National Cheng-Kung University.

During my research, I received crucial grant support from the National Endowment for the Humanities, the Emily Dickinson International Society, and Oberlin College. I was also helped by the kindness and professionalism of the librarians at the Frost and Jones libraries in Amherst and the Houghton and Widener libraries at Harvard. Special thanks to Margaret Dakin and the Amherst Archives and Special Collections for the image of Dickinson's dictionary.

Earlier versions of chapters 2, 4, and 6 were published in *The Emily Dick-*

inson Journal, and I am grateful for permission to reprint. This book carries the traces of helpful suggestions made by the editors at the time those essays were first written: Suzanne Juhasz, Gary Lee Stonum, and Cristanne Miller. The later stages of the manuscript benefited from two anonymous external reviewers at the University of Massachusetts Press and from Jennifer Bryan's osprey-like editing eyes, medievalism, and vim. As the book neared publication, it was further aided by Bruce Wilcox and editors Amanda Heller, Mary Bellino, and Carol Betsch. The image on the cover of this book is of *The Reading Girl*, a mid-nineteenth-century statue by John Adams Jackson housed in the main library in Mudd Center at Oberlin College. I am grateful to Sophia Yan for the photograph, and to the college and Ray English, Director of Libraries, for permission to use it.

I thank all the friends, colleagues, and students with whom I have confabulated about Dickinson. Those who have tried to think with me include Gary Lee Stonum, Joy Ladin, Paul Crumbley, Scott McMillin, Hsin-ya Huang, Yu-chen Lin, Shu-li Chang, Cindy MacKenzie, Richard Brantley, Jane Eberwein, David Porter, Min-hsiung Huang, Yu-ping Wen, Claudia Stokes, Bruce Holl, Roland Champagne, Willis Salomon, Fred Loxsom, Jim Guthrie, Cynthia Hallen, Marianne Noble, Melanie Hubbard, Becca Glaser, Katrin Welch, Emily Klim, Meredith Cohen, Jamiella Ortiz, Rose Garrett, Lucia Graves, Sophia Yan, Kathleen Tierney, Azadeh Pourzand, Rachel Auerbach, Brian Howard, Darcy Gervasio, Rachel Pole, Cori Winrock, Ben Zilber, and Danielle Koplinka-Loehr.

My whole family lies beyond the Plumb of Speech, but especially Hsiu-Chuang, Formosa, and Ginger. This book is for them.

Introduction

WHY IS IT, Ralph Waldo Emerson asked in "The American Scholar," that we sometimes feel a "most modern joy," and even an "awe mixed with the joy of our surprise" when we read poets from ages past? (58). He suggested that the answer lies in the way we "abstract" them from their time and bring them into ours: when we receive them as live voices, we enable ourselves to respond with strong thought and emotion. Sometimes we even find those old poets saying "that which lies close to our soul," just what we ourselves "had well-nigh thought and said" (58). In this book I argue that if we listen carefully and read creatively and contextually, we will find that Emily Dickinson can help us to see and think what we are well-nigh thinking and saying. The way she used the language of lyric poetry to respond to her most difficult personal and cultural challenges can help us respond to our own.

Many of us *are* reading Dickinson. While middlebrow nineteenth-century American poets such as Whittier, Lowell, and Longfellow find themselves all but consigned to irrelevance, the iconic Dickinson is a household name with a global readership. The Academy of American Poets chose her to represent National Poetry Month in 2005, and her poster-poet status continues to inspire everything from genuflection to sarcasm. Some treat her house in Amherst, Massachusetts, as a poetic tourist attraction where one may haunt the patron saint of otherworldly writers, while others see her in Adorno-style modernist terms as an elite, difficult, eccentric, yet salvific figure who triumphed over a disheartening world. Somehow, all at once, she manages to be the arch-poet of loneliness but also of intimacy, of mind but also of raw feeling, a classical wordsmith and an effusive Romantic. But moth or myth, albatross or inspiration, the most basic and widespread image of Dickinson is that of the reclusive, mysterious, brilliant poet.

Her popularity and reputation for cerebrality make it easy to suggest that she is resonating with contemporary thought but not to say how or why. For various reasons we have not yet taken Dickinson's full measure as a thinker either historically or as one particularly apt for our time. Reflecting the training of Americanists, the dominant schools in Dickinson studies have lately been feminism, historicism, psychoanalysis, religion, textual and manuscript studies, and various kinds of cultural and biographical study.[1] A small percentage of her critics have turned to philosophy and postmodern theories, or have written in a loosely poststructuralist vein; but it is telling that, as Gary Lee Stonum notes, even the author of "the most thoroughly deconstructive reading of Dickinson extant," David Porter, disliked the poet's poststructuralist tilt.[2]

Indeed, although the fact is not necessarily to be lamented, it is curious that nothing like a *Postmodern Dickinson* was ever written, not even by an opportunist or an acolyte during the heyday of literary theory in the 1970s and 1980s. By now one half expects to find such a title in the library catalog. But to examine Dickinson's status in the canon of twentieth-century philosophy and high literary theory, as Marjorie Perloff started to do, is to be surprised at her absence from it. This major poet never appears in the works of Foucault, Blanchot, Jameson, the entire Frankfurt school, Bataille, Baudrillard, Barthes, Lyotard, Nancy, Žižek—the list goes on.[3] In retrospect it is not obvious why, during his many years in the top American universities, the latter-day high king of allegoresis, Paul De Man, was not spurred by one of his Americanist colleagues to take up David Porter's argument that "the basic movement" of Dickinson's mind was "allegorical" (*Modern* 64). He might have found that her lyrics furnished some of the best tests for his deconstructive readings of the "vertiginous" referential aberrations of figural language, that she, the "poet of the omitted center," had wrestled just as hard as his Rousseau with the ways literature names "the presence of a nothingness" and was a technician of tropes comparable to his cherished Keats, Hölderlin, and Wordsworth (De Man, "Criticism" 18; Leyda 1:xxi).[4] And circumstances could easily have brought Jacques Derrida to ask whether the terms he so famously used for the absences at the center of the structures of Western metaphysics (essence, existence, substance, subject, transcendentality, consciousness, God, man) had counterparts, differently deconstructed for different (usually more immediate and pragmatic) reasons, in Dickinson's poetry: soul, infinity, immortality, self, nature, circumference, consciousness, God. Even many theorists specifically concerned with lyric poetry or women's writing—Kristeva, Irigaray, Cixous—have had nothing to say about Dickinson, a fact that also holds true for leading American philosophical critics such as Stanley Cavell, J. Hillis Miller, Richard Poirier, Cary Wolfe, and Geoffrey Hartman.

Perhaps none of this is to be lamented, either, for Dickinson has not lacked readers, and her robust critical tradition includes many of the ideas if not the firsthand assessments of these theorists. But why have so many accounts proliferated on her place in the history of poetry, women's writing, and American literature and so few on her role in the history of ideas or her strength as a thinker? Why has it been so easy for theorists, philosophers, and intellectual historians to tell their stories without Dickinson? Her general popularity has probably discouraged some from taking her as seriously as they would a Milton or a Mallarmé, and other likely reasons include Eurocentrism, sexism, and a general preference for prose writers.[5] Since intellectual history often plays out as the study of influence, Dickinson has been hurt by the manner in which her works were made public: almost nothing in her lifetime, and then piecemeal and sporadic publication until Thomas Johnson's edition of the complete poems in 1955. At bottom, of course, there is the widespread assumption that American philosophical and intellectual history—all that writing about the American Mind—can be coherently told without its creative writers. When Perry Miller envisioned his comprehensive three-volume *Life of the Mind in America: From the Revolution to the Civil War*, he made room for nine large categories—evangelism, law, technology and science, education, political economy, philosophy, theology, nature, and "the self"—but not poetry or fiction (327). More recently, Louis Menand's 2001 study *The Metaphysical Club: A Story of Ideas in America* deals exclusively with post–Civil War American thought but makes virtually no mention of the poets of the day.[6] Reflecting this widely held faith in the separation of disciplines, book reviewers and other readers rarely worry the question: Menand may be a professor of English, but *The Metaphysical Club* is about the history of ideas.

If the idea of exploring some of Dickinson's connections to philosophical thought does not seem controversial, then it may be harder to accept another of this book's proposals: that she is a poet especially suited to speak to postmodernity. After all, the most influential models of postmodernism's origins and ascendancy depend on notions of epochality, progression, and distinction from the "modern" age, and anybody guided by such ideas will find it odd to select as one of its important precursors—and downright awkward as one of its hermeneutically appropriate thinkers—a nineteenth-century poet. Not only that, but most prominent accounts of postmodernity also tend to endow its leading artists with keen historical awareness. This is true of the simplest and most common definition of all, that postmodernism, at least in most cultural spheres, is (true to its name) a sprawling late-twentieth-century reaction to the early-twentieth-century modernist burst of creativity and progress across the arts and sciences. When John Barth argues that creative writers' postmodern awareness depends on their sensitivity to the fact that certain literary practices have been "used up," that high modernism is over but that one can never return to earlier modes such as realism, he leaves little room to see Dickinson or any other nineteenth-century author as a contemporary voice. He lionizes twentieth-century figures like Jorge Luís Borges because they are aware of past and present states of creative writing as well as of wider movements in the history of civilization, and because that double awareness allows them to transform paralyzing "felt ultimacies" about contemporary life into creative masterworks like "Pierre Menard, Author of the Quixote" or "The Library of Babel," thereby renovating entire literary forms such as the short story. But Dickinson developed few complex descriptions or theories, poetic or other, on whether history was guided by class struggle or strong individuals, by God or by chance, and had relatively little to say about what historians consider the topics of the day—the Civil War, Reconstruction, democracy, slavery, abolition, suffrage, immigration, westward expansion.[7] From a Barthian perspective on postmodernism, it would not matter how illuminated she was by the bulletins she received from immortality, for she not only lived in the wrong century and neglected her own history, she also never set out to synthesize and transcend her literary tradition, if she had one, in anything like a Borgesian mode.[8]

Or, to take another well-known example, when Fredric Jameson uses periodizing hypotheses to produce a Marxist dialectic running from nineteenth-century realism to modernism to postmodernism (the beginning of which he puts in the late 1950s), he ties literary modes to economic engines in a way that embeds both in their historical moment. Postmodernism is then not one set of stylistic options to compare to others but the "cultural dominant" of a time determined by late capitalism and American military and economic hegemony. Owing in part to "consumers' appetite for a world transformed into sheer images of itself," postmodernity has become a time of imitation, of parody and pastiche, the two basic modes by which the "mannerisms and stylistic twitches" of earlier styles are reused. Parody produces an "imitation which mocks the original" with anything from satirical intent to secret sympathy, while pastiche takes place as more "neutral" quotation (284). While modernism inspired a lot of parody, thanks to the strong, idiosyncratic styles that dominated it,[9] in postmodernity pastiche has come to the fore.

Regardless of how one perceives the relative strength of imitative modes in contemporary culture, there is again little room in this theory to experience a nineteenth-century poet as a strong and immediate voice. She enters Jamesonian hermeneutics as a predecessor artist with a signature style, and to feed her into one of his books is to watch her transmogrify into an irresolute prototype of his Wallace Stevens—one of the few poets Jameson mentions en passant as he builds the literary portion of his machine with French and English prose—whose "peculiar way of using abstractions" stands as a canonical example of modernist authorship (284). (Without saying exactly why, Jameson does nominate Marcel Duchamp, Raymond Roussel, and Gertrude Stein as three "outright postmodernists" *avant la lettre*.) Such a Dickinson could never act on a twenty-first-century person in the way Emerson described, for she could never match the transformative power of all the combined forces of late capital. She is to be quoted, nostalgized, pastiched, ironized—anything but heard as if she were in the room. In similar fashion if on less Marxist grounds, a good deal of twentieth-century criticism positioned Dickinson as a better modernist than postmodernist. Writing in 1929, Anna Mary Wells cited the poet's "flippancy" in matters of religion, her "epigrammatic brevity," and her "unexpected mingling of sardonic wit with sentiment" as evidence that the "attitude of most of Emily Dickinson's poetry is closer to what we choose to call modern than to the general conception of what people were thinking in the eighteen-nineties" (243). The critical path to Wells had already been cleared by readers such as Elizabeth Shepley Sergeant and Amy Lowell, who hailed Dickinson in the 1910s as an early imagist, and many others have since emphasized her opposition to bourgeois dimity convictions, her iconoclastic habits with syntax and rhyme, and the other explosive and unconventional traits that align her so well with the modernism of Marianne Moore, Pound, Picasso, Joyce and company.

Not only is the idea of Dickinson qua honorary postmodern counterintuitive on all these counts, but also, from the point of view of cultural embeddedness, even the modernist options can be made to look like a stretch. By 1923 Herbert Gorman was already feeling distanced: "The conditions which made her," he explained, "the philosophical atmosphere in which she came to maturity, have vanished" (54). Similarly, Allen Tate in 1932 thought that Dickinson's writing reflected an "ingrained philosophy," a "settled attitude" that was even then "almost extinct," and suspected that few people could ever hope to understand her on her own terms (153). And today, of course, it is even easier to name circumstances, from our side of history or hers, that make Dickinson seem remote and her popularity an effect of cultural exoticism or canonical inertia. A short list might include terrorism, the war in Iraq, postcolonialism, global warming, overpopulation, genocide, AIDS, computers and other technology. What do such issues have to do with nearly two thousand lyrics written—before radio, telephones, airplanes, two world wars, penicillin, nuclear energy, and so much else—by a quirky Puritan on subjects like nature, bees, flowers, time, sunsets, ecstasy, solitude, consciousness, fame, love, pain, madness, and faith? Or from her side: Dickinson lived her life unmarried in a small college town socially regulated by Victorian moral codes and a waning but reactionary Calvinist culture; women did not vote and had few professional avenues. Her basic educational requirements included now forgotten books—at the time they were *text*books—such as Edward Young's *Night Thoughts*, James Thomson's *The Seasons*, and Isaac Watts's *Improvement of the Mind*, and much of what she read for pleasure is similarly beyond cultural recall: Ik Marvel's *Reveries of a Bachelor*? Elizabeth Phelps's *The Gates Ajar*? Lady Georgiana Fullerton's *Ellen Middleton*? Proceeding this way, one can make the barriers appear insuperable and Dickinson—to borrow one of her words—retrieveless.

Yet some strains of postmodern theory are more promising suitors, notably those less attached to the way artists reflect larger historical forces or thematize them in their work. Aspects of Dickinson's writing have been found to anticipate phenomena as different as LANGUAGE poetry, Bakhtinian heteroglossia, deconstruction, and Lacanian theory. Her techniques of distilling "amazing sense" from ordinary experience and "italicizing" epiphanic moments suggest that she would be a good test case for the influential theses on the sacred in everyday life propounded by the Collège de Sociologie in the 1920s and 1930s and later reinvested in postmodern thought. Dickinson also seems like an ideal companion thinker for many of the now classic post-

Cartesian, postmodern paradoxes of human agency "after the subject" (in Jean-Luc Nancy's phrase) articulated by, among many others, Donna Haraway.[10] To be a human self in the age of cybernetics and cyborgs, she writes, is to "be autonomous, to be powerful, to be God"—precisely Dickinson's recurring fantasy-idea of a self that is autonomous, columnar, and tough as a diamond in a Bolivian mine (476).[11] Yet, Haraway continues, it is *also* to be "involved in a dialectic of apocalypse with the other" (476). And that is a dark side of agency that Dickinson articulated—better than her more famously self-reliant peers—in a stream of poems about the ways humans can be hesitating fractions and rebellious syllables to and for one another, wrecks in the Noons of the Other and drops absorbed in the sea.

Jean-François Lyotard invites another kind of conversation with Dickinson when he describes modern and postmodern artists as attempting to "present the unpresentable," that is, work plastically with concepts the mind finds rational but impossible to put into adequate sensuous form, for example, infinity, God, or death. He sketches a difference between moderns and postmoderns in the way they negotiate this Kantian tension: modern artists nostalgically regret the loss of the unpresentable and therefore allow themselves the "solace" of beautiful, pleasing forms, while postmoderns "deny themselves" the consolations of beauty and put forth new presentations "not in order to enjoy them but in order to impart a stronger sense of the unrepresentable" (*Postmodern* 81). That Dickinson's poetry trades in the "unpresentable" is clear just from its thematic obsession with things that refuse to reveal themselves to her: God, heaven, Nature, death, mind, and ecstasy, to name a few. As to whether she treats those topoi in one or the other Lyotardian mode, both cases can always be made: by simultaneously distrusting and yearning for the heavens she could not reach, Dickinson both regrets and intensifies their unpresentability. On the level of form, of course, she has always been understood to soothe as well as "injure" presentation, to give both pleasure and pain to readers with her jingles, riddles, slant rhymes, bewildering dashes, and distorted syntax.

More generally, Dickinson's oeuvre is interpretable as an early, intense response to the fragmenting epistemological conditions Lyotard identified in *The Postmodern Condition* as attending the weakening of authoritative Western narratives of history, God, nature, the self. In the way she refused either to endorse or reject many of the authoritative and explanatory vocabularies of her time—from Whig politics to mental philosophy to manifest destiny to dictionary definitions to Christianity to chemistry—she exemplifies the attitude Lyotard describes as most definitive of postmodernism: incredulity toward metanarratives.

These very few examples represent postmodernity neither accurately nor exhaustively. In fact, because "postmodernity" admits so many descriptions, it seems unlikely that the best new narratives about Emily Dickinson will be produced simply by swinging her through the academic categories that pullulate beneath the contested umbrella term. Yet the preceding discussion is of more than calisthenic benefit if it demonstrates that while there is little value in molding definitions of postmodernism to fit an elusive author, and still less in arguing for or against Dickinson's status as "relevant" or "postmodern" in any permanent sense, there are productive conversations to be had.[12] I hope it also makes clear that we cannot hold out hope for a theory of the "Dickinson postmodern" along the lines of Gary Lee Stonum's elegant "Dickinson sublime." Later we will see how Stonum, building on the work of Thomas Weiskel, was able to historicize Dickinson's poetics of the sublime and show precisely how it differed from an "orthodox romantic" version. In the case of postmodernism, however, we lack a baseline orthodoxy.

Thus if Dickinson's connection to postmodern thought deserves to be explored further, it cannot be in order to put on a pyrotechnical theory display, retrofit an argument to guess what she might say about today's news, or turn out a *Dickinson Soup for the Postmodern Soul*. No, the best reasons to think about a "postmodern" Dickinson are more pragmatic and scholarly: certain strains in postmodern thought can help make visible central aspects of her poetry, and her poetry has the power to illuminate and respond to contemporary situations.

What kind of situations? In chapter 1 I argue that if we accept the antifoundational and "post-metaphysical" arguments presented by thinkers like Richard Rorty and Gianni Vattimo, then Dickinson becomes an important companion thinker for us on a wide range of questions, from hermeneutic ones about language games, vocabulary selection, and self-creation to existential ones about how to think of loneliness and death. Ultimately all this is more than a matter of taxonomy and nomenclature, for to the extent that we accept Dickinson as a viable philosophical interlocutor for our moment and agree to try her out in postmodern roles—for example, the Nietzschean accomplished nihilist, the Nancian finite thinker, the Vattimian weak thinker, the Rortian liberal ironist—we add to the traditional expressive functions of her poetry a valuable, timely, and interpretable layer of philosophical inquiry.

The poet, asserts Emerson in "Circles" without arguing the point, "smites and arouses" us, "breaks up" our "whole chain of habits," and opens our eyes to our own "possibilities"—but in what forms of language do we consolidate, think through, and converse with these possibilities (409)? If Dickinson is to be compelling—not just credible—in philosophical roles, it is on the condition that we solve the "incommensurable discourse" problem between the philosophers and the poet. However pied philosophical prose may become, it can never be confused with her unique lyrics, and a translation strategy or interpretive discourse of some kind is needed to enable a meaningful dialogue between them. Every hope of a practical result for this study depends on this, but nothing guarantees in advance that it will be easy or even possible.[13] Among other things, Dickinson presents the paradox of a writer who self-consciously maintained a strong, hierarchized distinction between poetry and prose and yet, as we will see in detail in the next two chapters, also turned poetry to the prosaic, traditionally philosophical purposes of phrasing and responding to difficult questions.

I immediately set aside the options of searching for a metadiscourse or *reine Sprache* into which everything might be translated, of trying to "rephrase" the poetry in the prose of postmodern language games, or of producing what Jacques Derrida would call "transcendent" readings of the poems, that is, those that move quickly "beyond interest for the signifier, the form, the language . . . in the direction of the meaning or referent" (*Acts* 44). As Derrida says, in any reading of any text the moment of transcendence or rush to stable meaning is ultimately "irrepressible," but the ways this impulse can "be complicated or folded" can become the more important contribution to thinking. He argues that it is in fact "in this play of foldings that is inscribed the difference between literatures, between the literary and the non-literary, between the different textual types" and makes a useful broad distinction: if the specificity of a philosophical text can often be defined as its "project of effacing itself in the face of the signified content"—the attempt to neutralize the semantic consequences of style and form—then the "philosophical force" of lyric poetry comes from its countervailing ability to suspend "the 'thetic' naivety of the transcendent reading" and to provide "'phenomenological' access to what makes of a thesis a *thesis as such*" (*Acts* 45, 104, 46). I argue that this is true par excellence of Dickinson, that the way her lyrics both postulate and complicate thetic language can tell us a great deal about how we originate and converse with theses, truth claims, beliefs, vocabularies, attitudes, and interpretations in a post-metaphysical age.

Moreover, I agree with Derrida that if lyric poetry has provocative philosophical force, then it is not "hidden in the text like a substance" but must be developed "in response, in the experience of reading" (45–46). The goal of this book is therefore not to pry out finished products—information, opinions, beliefs—hidden in the poetry but to explore the thinking of which the poetry is the necessary byproduct. The translation I wish to perform between Dickinson's lyrics and certain dialects of philosophical prose thus requires constant attention to those poetic features that stage, fold, voice, interrupt, or complicate the movement toward singular meaning.

As a practical matter, anyone who would converse with Dickinson today needs to know as much as possible not only about her unique poetics but also about the historical conditions of her vocabulary. Only by attending to the way she acquired, negotiated, and deployed her poetic forms and words will we be able to think with her. Thus, while the idea of a "postmodern" Dickinson may suggest ahistoricism to some readers, just the opposite attitude is required in order to pick up the gauntlet Derrida has thrown down: the "best" possible reading consists in "*giving oneself up to* the most idiomatic aspects of the work while also *taking account* of the historical context" (68). Fortunately there is enough regularity in Dickinson's poetics that a single close reading can give a strong preliminary sense of the accent with which she spoke lyric language, how she used it to think, and how it might contribute to contemporary philosophical inquiry. I begin with the following 1863 poem in part to draw attention to three important and typical elements that I will explore further in the book: the poem originates from a secularizing and post-metaphysical theoretical perspective, features a speaker radically *redescribing* a central meaning-giving practice of her culture (prayer), and takes place as a metacommentary on the poetics of conversation:

> Prayer is the little implement
> Through which Men reach
> Where Presence - is denied them -
> They fling their Speech
>
> By means of it - in God's Ear -
> If then He hear -
> This sums the Apparatus
> Comprised in Prayer -
>
> *(Fr623)*

The first three lines form a prose sentence resembling a proverb or dictionary definition: *Prayer is the little implement through which men reach where presence is denied them.* The "little implement" metaphor construes prayer through the kind of de-spiritualizing, anthropological perspective that usually suggests irony, criticism, or humor, but here it is hard to tell: it may be comforting, since it captures the mysteries of human-divine communication in an intimate, domestic image, or trivializing, because it reduces prayer to a utilitarian function and raises doubts about the ability of a "little implement" to deal with something as serious as the denial of God's presence. By itself, the image optimistically suggests that men *can* reach God, and these lines are in fact often removed from the poem and quoted that way. Lines four and five, however, which form another complete prose sentence, are more irreverent and insulting. They characterize those who pray not as worshippers with rich spiritual lives who thoughtfully interact with God but as "Men" who desperately "fling their Speech." And it is very much "they," not "we," "you," or "I," who do this flinging: the speaker's voice is that of the ethnographer persona Dickinson often adopted to redescribe her community and thematize her differences from it.[14] The next line—"If then He hear -"—is pivotal: the logico-deductive formula of "if X then Y" is left hanging on the second half, the consequences: If then He hear, *then what?* The thesis is suspended, and the speaker, in a gesture of divine absencing, gives us only a dash and then, seemingly, nothing -

But we very much wanted an answer to that. The poem has so far proceeded with two satisfyingly complete sentences and thoughts—and a glance shows that it ends with a couplet—so we expect a clean finish to line six, too. Since the question of the efficacy of prayer is a classic one, we also expect a view on whether or not the little implement works. Any answer will do, for no matter how atheistic, agnostic, or faithful it may be, it will fall into a family of responses that everyone knows: "yes, prayer works," "no, it does not," "only in some circumstances," or "nobody knows." These opinions are all sanctioned by tradition, metaphysically comforting, and negatively present in the poem as thoughts ignored or evaded. As it cuts across the usual metaphysical positioning by rejecting both its set of responses and its modes of presentation, the abruptly lyricized, performative silence starts to acquire an unsettling, post-thetic philosophical edge.[15]

Starting with line six, then, we cannot continue listening to the prose we have been hearing, for it has been suddenly interrupted or folded back upon itself. Now, requiring an active response from the reader, the words have taken a non-negligible lyric turn, become hermeneutically conversational, and we must interpret. Thinking it through, we may suspect that the speaker has decided to parallel divine unresponsiveness, to dramatize prayers going unanswered in order to transform a comfortably comprehensible *concept* of "divine absence" into an uncomfortable *experience* of it. In fact we may feel several kinds of denied "Presence": as the transparent, linear prose evaporates, so do the Godlike author/speaker and the illusion of a single, authoritative interpretation. We may hold out hope that the last couplet will reinstate a theocentric experience of reading, but after the disorienting offer and withdrawal of presence in line six, we receive an unsatisfying and skeptical thesis: there is very little to know about the "Apparatus" of prayer, and that is all there is.

If the poem represents a forward movement of thought, a thesis-generating sequence that the speaker wishes to reproduce even as she forces the reader to participate in creating it, then the shift in vocabulary from the "implement" to the capitalized "Apparatus" reveals a crucial commitment to figural language as a means of analytical redescription. A little implement is unobtrusive, inexpensive, and simple, a part of what Heidegger calls the everyday world of references and assignments. "As a rule it is the use-objects around us that are the nearest and authentic things" (*Poetry* 29). Prayer, in this sense, is like a broom, ladle, or leash, always ready to hand, authentically itself, available to extend the "reach" and capability of everybody, not just a chosen few. As an "Apparatus," however, prayer becomes complicated, scientific, and technological, the product of a developed conceptual system that grounds its meaning and function, like a hydraulic press or eudiometer that only learned initiates can use. First presented in the universalizing terms of everyday utility, then as part of the restricted techno-scientific world of experiments and labs, prayer is never resolved into a definition that subsumes or merges both options. The speaker's self-confident tone in the closing couplet seems unearned, for surely these contradictory tropes cannot represent everything there is to know and say about prayer.

On the basis of these metaphorical implications, a reading along the lines of Paul De Man would develop competing interpretations of the poem, show that it is impossible to choose between them, and then speculate on the epistemological or existential consequences of that undecidability.[16] Such a method depends on the reader's initial willingness to posit the kind of metaphysical framework of unitary, freestanding, nonconversational meaning that the discovery of aporia and critical deconstruction could then proceed to destabilize. But since I recognize in Dickinson both a preexisting suspicion about the metaphysics of presence and a respect (worked deeply into the poetic fabric) for the hermeneutic contribution of the reader, in this book I do not stage such interpretive impasses as gateways to abyssal reductio ad absurdum discussions. Instead I identify them as decisive moments in the conversations readers have with texts and with themselves, fulcra on which theses are balanced and questions formulated, sometimes unfairly and reductively, as in the self-evidently false binary of considering prayer as "either" an implement "or" an apparatus. To anticipate a Dickinsonian distinction I examine in chapter 2, such moments force interpreters not just "to think" but to "try to think," to integrate into thought the defiantly non-thetic structures and textures of lyric processes. Because "Prayer is the little implement" abounds in such moments, it will help to look in an introductory but emblematic way at how it uses three categories of Dickinsonian lyric expression: syntax, voice, and meter.

Syntax. Maybe we can solve the problem of line six by taking it as a prose clause, one that is troublesome only because it has the ambiguous syntactic function of a squinting modifier. After all, it can be tacked on to the end of the preceding sentence—"they fling their speech by means of it in God's ear, if then He hear"—rendering it a sarcastic aside. (He probably does not hear.) Or it may introduce the last two lines: "If then He hear, this sums the apparatus comprised in prayer." (If God does not hear, then you do not have the whole of the apparatus of prayer.) Or maybe we can interpret the poem by identifying the agency hidden in the passive construction in line three— "Presence - is denied"—a typically Dickinsonian way of raising questions about causality: Who or what denies presence, and why? Or again maybe the problem is the antecedent of the word "This" in the phrase "This sums the Apparatus / Comprised in Prayer." Spoken softly and pensively, this "This" refers to the whole poem's description of prayer: "all of this, everything I have said in this poem, is all we can know of prayer." Spoken loudly and urgently, however, it can refer specifically to the performance of the process of God's absencing in line six, along with the reader's attendant feelings of deprivation: "*This*, what you're feeling now, see what I have just done to you? Now *that* is what the experience of prayer is all about."

Voice. Well beyond the options of loud and soft, this poem can be voiced as argumentative, sassy, humble, matter-of-fact, pensive, and resigned, among other options. Thus the reader has wide latitude to interpret the strength and tone of its irony; it works as anything from a lighthearted Horatian satire to a biting Juvenalian-Nietzschean critique. In fact, readers who wish to hear a meditative, soulful, humanistic poem might back up and preface it with an overture: *Is it not poignant and touching to think that prayer is the little implement* . . . Or for those who prefer an abrasive, dismissive statement: *I know you won't agree, but I don't care what you think. The truth is that prayer is the little implement* . . . And one need not listen for a unitary voice or tone at all. By the end of the poem, those readers who began by tuning in to the voice of a social scientist with a big ego may lose their confidence in her, for in retrospect the amiable gesture of using domestic metaphors to describe prayer can easily seem compromising or condescending. The increasingly alienating and didactic vocabulary—the noun "Apparatus" but also the verbs "comprise" and "sum"—suggests that this particular ethnographer may be insensitive, judgmental, and disingenuous, hiding behind vocabulary and furnishing an excellent example of how *not* to redescribe. What began as a seemingly benign attempt to produce a good Aristotelian metaphor, to bring the unfamiliar into the familiar and examine it with charity and honesty like a good Rortian liberal ironist, will ultimately feel to some readers like an exercise in procrustean lexical imposition. The fact that, like a tautological dictionary definition, the poem begins and ends with the same word only reinforces our sense of being forced either to cut Gordian interpretive knots—for example, by assigning a voice to the poem or choosing a syntactic pattern—or to remain within a circle of very small circumference, to accept that no more can be said about prayer.

Meter. A great many of Dickinson's poems use variations on what is called "ballad," "hymn," "folk," or "common" meter, a regular, iambic 8/6 syllabic pattern that makes it easy to pause two beats at the end of every trimeter line to create the feel of steady tetrameters.[17] But here the alternating tetrameters and dimeters feel like a curt, clipped compromise, especially since the third, fifth, and seventh lines each contain only seven spoken syllables. To create the feel of tetrameters in those lines, one must find somewhere to pause, which is not easy, and even then the dimeters pose a problem: one does not hold a pause for four beats, but it is hard to read those lines without pausing at all. And line six, again: Is it dramatic, with a long pause at the end? Does the wildly unexpected rhyme of *hear / Ear* in lines five and six signal a rupture? A closure? A transition between tones or voices? If a form-follows-function beauty guides this close-shaved meter, it is only in the restricted sense that a poem characterizing prayer as a dysfunctional conversation forces its readers to fumble their way thinkingly into it. Indeed, if Lyotard is right that denying oneself the "solace of good forms" and making presentation suffer are postmodern traits, then this poem reveals a contemporary Dickinson quite comfortable with uncomfortable thought and expression (81).

What does a poem like this give us to think, and how does it help us think it? First, since it takes place as an answer-that-does-not-answer, it gives us the question itself and invites us to try to ask and answer it better, all but forcing us to make, and assume responsibility for, a host of contingent interpretive decisions. Like many of the religious poems, this one begins in a traditional, almost scholastic register, with the kind of perfectly stable metaphysical question—"What is prayer?"—that may mean everything or nothing to a given reader. Dickinson herself, of course, heard this question asked and answered all her life. On October 26, 1856, for example, Edward Dwight preached a sermon in Amherst on Luke 11:1 titled "Prayer." In the positive terms typical of mid-nineteenth-century Amherst he described the consciousness of a man praying: "He will perceive an unseen Presence *always* accompanying him . . . he will be conscious that his own finite being is completely surrounded with the being of One beyond comparison greater" (Leyda 1:345). Dickinson, lacking faith in unseen, unchanging presence and pure linguistic referentiality, cannot seek out and name a single, confident truth about prayer, a "prayer is . . ." Instead she activates, in compressed lyrical form, an unresolved dialectic between the two unattractive entities of a sardonic, secular, scientific consciousness and a flailing, hapless Christianity. Discouraged from fully identifying with either pole of the dialectic, readers are thrown into "Prayer is the little implement," given the reins, and challenged to improve on the results. Redescribing, analyzing, and performing prayer, this short lyric offers terms, frameworks, and signifying strata for continued thinking even as it profoundly weakens the metaphysical form of the original question.

This reading helps make initial sense of the seemingly paradoxical claim that Dickinson is a valuable interlocutor and companion thinker for postmodernity, that she has as much or more to say to the twenty-first century as she did to the nineteenth. For to say that she is a poet for our time is to suggest that her poetry reveals different expressive powers and hermeneutic functions for post-metaphysical readers than for those who leave unquestioned the assumptions of strong thought, that her signature habits of expression are potentially more accessible and stimulating now than in any place or time where transcendence, science, religion, and poetry have been thought to have stable metaphysical foundations. It is therefore to say as well that we are sympathetic to her decision to write poetry that responds to the human condition of finitude and exposure, where capitalized "Presence" is "denied." [18] Such poetry shares impulses with an epoch that understands why Heidegger's *Being and Time* begins, as Vattimo notes, with the impossibility of construing human existence within the categories of traditional metaphysics, and especially not within "the thinking of Being as presence and objectivity" (*Beyond* 29).

This reading also promisingly suggests that neither prose paraphrase nor maladroit thetic positioning is required to place Dickinson's lyrics into philosophical conversation. On the contrary, by offering or allowing so many partial, interruptive, and supplementary semantic assignments to prosodic and other phenomena ordinarily deemed obstructive to, or negligible in, philosophical prose—voice, syntax, imagery, meter, tropes, rhyme, consonance (those eight "p" sounds in "Prayer is . . ."), and so on—the poems expand and transform the hermeneutic field. They incorporate analytic, deductive, distinction-making modes of reasoning, expose their contingencies, and try to think with and beyond them, encouraging us not to select or point to independent interpretations but to create new ones in collaborative hermeneutic events. For readers, as we will see, the poems' topics and techniques tend to create the kind of philosophical challenges that characterize pragmatism in a post-metaphysical age.

Few readers will come to or emerge from "Prayer is . . ." satisfied with the metaphor of "a little implement" or an "Apparatus," but those who have other ideas on the topic—it is hard not to think of Edward Dwight—must negotiate the poem's testimonial, argumentative, and stylistic textures. (One wonders exactly how many of Dickinson's contemporaries were ready to converse with such poems rather than simply agree or disagree with them.) By contrast, those who have no fixed opinion on prayer will find themselves introduced to an abundance of ideas and voices that organize but do not decide on many possible answers. The poem is potentially for everyone and, despite its seeming opinionatedness and decisive opening copula, reflects a thoroughgoing hermeneutic humility.

From this perspective, Dickinson's frequent poetic use of a seemingly all-inclusive "we" and of absolutist-sounding openings like "There is . . ." seem less legislative or imperial than propositional, as if they were indices of her willingness to share her best thinking on even the most private emotional or mental experience. Little concerned with winning adherents and fame or proving distinctiveness from predecessors, Dickinson wrote poems that remain conversationally experimental: they ask questions, hypothesize, present, test, and extend observations in the confined times and spaces of the short lyric. As we will see, there can be little doubt that she herself—if for some readers only in the guise of a Foucauldian author function—was optimistic about, and deeply invested in, the lyric's philosophical promise.

In short, proposing themselves as a new kind of implement or apparatus, Dickinson's poems exhibit many of the traits we look for in our best companion thinkers: they reflect an almost orgiastic capacity to initiate, posit, or offer thought; they say something serious but succinct—a pair of eighteen-word stanzas in the example of "Prayer is . . ."—on difficult and common problems; they step back from the personal situation and try to comment from a general perspective; and they use everything available to pursue their thought, from library to vocabulary to the overflowing toolbox of lyric techniques. The truth that emerges from reading such poems is never a fixed position but always a singular event of shared thought.

As has been suggested, it is not possible to understand the philosophical force of these Dickinsonian events without paying careful attention to "the signifier, the form, and the language" she used. And if we recognize with David Porter that "historical contextualizing or biographical storification does not equip readers to retrieve the controlling syntactical logic in the problematic poems" ("Unrevised" 14–15), then the opposite is also true: knowledge of the poetics does not let us see and learn from the way she used poems to respond to external contexts, to intervene in surrounding vocabularies. Since, for those seeking to negotiate postmodernity's language games, Dickinson becomes an increasingly valuable companion thinker the more we learn how she responded to her own, to understand her significance today—to make Emersonian abstraction work—is necessarily a maieutic process requiring both historicism and close reading.

In chapter 1, "Dickinson and the Hermeneutics of Conversation," I describe why a lyric poet like Dickinson makes a particularly good conversation partner for a postmodernity defined by Richard Rorty's neo-pragmatism and Gianni Vattimo's "weak thought." Rorty and Vattimo both elevate conversation to new philosophical stature by playing it off against metaphysical modes of reasoning and argue that certain kinds of conversation provide the best contemporary mode for the exchange of interpretations. Although Dickinson shared many of the post-metaphysical and anti-foundational attitudes of Rorty and Vattimo, her lyrics, guided by an Eco-style poetics of openness and a conversational "hermeneutics of friendship," also provide rigorous challenges to the arguments they make about poetry, vocabulary selection, reading as conversation, and other leading postmodern questions. The chapter concludes by showing how, from the perspective articulated by Vattimo, Dickinson's famously contested, poetized relationship with Christianity can contribute to ongoing philosophical conversations about secularization.

Chapter 2, "Trying to Think with Emily Dickinson," shows how dominant Dickinson found the category of thought, how committed she was to certain projects of thinking, and why she needed lyric poetry—not thought alone, nor other kinds of writing—to address them. This chapter examines the relationships Dickinson established between thinking and writing and pays special attention to her Baconian experimentalism, her correspondence with Thomas Wentworth Higginson, and the important lyrical subgenre she invented: the "try-to-think" poem.

Chapter 3, "Dickinson and Philosophy," demonstrates how enracinated Dickinson was in her philosophical culture and shows how her mind was formed by exposure to strong but opposing philosophical vocabularies. On one side were the Lockean materialism and Scottish Common Sense that dominated her schoolbooks in logic and mental philosophy (Hedge, Watts, Stewart, Brown, and Upham), and on the other were the Kantian themes and modes of apprehending the supersensible that circulated throughout Transcendentalism. In the ways Dickinson received and negotiated the tensions between these vocabularies and bodies of thought, we can glimpse both the origins and the postmodern significance of many poems.

Chapter 4, "Amherst's Other Lexicographer," treats Dickinson's creative responses to dictionary definitions, aphorisms, and various other "strong" metaphysical forms of language that saturated nineteenth-century America. Dickinson wrote over two hundred "definition" poems—many during the famous Webster–Worcester "War of the Dictionaries"—and her lyrical lexicography mimes but also redefines the entire genre, reflecting and inflecting national controversies over the control of English words and their meanings.

Chapter 5, "Through the Dark Sod: Trying to Read with Emily Dickinson," studies paradigmatic scenes of childhood reading in some of Dickinson's most cherished books—*Jane Eyre*, *Aurora Leigh*, and *The Mill on the Floss*—to speculate on sources for her understanding of hermeneutic encounters and her aggressive reinterpretations of American culture. Although Dickinson's interest in these *Bildungsromane* has been examined from biographical and feminist perspectives, an analysis of the hermeneutic models they employ reveals something very new. These books problematized the links between girls' reading and their expectations for life in ways that opened up possibilities for Dickinson to develop her lyricized hermeneutics of friendship, charity, and conversation.

Chapter 6, "With Bolder Playmates Straying: Dickinson Thinking of Death," builds on the previous chapters and examines how Dickinson, after a lifetime of thinking with and against the language games of her culture, joined her hermeneutics to her existentialism and innovated a neo-Kantian poetics of the sublime in order to converse with her culture and herself about death. A close reading of a late, little-known death poem shows her reworking the Romantic vocabulary of the sublime emerging from Kant, Wordsworth, and others in ways that predict twentieth-century articulations by Jean-François Lyotard and Jean-Luc Nancy. It also shows Dickinson adapting ideas of childhood, play impulse, and "naïveté" from the German Idealism of Friedrich Schiller to produce a logic of sacrifice and sovereignty along the lines of Georges Bataille. In a postmodernity in which, as Sherwin Nuland has argued, those "who think most clearly about death are usually such as philosophers or poets, not physicians" (62), this post-metaphysical fortitude and hard-won, self-reliant poetics make it especially valuable for us to try to think with Emily Dickinson.

1

Dickinson and the Hermeneutics of Conversation

> I know that the world I converse with in the city and in the
> farms, is not the world I *think*.
>
> EMERSON, "Experience" (1844)

> My best Acquaintances are those
> With Whom I spoke no Word -
>
> EMILY DICKINSON (1865)

"SERMONS ON UNBELIEF ever did attract me," wrote Emily Dickinson in 1854, and this iconoclastic inclination, combined with her hermeneutic humility and awareness of the embeddedness of thought in and among vocabularies, broadly aligns her with twentieth-century anti-foundationalist thought (L176). Because she so often experienced "presence denied" not only as deprivation but also as opportunity, we can consider her a member of the nineteenth-century avant-garde of "accomplished" nihilists in the sense Gianni Vattimo derives from Nietzsche: thinkers who understand, first, that when God dies—becomes an unnecessary hypothesis—the possibility of foundational truth dies too, and second, that the resulting nihilistic possibilities can be more than just passive or reactive. They can be positive, creative, and poetic in the widest sense. Approaching questions from the perspective of losing or having lost faith in absolutes and "doctrines," Dickinson accomplishes her nihilism by poetizing language in the interest of self-interpretation and self-creation.

Suggestions of Dickinson's anti-foundationalist and post-metaphysical attitudes abound in the criticism. She stands out among her contemporaries, says Shira Wolosky, for the way she withstands "the impulse to defend and explicate suffering in terms that claim for it metaphysical justification and redemptive value" (*Public* 118). Joanne Feit Diehl argues that Dickinson understood but could not share Emerson's naturalized Romanticism because for her, nature was a "deceptive text that cannot be read right" (*Romantic* 10). Harold Bloom hyperbolically salutes her proto-Nietzschean perspectivalism, arguing that "Dickinson's 'Tint I cannot take' poem knows, as no other poem in her century knows, that we are always besieged by perspectives" (305). For Bloom, Dickinson's "entire art at its outer limits" is to "think and write her way out of that siege" (305). Resisting metaphysical explanations for human traumas, worrying over the "Graspless manners" of landscapes and other natural phenomena that look as if they had just "repressed / Some secret," beset by perspectives and trying to think, Dickinson has much to talk about with a postmodernity leery of absolutes and metaphysical foundations (Fr696). Thus, although the search for good conversationalist precursors is usually pursued by and for thinkers inside specific disciplines—philosophers being famously in-house—in this chapter I present some of the ways in which contemporary dialogues can benefit from Dickinson's poetry.

Of the many philosophical approaches and vocabularies innovated or resurrected in postmodernity, Gianni Vattimo's *pensiero debole* (weak thought) and Richard Rorty's neo-pragmatism share enough with Dickinson to enable a good conversation. Like other thinkers associated with postmodernism, both Rorty and Vattimo argue that we have reached a point at the end of Western metaphysics where knowing and producing new knowledge are a matter neither of discovering permanent truths and unshakeable foundations nor of aligning natural language better with the nonhuman world.[1] In broad accord with the Nietzschean-Heideggerian critiques of the way philosophy tried to establish logic, scientific analysis, and objectivity as both base and summit of human thought, they argue that instead of increasingly accurate representations of observer-independent states of affairs—"world-pictures"—what we have, and can only have, is ongoing dialogue. We tend now, as Vattimo puts it, to accept that the human subject "is not the bearer of the Kantian a priori, but the heir to a finite-historical language that makes possible and conditions the access of the subject to itself and to the world" (Vattimo, *Beyond* 8).

The pragmatic, Deweyan Rorty thus salutes what he sees as the decisive attempt by the hermeneutic, Nietzschean Vattimo to set aside such once compelling topics of conversation as "unconditional moral obligations, universal validity claims, and transcendental presuppositions of rational inquiry" (Foreword xii). Asked in a 2005 interview what exactly he meant by calling our current culture "post-metaphysical," Rorty redescribed it as "poeticized" because it has rejected the traditional metaphysical position that one can find "an ahistorical, transcultural matrix for one's thinking, something into which everything can fit, independent of one's time and place" (Rorty, *Take Care* 46). Rather than looking to God, nature, reality, or history to tell us what kind of world it is already, we understand that we are more poetically responsible for creating it (46).

If Vattimo is right that being thrown into a finite-historical opening is "always inseparable from an active participation in its constitution, its creative interpretation and transformation" (*Beyond* 83), and Rorty is right that to "create one's mind is to create one's own language" (*Contingency* 27), then we do both when we converse with our heritage through reading.[2] Reading helps enable us to pursue the kinds of projects Rorty denominates "edification": the hermeneutic and redescriptive activity of making connections between ourselves and others, between our culture and other historical periods, or between our chosen theory or discipline and others that seem "to pursue incommensurable aims in an incommensurable vocabulary" (*Mirror* 360). Edification can also take place as a more inventive process, for example, the " 'poetic' activity of thinking up . . . new aims, new words, or new disciplines," and this can lead to "the inverse of hermeneutics: the attempt to reinterpret our familiar surroundings in the unfamiliar terms of our new inventions" (360).

Vattimo agrees that the best and most useful thinking is no longer demonstrative but edifying, and the interpretation of truth has become primarily hermeneutic—drawn from engagements with one's intellectual heritage—rather than logico-deductive ("Weak Thought" 452).[3] He sees Nietzsche and Heidegger as especially indispensable precursors because, unlike Habermas, Levinas, and others sympathetic to post-metaphysical approaches, they bring traditional Western metaphysics to closure without erecting new systems or foundations or reintroducing "strong" criteria such as absolutes, moral imperatives, or Cartesian rationality.[4] They "weaken" strong metaphysics not by overcoming it, erasing it, or substituting for it but by muting its imperatives and historicizing it. Vattimo finds it all but impossible, in the wake of Nietzsche, to continue thinking of "clear and distinct ideas as the model for truth, or of the experience of the true as the incontrovertible certainty of consciousness before a given content" (*Beyond* 87). Although some critics have tried to align Dickinson with strong metaphysical projects—Charles Anderson has argued that the reason she wrote so much about the nature of the mind and consciousness was "to identify and define the Self" (*Stairway* 33)—we will see that there are far too many weak hermeneutic features in her writing to do so.

Explaining his own conception of poetized truth, Rorty argues in the same vein that when thought recovers from metaphysics and no longer aspires to secure the foundations for all disciplines and inquiries, it must, like the later work of Wittgenstein, Heidegger, and Dewey, become therapeutic and edifying rather than systematic (*Mirror* 6). He describes the act of interpretation under these conditions as "more like getting acquainted with a person than like following a demonstration," and contends that what matters most is the way we constantly acquire new ways of speaking and remake ourselves "as we read more, talk more, and write more" (319, 359). Human beings are talking animals who use marks and noises, so being rational does not mean possessing a perfectible faculty of logic or truth-identifying apparatus. It means being "conversable," that is, capable of meaningful conversation.

Vattimo, citing the way Marx, Nietzsche, and Freud have "led us to doubt all that appears to us the most obvious," assigns philosophy the task of making persuasive the preference for intersubjective, interlinguistic conversability ("Weak Thought" 453). Powerful institutions such as "the papacy, an empire, newspapers, the media" may carry on trying to "define objective truths," but philosophy must show that truth itself "is conversational," for it is only "within conversational frameworks" that "preferences (as opposed to objective truths)" can be delineated," only within "conversation that preferred interpretations can be proposed" (453).

Clearly, if we want more than just repetition, confirmation, or distraction from our reading, if we want good, edifying conversations, then we must strategize our reading lists. If the "cultural space left by the demise" of strong metaphysical epistemology is not to be filled up anew with dreams of a "permanent neutral framework" beyond the range of contingent conversation, if we are to free ourselves from the vocabularies of the authorities who got to us first, then we must think carefully about which authors and texts reflect the fewest foundationalist illusions (*Mirror* 315–16). Could Dickinson's lyrics be among those that can help us recognize, appropriate, and redescribe the conditions of our contingency?

The point is not immediately obvious, for one might agree with the idea of truth as conversational and still wonder why philosophers should open their conversations to poetry. If a "philosophical requirement of hermeneutics," as Jean-Luc Nancy says, is "a precomprehensive anticipation of that very thing which is the question to be comprehended," then a lot depends on how thinkers approach and expect to participate in poems (*Sharing* 213). Traditionally, many readers have seen the lyric as uniquely adapted to times of noncomprehension and emotional desperation: acute grief, trauma, joy, ecstasy, dread, love. These are the moments when reasoned conversation becomes unreasonable, when sense becomes senseless and answers cannot be found for traditional questions. Why do I feel so lonely? What happens when we die? Why do I feel no presence of God? What is prayer? Why am I exhilarated by nature? Poets tend to address such questions differently from philosophers, and readers return to lyric poetry because of the way, both despite and because of its formal constraints, it resourcefully negotiates the extremes of emotion and cognition. Self-aware about the limits of being, thought, and expression, it can, even at its most difficult, seem more lucid and truthful than the philosophical prose that so prizes those qualities.

If the texture of poetry can complicate theoretical conversations, then it can also facilitate them by avoiding what Nietzsche excoriated as philosophers' uncompanionable traits, obstacles such as longwindedness, grandiose architectures of thought, and needlessly technical vocabulary. Poets, little worried about constructing armored intellectual positions or transferring their thought undisturbed to others, uninterested in the defensive intellectual projects of constructing logical sequences or making language "correspond to reality," tend to reach us non-didactically, as fellow travelers offering their thought. They may strike any attitude—serious, unintelligible, anguished, charming, disconcerting—but in their presence it can become possible to reach the key conversational point of being ready to rethink what we knew, either in the limited sense of reconsidering beliefs and trying on redescriptions or in the deeper one of rethinking how and why we rethink and redescribe at all. Poets, bursting and rendering visible the limits of prose, can prepare us to see and compare vocabularies and language games, to "redescribe ourselves, our situation, our past," and "compare the results with alternative redescriptions which use the vocabularies of alternative figures" (Rorty, *Contingency* 77).

Here it is worth noting a few reasons why it makes sense to think of Dickinson's lyrics as experiments in redescription: she warned Higginson that her lyric "I"s were only ever "supposed persons"; she wrote straightforwardly redescriptive poems like "'Arcturus' is his other name"; she often chose intrinsically redescriptive forms such as riddles and definitions; and she spoke of poetry as a language that redescribes ordinary experience in order to reveal the "amazing sense" within it (L268). Next, to understand how such Rortian redescriptive modes might also serve "weak" philosophical purposes à la Vattimo, it helps to recall how they were voiced. If, on the one hand, Dickinson's wide array of personae can be seen as a form of strength, a Whitmanian, elastic ability to identify with and draw power from multiple perspectives—Jane Eberwein lists "boy, queen, bride, sailor, languishing sentimental maiden, or hysterical gothic victim" (*Strategies* 126)—then, on the other, so much of this role playing ultimately speaks from weakness that Dickinson biographer Alfred Habegger names the "childish female" voice, the one that implicitly acknowledges its own "disabilities and 'lowness,'" her most characteristic (370). "Issuing from a position assumed to be powerless, this voice does not command or moralize in the fashion of so many Victorian voices, even Whitman's. It is a noncitizen's voice, disenfranchised and always aware of its lack of standing in debate or the arts of persuasion" (370). But while Habegger sees this voice forced to "resort to the personal, the perceptual, the divine" in order to speak (370), I emphasize, with Eberwein, that it is also often a strategy, adopted in conditions of weakening metaphysics, to negotiate keenly felt limitation and contingency. And as we will see in chapter 5, she found inspiration and models for this in the texts she loved best.

Because Rorty and Vattimo follow Gadamer in preferring an ideal of ongoing interpretation and *Bildung* to one of fixed truth or knowledge, their philosophies reserve a central place for literature and poetry. In fact Vattimo's description of the way philosophical hermeneutics has evolved to embrace aesthetics suggests that it may be poised to incorporate more poetry. Today, he argues, hermeneutics tends to be neither a "view from nowhere" of the "perennial conflict, or play of interpretations," nor a claim about the essential interpretive structure of humanity; rather it is the "philosophical theory of the interpretative character of *every* experience of truth" (*Beyond* 8, 7). And since this theory is itself located in history, we should prefer it to metaphysical and objectivist theories for reasons of historical legacy, not because we think it mirrors reality (10). Vattimo notes that although hermeneutics has traditionally taken specific disciplinary forms—"biblical, juridical, literary or even simply general" (4)—interpretation is no longer seen as confined to specialties. So to the extent that contemporary hermeneutics considers and combines many textual fields and replaces traditional correspondence notions of truth—"the appropriation of a thing via an adequate representation"—with others that are more "aesthetic" than "cognitive-appropriative" (notably the Heideggerian truth as "dwelling"), the discipline seems to open itself to lyric poetry (86).

Yet while their philosophical frameworks theoretically postulate roles for the lyric as a pragmatic, redescriptive, hermeneutic resource for a post-metaphysical age, neither philosopher pursues the idea very far. Vattimo delineates two options: it is always possible to extract philosophical theses from poetry, he points out first, but this is a vacuous procedure because the "truth of art" lies neither in "what the artists and poets say" nor in paraphrase (70). Instead he recommends interpreting truth as "the ontological significance for the history of the meaning of Being that can be perceived in the destiny of art and poetry in the epoch of the end of metaphysics" (70–71). He reinforces this Heideggerian framework with another Heidegger thesis—that poems and other artworks are "the setting into work of truth"—and advocates a method for interpreting them in the history of the meaning of Being. Since we are today living in the "epoch of the end of metaphysics," from the standpoint of hermeneutic ontology the most important thing is the observation that "the poets to which the philosopher can turn" are those who "speak of the essence (the *Wesen*: the historico-ontological destiny, not the eternal nature) of poetry" (69). By maintaining the Heideggerian assumption that one can understand epochs by reading major thinkers and poets into the history of the meaning of being, Vattimo endows poetry with a continuing ontological significance.

At the same time, and despite Vattimo's sensible warnings against interpreting the "essence" of poetry metaphysically as an "eternal nature" with immutable properties, from a pragmatic point of view his program limits interpreters to treating individual poems as reflections of (or ideally *on*) the "historico-ontological destiny" of poetry or poiesis as such. It is therefore not surprising that Vattimo never produces anything like close readings of lyric poems: the kinds of conversation he envisions with poetry are so specific to hermeneutic ontology that they preclude more focused, pragmatic instances of Emersonian abstraction.

Rorty provides similarly latent but undeveloped connections between philosophy and poetry. At first glance, the high cultural and intellectual significance he consistently awards to Bloomian "strong poets" and their ability to create new, potentially edifying metaphors suggests that he would also welcome lyric genres. And yet despite his recurring rhetoric of "poeticized" truth, the opposite is true: he argues that the turn away from metaphysically based epistemology and philosophy must be "toward narrative," for such a move would emblematize "our having given up the attempt to hold all the sides of our life in a single vision, to describe them with a single vocabulary" (*Contingency* xvi). True to his word, his examples of successful redescription and of new metaphors literalized and accepted as truths are virtually all drawn from prose narratives, the chief examples in *Contingency, Irony, and Solidarity* being Orwell, Nabokov, and Proust.

A lot remains to be done to realize the potential for lyric poetry's contribution within Rorty's and Vattimo's post-metaphysical, pragmatic, hermeneutic philosophies. To begin to do so, it is not necessary to posit any ahistorical properties to poetry or otherwise belabor the question of genre; a few pragmatic observations are enough. The way in which Dickinson critic Margaret Dickie distinguishes the lyric from novels, for example, strikingly positions it as a constructive interlocutor for today's post-metaphysical readers.[5] Unlike novels, she argues, lyrics like Dickinson's tend not to "mythologize the individual as a readable organization" or to turn isolated or fragmentary moments of experience into conceptual coherence ("Lyric Self" 541). On the contrary, they transform that kind of coherence into discrete experiences and restore "with words the contingency of the self that has been lost" (541).[6] Put in historical context, the particular status of Dickinson's lyrics as formal vehicles for contingency become even clearer: "Despite Poe's claim for its importance, the lyric was a woman's form, considered insufficient to express the grandness of America and the American individual, the central mission of the nineteenth-century literary establishment. This insufficiency of form was coextensive with the insufficiency of a self conceived as incomplete, unsure, recalcitrant, and—it must be admitted—female" (539). The simple fact that Dickinson committed her creative and cognitive energy to a lyric form *in statu nascendi* suggests that she intended to, and guarantees that she did, preserve the kind of contingencies on which so much postmodern thought has seized.

The ones Dickie mentions are reflected especially well in Dickinson's profoundly conversational, other-dependent conception of poetry. Hundreds of poems were sent to friends, family, and acquaintances as part of a lifelong dialogico-epistolary economy, and many of them collaborate or compete with real or implied readers. Typical conversational devices include quotation marks, reported speech, stichomythia, real-time narration, listener feedback, interruption, turn taking, shared allusions, puns, and other wordplay. One large group of poems analyzes or comments on specific kinds of conversation partners—"Talk with prudence to a Beggar" (Fr118), "I fear a Man of frugal speech -" (Fr663)—and others stage conversations between lovers, friends, spirit and body, the heart and the mind, natural phenomena, and other entities: "The Skies cant keep their secret" (Fr213); "You're right - 'the way *is* narrow -'" (Fr249); "Death is a Dialogue between" (Fr973); "You said that I 'was Great' - one Day -" (Fr736); "'Why do I love' You, Sir?" (Fr459); "'They have not chosen me' - he said -" (Fr87); "I asked no other thing -" (Fr687); "Going to Heaven!" (Fr128); "I'm Nobody! Who are you?" (Fr260). There are many more, for Dickinson's poetry overflows with extreme or limit-case scenarios. In fact, it is not always necessary to speak in order to talk with others:

> We talked with each other about each other
> Though neither of us spoke -
> We were listening to the Seconds' Races
> And the Hoofs of the Clock -
> Pausing in Front of our Palsied Faces
> Time compassion took -
> Arks of Reprieve he offered to us -
> Ararats - we took -
>
> *(Fr1506C)*

This conversational "we" turns down a boisterous ark in favor of a quiet, long-distance conversation between isolated mountain peaks.

Besides the poems that thematize conversation, a great number can be construed as responses to offstage interlocutors, as is clear from the way they invoke dialogical settings, techniques, and dynamics beyond the ones already noticed in "Prayer is the little implement." These include many "think-again" or "double-take" structures that fold thought back upon itself as if in reply: "For Death - or rather / For the Things 'twould buy -" (Fr644B). "What was *that*?" is the provocative question that seems to originate some conversational poems: "It was not Death" (Fr355); "It was not Saint" (Fr1052). Often the poems' very brevity can be interpreted as a way of not trying to say everything, of creating time for dialogue, for the reader's breath "to straighten" and brain "to bubble Cool" so as to prepare a response (Fr477A). Marianne Noble points out that in the opening line of "Struck, was I, nor yet by Lightning -" (Fr841), the words "'nor yet' seem to refer back to a previous remark by someone else" (179). Her paraphrase emphasizes the energy of dialogue—"I tell you I was *struck*, and it wasn't simply by lightning"—and her observation that the poem's insistent tone implies a listener holds true for many others (179).

The philosophical value of Dickinson's conversationalism becomes clearer when we see how it is conditioned by the poems' unfinishedness. Since Dickinson's creative process rarely eventuated in final or monological expression, her writings can be seen as "open works" in the sense of Eco, as "texts" in the sense of Barthes, and as thoughtful responses to what Blanchot, Nancy, and Lacoue-Labarthe have, in different ways, called the "fragmentary exigency."[7] Eco, for example, distinguishes between the banal kind of openness exhibited by any work of art in its ongoing susceptibility to new performances and interpretations and a more radical kind in which the work is "passed on to the addressee in an unfinished state" (*Open* 4). Here the artist not only understands the implications of leaving works unfinished but also turns unfinishedness into a "positive aspect" of the production, thereby creating an openness that is "intentional, *explicit*, and extreme" (5, 39). The important difference is thus between the reader who is free to choose among myriad interpretations of a work and the one who absolutely must do some of its "organizing and structuring," who fully collaborates in "*making* the composition" (12).

Dickinson's poetry can generally be thought of as "open" in the latter, more explicit sense. Even if we treat the poems conservatively as discrete aesthetic objects, we find ourselves constantly forced to ask and answer questions about the topic, scene, addressee, and other contexts that precede, surround, and follow them. This is a poet, notes Eberwein, who often left out much of what "her readers want to know: things like what condition the speaker actually describes, how she got there, and how she emerged" (*Strategies* 141). Indeed, as we will see in detail in chapter 4, many of the poems that seem most dedicated to closed forms and unitary meaning, such as the riddles and definitions, remain profoundly open.

To look at the manuscripts of the poems is to confirm this diagnosis. They enable Marjorie Perloff to celebrate the way Dickinson predicts "the 'differential' poetics of our own time—'differential' in that there is not one 'correct' or even preferred text but a variorum set that allows the reader to consider alternatives." Dickinson's "poetics of process," Perloff finds, prepares for "much more reader involvement than does the Modernist aesthetic of the *mot juste*'" and transfers "poetic authority" from the poet to the reader much more than do the styles of Celan, Wordsworth, and Yeats.

Gary Lee Stonum finds an affective openness as well. He points out that although Dickinson distributed poems in letters throughout her life to dozens of different readers, she never once hinted at how they should receive or respond to them. He concludes that she conceived of her poems not as "ends in themselves," existing in some "esthetic space ideally transcending other aspects of life," but rather as "rhetorical stimuli" intended "to stimulate the reader's mind without necessarily determining it" (*Sublime* 66, 147). Such writing encourages a reader's "sublime empowerment" but, unlike much Byronic-Romantic poetry, and in a way that reflects deeper structural openness, never asks that we submit to the authority of the poet or person. With Dickinson we need never take that "first identifying step" (147).[8]

From a feminist perspective, Karen Oakes shows that Dickinson's poetry denies both "the traditionally feminine, passive, and inferior role which Trilling's masculine artist characteristically assigns to the reader" as well as the critic's usual role of evaluative outsider claiming an objective viewpoint (201). She finds that Dickinson even disables any of her own "artist's assumptions about a reader's role" that may provoke the latter posture (201). For Oakes, all of this tends to equalize the author and reader but also constitutes a difficult "balancing act": just as the poet "fears obliteration while she seeks interaction and closeness," while the reader is expected to participate so deeply "in the recreation of a poem-as-process" that interpreting becomes a self-risking activity (201). To join one's thought to some poems is to forfeit rationality and autonomous selfhood.

In short, Dickinson's poems are open, dialogical, differential, and deferential—each in an extreme way. From this perspective, Paul Crumbley is right to speak of the poems as profoundly dialogical in the Bakhtinian sense, as "loci where discontinuous speaking selves" come forth and coexist (*Inflections* 30). With remarkable freedom and hermeneutic authority, a reader in their presence faces Perloff's postmodern textual multiplicity, Stonum's highly affective but unheroic and unromantic lyrical encounter, and Oakes's egalitarian but perilous self-involvement, all while trying to make the kinds of basic decisions we saw in "Prayer is the little implement."[9] The result is a postmodern condition à la Vattimo and Rorty: Dickinson's readers are poetized and post-metaphysical, both gifted and burdened with radical hermeneutic responsibility and conversational control.

Critics who accept these formal features and do not wish to default unthinkingly to one position or another must find a way to respect Dickinson's programmatic openness.[10] One might, for example, try to understand the development and purposes of this reader-oriented poetics by tracing its origins (in, say, Dickinson's biography, psychology, or literary heritage) or else simply accept the invitation to autonomy. I take Susan Howe's reading of Dickinson as a LANGUAGE poet, Camille Paglia's of her as "Amherst's Marquis de Sade," and Jerome McGann's of her as a graphic artist to be examples of critics sprinting away with a baton received from the author.

In this book, however, I have chosen a pragmatic method emphasizing, to different degrees in different chapters, close reading and historicized hermeneutics. The rest of this chapter elucidates some of the ways Dickinson's poems converse with—confirm, complement, correct, and supplement—the philosophies of Rorty and Vattimo, precisely on the topic of conversation. If we acknowledge that Dickinson can be described in general terms as a conversationalist and an open-form poet, then individual poems become valuable for the ways in which they elaborate specific varieties of conversation and pose specific problems for the philosophers. To see how we might bring forth Dickinson's contributions, it is useful to turn now to Rorty's best model for contemporary conversation: the liberal ironist.

Noting broad generic distinctions between poetry and kissing cousins like philosophy and fiction is not enough to address a basic post-metaphysical problem: If our descriptions of everything are not demonstrably grounded in the real but instead result from epistemologically soft conversations with people and texts, then why should we prefer one description, or one text, over another? Rorty vivifies this grand predicament with a character he consistently genders female and calls the "liberal ironist."[11] She is his heroine of postmodern interpretation because she manages both to accept the dissolution of metaphysical illusions, the kind that still deleteriously saturate so much thinking, while also remaining a thoughtful, tolerant, good person. She fulfills three key conditions. She "has radical and continuing doubts" about her "final vocabulary"—the words she uses to justify how she lives, what she does, and what she believes—and her self-doubt stems from the way "she has been impressed by other vocabularies, vocabularies taken as final by people or books she has encountered" (*Contingency* 73). She also recognizes and accepts that arguments phrased in her present vocabulary can "neither underwrite nor dissolve these doubts"; and lastly, to the extent that she "philosophizes about her situation, she does not think that her vocabulary is closer to reality than others, that it is in touch with a power not herself" (73).

For Rorty's liberal ironist, human conversation is the preferable alternative to misguided, overconfident epistemology in the matter of the ironist's vocabulary selection. For Vattimo it is the mode in which interpretations can best be proposed and reinterpreted during a post-metaphysical epoch. But what about Dickinson? What aspects of conversation were most important to her, and what was her idea of good conversation? Although her writing exhibits such openness that this question could be addressed through almost any set of poems, it makes practical sense to break into the hermeneutic circle with some that are "metaconversational," that is, that go beyond representing conversations to assessing and analyzing them.

I begin with a poem that characterizes good conversation by denouncing its opposite:

> They talk as slow as Legends grow
> No mushroom is their mind
> But foliage of sterility
> Too stolid for the wind -
>
> They laugh as wise as Plots of Wit
> Predestined to unfold
> The point with bland precision
> Portentously untold
>
> 6 Predestined to] <Retardedly a><I>interlined above
>
> *(Fr1732)*

Whoever these unattractive "others" may be, it is unpleasant to listen to their bovine talk and laughter. The speaker assumes the kind of supercilious anthropologist's voice that preempts any conversational "we" from forming: each stanza opens with field notes on how "they" talk and laugh. She gives no outward reasons to explain the poor conversation (say, by classifying her objects of study as ill bred, uneducated, senile, or pompous), but her description implies the analysis: since painful conversations are "slow," "sterile," "stolid," and "bland," we know that good ones must be quick, fertile, nimble, and spicy. Mushrooms grow instantly, unseen, and abundantly, but these people take centuries to say anything, and their minds are filled with the "foliage of sterility."

The second stanza continues trying to raise the conversational standard. Beginning with a scathing pun—"Plots" of wit suggests canned, planned narratives and squares of space—the speaker castigates the "they" further for their overlong stories in which the main point is "Portentously untold," that is, annoyingly withheld. A series of special effects then separates the speaker's style from that of the plodding clods: along with the vivid images of mushrooms, barren branches, and wind there is consonance ("mushroom" / "mind," "sterility" / "stolid," "wise" / "Wit"), internal rhyme ("slow" / "grow"), and, most dramatically, an explosive, frustrated spluttering of seven "t" and five "p" sounds in the second stanza alone: "Plots," "Predestined," "point," "precision," "Portentously." With her proliferation of polysyllabic terms and tropes, the speaker outperforms the unedifying dullards.

Poems like "Prayer is the little implement" and "They talk as slow as Legends grow" reveal a rather ruthless Dickinson dissecting and dismissively redescribing some of her culture's practices. The following poem, however, typifies those that give more positive and collaborative answers to the question of how conversation can edify:

> He was my host - he was my guest,
> I never to this day
> If I invited him could tell,
> Or he invited me.
>
> So infinite our intercourse
> So intimate, indeed,
> Analysis as capsule seemed
> To keeper of the seed
>
> 5 intercourse] interview   7 as] like
>
> (Fr1754)

Over time, this speaker has grown extremely close with an unspecified "He" who, across Dickinson's poems, may be many things: a friend, lover, God, disputant, bird, enemy, haunting or attractive idea, book, or part of the speaker's self. Yet the past-tense narration signals that the immediate, interactive part of the relationship has either ended or moved to a new stage, and what remains is a kind of mid- or post-conversational meditation.

Back-and-forth clauses echo through the first stanza—"He was my host," "he was my guest," "I invited him," "he invited me"—as the separate subject positions dance through pronouns: "He," "my," "he," "my," "I," "I," "him," "he." The second stanza, however, thematizes the conversational "we" of which the speaker is a part ("our intercourse") and muses over the origin and evolution of the now precious relationship. Disparate aspects of once separate selves—perhaps vocabularies, perspectives, bodies, consciousnesses—have mixed to form an intimate, infinite conversation. So on the simplest level, the dash and the comma in the first line translate to question marks—my "host?" my "guest?"—and the whole poem to light nostalgia: *Just imagine, He and I are so close now, so intertwined, that I cannot even recall how it all began.*

Yet from another perspective, suggested in part by the final simile on the uselessness of "Analysis," the poem is more complicatedly philosophical, and the question about the original "invitation" has enough metaphorical depth to raise the postmodern issue of agency: am I "invited" by a vocabulary, a person, a book, or do I "invite" them into my life and thought? When am I guest and when host to the influences that shape me?

At first, guest/host roles provide the capsular protection that allows the "seed" of conversation to grow between separate entities. These social assignments evolve as intimacy increases, however, and while they do not vanish, they become misleadingly restrictive, ultimately losing the ability to categorize the complex together-separateness of "I" and "He" selves held together in and by conversation. The poem in this sense represents the expiration of a binaristic vocabulary about conversation—I/He, guest/host—and the fact that the speaker hesitates between the terms "intercourse" and "interview," with their suggestions of sexuality and diverging etymological connotations of "running between" (*inter-currere*) and "seeing between" (*inter-videre*), proves how difficult it is to redescribe this non-fused yet non-separate conversational state. And although the speaker begins by asking a traditionally metaphysical kind of question—What really happened, which of us played host first?—the fact that she ends by dismissing it as irrelevant further suggests that she has reached a more post-metaphysical position: the intercourse of which she is a part cannot be encompassed by an independent vocabulary or logic.

Above all, since conversation is the poem's topic, its own performance as a piece of intimate writing stands out. In the second stanza, just when a conversational "we" is invoked, the language play suddenly multiplies: there are six words in the poem beginning with "in"—"invited," "invited," "infinite," "intercourse," "intimate," "indeed" (seven if we include the variant "interview")—and it all reads like an in-joke, as if the speaker were innovating with Latinate vocabulary for a private initiate. The result is an odd but thorough Rortian redescription: the speaker draws on the performative aspects of shared language to redescribe those very things. But this kind of description, relying as it does on sparks of playful lyricization, implicitly redescribes Rorty's prosaic conception of the practice.[12] Comparing this kind of rhymed, rhythmic, confidential conversation to more routine exchanges of language, postmodern readers may construe the poem as a rhetorical invitation—not an argument—to prefer it to them.

For reasons that might be called emblematically postmodern, poems like this are hard to interpret. The history of linguistic interplay between "He" and "I" is at best partially intelligible for those who, like the poem's readers, merely "overhear" some of the conversation. We suspect that only He can respond knowingly to the inspirations of his ingenious interlocutor, and this circumstance may unfortunately hold just as true for many of the transcripts of conversation we receive from the history of literature and philosophy. Ultimately, the poem's important question is not the chicken-or-egg metaphysical one about the historical facts of the original encounter but the hermeneutic one of whether sustained conversation can—perhaps through a process of interpersonal lyricization?—originate richer descriptive language.

Like Rorty and Vattimo, then, this speaker prizes conversation, especially the intimate, infinite kind that lasts long enough to suspend or renovate sociohistorical protocols. But by contrast with Rorty, who tends to depict his ironist as a disembodied soul freely meeting and choosing vocabularies and descriptions, she attends more to the ways social cues and local or even private language games can determine conversations. The difference is not absolute, but it implies a significantly different framework for the philosophical question of vocabulary selection. This question is crucial for Rorty because, he argues, we are today increasingly aware of participating simultaneously in different language games. And to the extent that we are no longer willing to appeal to truth, reason, God, nature, reality, the dialectic of history, or any other divinized entity to decide which vocabulary to privilege, we tend instead to compare language games and vocabularies to one another, not to "reality."

What we have come to realize, says Rorty, is that when we take specific examples, such as "the vocabulary of ancient Athenian politics versus Jefferson's, the moral vocabulary of Saint Paul versus Freud's, the jargon of Newton versus that of Aristotle, the idiom of Blake versus that of Dryden," it becomes very hard to "think of the world as making one of these better than another, of the world as deciding between them" (*Contingency* 5). From the perspective of such broad discourse tectonics, the language game of arguing about which sentences within any single game are falsifiable or more or less "true to reality" can seem parochial or pointless, and to recognize this is, for Rortian liberal ironists, a great philosophical advance because it releases them from time-wasting efforts at making language "correspond" and concentrates them instead on the problem of how to compare language games.

Even putting aside the likelihood that any theoretical language complex enough to be considered a "vocabulary" might be self-contesting or "textual" in the senses of Derrida or Barthes, and therefore prima facie difficult for an anxious ironist to shuffle about as an all-or-nothing, freestanding option for self-description, a large group of Dickinson poems raises other questions about the way we come to, appreciate, and acquire new vocabularies. Like Rorty, they insist on the experiential and perspectival situatedness of conversational language. But they also suggest that Rorty's model mistakenly diminishes or obviates the roles of the other in the give-and-take of conversation and redescription.

The 1863 "Strong Draughts of Their Refreshing Minds" gives a more detailed view of reading as conversation and directly addresses the question of how it affects the reader's mind. Using figural language to describe how engaging with the "strong" minds of one's heritage can transform one's own, the speaker opens with a suggestive pun on "draughts" as both "drinks" and "sketches":

> Strong Draughts of Their Refreshing Minds
> To drink - enables Mine
> Through Desert or the Wilderness
> As bore it sealed Wine -
>
> To go elastic - Or as One
> The Camel's trait - attained -
> How powerful the stimulus
> Of an Hermetic Mind -
> (Fr770)

To share minds is to mix strong drinks. Because Dickinson stood well apart from cultural codes warning of the corruptive powers of alcohol and many kinds of reading, it is not surprising to see that the two main effects of this process are fortifying rather than disabling. Where Rorty emphasizes the attractive coherence of the vocabularies to which his ironist is exposed even as they fail to correspond to reality in any permanent, foundational sense, Dickinson's alcoholic metaphors redescribe that attractiveness as the more Foucauldian result of their power and influence. Yet even as she recognizes the dangers of getting drunk on someone else's thought, the speaker defends the thesis that conversations with strong minds improve mental resilience: absorbing another mind relaxes the rigidity of one's own and allows it to "go elastic" through the desert or wilderness. At the same time, it provides one with the "Camel's trait," the ability to preserve a life-sustaining resource over long, barren stretches of time and distance. In both cases, reading powerful sources gives the mind powers that are useful when it is a matter of survival, when one is thrown upon one's own resources, and the biblical landscapes of "Desert" and "Wilderness" suggest that this kind of conversation is especially valuable for the lonely or abandoned spirit. If we hear or read enough of the right things in advance, we will make it through the desert by ourselves.

Reading is thus a life-preserving activity, a form of conditioning, a prophylactic. But to understand what powers are carried in the sealed wine of another mind or text and how they are transmitted and used, we must look still more carefully at these elastic and camel metaphors and try to reach the movements of thought that originally produced them. First, if sharing another mind enables one to "go elastic" through a trauma—an intellectual, spiritual, emotional, or psychological wasteland—then the going may be imagined: life's most arduous journeys may take place in the mind (where it may be nobler to suffer, as Hamlet thought). In this sense, sharing thought through reading would elasticize the mind by delivering events beyond those one has already met. At the same time, going elastic may also mean traveling through life with the mental, emotional, or spiritual ability, gained through exposure to strong minds, of being able to spring back into shape no matter what happens. This matches the definition for "elastic" given in Dickinson's 1844 Webster's dictionary.[13]

But these interpretations of the mind being "elasticized" by reading are immediately qualified, perhaps even contradicted, by the second striking figure: "Or as One / The Camel's trait - attained -." Instead of conjuring a mind circumferentially expanding and contracting, this image implies a rigidifying process in which reading produces a self that is increasingly individuated, self-reliant, and *in*elastic. In this conversational model, drinking others' minds transforms us into self-sustaining ships of the psychological desert, and the things we read are carried along inside, *other than* the self but precious and nourishing *for* the self, potentially forever. Such readings presumably include the memorable parts of texts, the beloved passages and details, the magnificent ideas and uses of language, the Rortian vocabularies, in short, all the wise and beautiful things we were well-nigh thinking and saying ourselves. Installing an eternal, internal fountain of intoxicating auto-edification, such reading would strengthen our memory, stamina, and independence.

Thus we have two opposing fantasy-answers to the question about radical self-reliance that Dickinson pondered throughout her life: Without love, God, or even food, is it possible to become impervious to pain and subsist—thrive, even?—on thought, a crumb of bread, air, or reverie? The camel self is a columnar yet mobile being with only an occasional need to drink at the source of another mind, and the elastic self is chameleonlike and adaptive, not a self at all, really, but a mirage-self, a responsive and absorptive agency.

It is not easy to reconcile these two visions of the edifying effects of shared thought, and the poem makes no explicit attempt to do so. Both interpretations come together in the last two lines, where, to make reader-oriented matters worse, there emerges an unresolved tension between the plural "minds" of the first lines and the isolated "mind" in the last. Although at first the closing couplet's aphoristic shape seems to promise a clear conclusion— "How powerful the stimulus / Of an Hermetic Mind -"—ultimately it only focuses the main interpretive problem into an undecidability: *Whose* mind is hermetic and powerfully stimulating? Is it the strong and refreshing mind embodied in the book I am reading? Or is it my own mind, strong and refreshed thanks in part to that book? Those who think of human agency in camelized terms have license to interpret it as the speaker's: newly fortified, delimited, Cartesian, and tough. For those who prefer the more conversational vocabulary of elasticity, that mind will be someone else's, perhaps a book's, continuing to influence, stimulate, and shape us in ways we do not fully understand or control.

Either way the poem synopsizes a dialectical debate between "strong" and "weak" conceptions, between "self" understood as metaphysically grounded, defined, and self-present on the one hand, or ungrounded, permeable, fluctuating, and self-obscure on the other. Vattimo reflects a postmodern preference for elasticity when he argues that in today's media society "the ideal of emancipation modeled on lucid self-consciousness, on the perfect knowledge of one who knows how things stand (compare Hegel's Absolute Spirit or Marx's conception of man freed from ideology), is replaced by an ideal of emancipation based on oscillation, plurality and, ultimately, on the erosion of the very principle of reality" (*Transparent* 7). From this perspective, Dickinson's landscapes of wilderness and desert can be taken as psycho-geographical sites of postmodern loneliness, detachment, and wandering, and this specific poem as a kind of litmus test for agency in the age of ontological weakening: To what extent does anybody now adhere to a theory of "self" as camel or elastic, and why? Because the poem is open and unresolved, and because it preserves both strong and weak answers to the question of how we are influenced by other minds, books, or thoughts—in short, the traditions to which we are exposed—the closing remark about the power of other minds and texts forever to stimulate us can be interpreted as a decision in favor of hermeneutics, the ongoing interpretation of one's cultural inheritance.

Christianity was the most powerful of Dickinson's inherited vocabularies, and—as is amply demonstrated by the rich critical tradition on her religious culture—the source of some of her most sustained conversations and redescriptive efforts.[14] But the Christian tradition also has a particular importance for post-metaphysical thinkers like Vattimo, and his discussion of its status in postmodern thought sheds retrospective light on both Dickinson's hermeneutics and the way we might now converse with her poetry.

That Dickinson conversed innovatively with her Christian heritage is a commonplace, although the premise continues to lead to contradictory conclusions. Some readers assume that because she took part in the conversation, she maintained a Christian outlook, however contested, while others privilege the conversation-stopping force of her redescriptions. Eberwein notes that among the people who were close to Dickinson and tried, as she did, to piece together the human and the divine, most ultimately managed, as she did not, to find "formulaic resources of fulfillment represented in her community by the Congregational church" (*Strategies* 69). Eberwein concludes that the poet ignored "alternative theological, philosophical, scientific, or psychological systems for overcoming the mortal privations that dominated her consciousness" and struggled instead to work out, within a religious vocabulary she did not entirely trust, "her own strategies for growth" (69). I argue, however, that Dickinson made more than passing use of these other vocabularies, even though they too often proved disappointing. From a point of view shared by accomplished nihilists and Rortian pragmatists, the ability to create with the very languages one perceives to be defective is both rare and valuable.

Today, of course, thinkers across the spectrum from atheist to evangelical can be found who characterize the postmodern era by the way it respects secular and anti-foundationalist language games. According to Vattimo, however, and crucially for the specific case of Dickinson, this post-metaphysical ascendancy emerged and is inseparable from the history of the relationship between Western metaphysics and Christianity. In a line of thinking strikingly unlike that of most other postmodern theorists (including Rorty), Vattimo holds that Christianity paved the way for the dissolution of metaphysics by offering a profound alternative to world-picture metaphysics (*Future* 43–54; *After*, passim) He sees Kant as the historical turning point where strong metaphysics began to stop resisting the "weak" possibilities inherent in Christianity, and concludes that the Nietzsche of the death of God and the Heidegger of *Ereignis* are the most radical heirs of the anti-metaphysical principle that Christ brought into the world.[15] His critique of his two master thinkers on this point helps explain why Dickinson's poetry—a poetry of shared thought that rebelliously used the resources of her Christian heritage to help dissolve absolutes—is a valuable resource for post-metaphysical thinking: "Nietzsche and Heidegger remain captive to Greek objectivism and refuse to develop fully the implications of Christianity's antimetaphysical revolution. These cannot be fully developed without recourse to charity. In other words, only friendship, explicitly recognized as the decisive truth factor, can prevent the thought of the end of metaphysics from lapsing into a reactive and often reactionary nihilism, to use Nietzsche's expression" (*After* 111). Thus Vattimo's hermeneutics recasts the charity introduced through Christ as an epistemological criterion. Friendship is a decisive truth factor when truth is seen not as the adequate capture of a nonhuman reality by a set of linguistic symbols but as a linguistically mediated event shared by human beings thrown together in historical contingencies.

Vattimo's wider framework helps us position Dickinson more precisely. Analogizing from the method employed in Weber's *Protestant Ethic and the Spirit of Capitalism*, he argues that Christian forms of interiority led to a postmodern community characterized by interpretation, irony, and charity. If capitalism can be seen as adapting certain aspects of the Bible and Christian culture rather than simply opposing or affirming them, then so too can postmodern, secular thought, which takes place during a time in which religion has flourished. The most important structural features of secularization, so often limited to deism and the wider Enlightenment project, are thus better understood as interpretive applications of the biblical message that situate it beyond the strictly "sacramental, sacral, or ecclesiastical realm," that is, precisely where a lyric voice like Dickinson's, which both reflects and contests Christian ideas, is prepared to speak and be heard (*After* 45).

In fact, a letter to Joseph Lyman, in which she describes her reading of the Bible, can be taken as a representative episode in Dickinson's long career as both a secularizing hermeneut à la Vattimo and a liberal ironist à la Rorty:

> Some years after we saw each other last I fell to reading the Old & New Testament. I had known it as an arid book but looking I saw how infinitely wise and merry it is. Anybody that knows grammar must admit the surpassing splendor & force of its speech, but the fathomless gulfs of meaning those words which He spoke to those most necessary to him, hints about some celestial reunion—yearning for a oneness— has any one fathomed that sea? I know those to whom those words are very near & necessary, I wish they were more so to me, for I see them shedding a serenity quite wonderful & blessed. (*Lyman Letters* 73)

Dickinson recognizes the Bible as providing language that other people find "near & necessary" to describe their lives—strong metaphysical terms that gather a community around a promise of "oneness" and shared essence— but she is anguished at being unable either to accept or to undermine it. She, like Vattimo, mutes the strong metaphysical aspects traditionally attributed to the Bible, such things as moral foundations, absolute truths, representations of law and commandment, or claims to describe the soul and universe accurately. Unable to think or argue her way into a necessary relationship, whether logical or emotive, with this book, she is struck more by its practical qualities: its philosophical importance stems more from being conversationally "wise" and "merry" than metaphysically incontrovertible or true to reality. Indeed, disappointed at finding herself inexplicably magic-proof, she especially admires the paradoxical way its air of prophecy, its "hints," and its "fathomless gulfs of meaning" manage to produce serene inner experience in so many other readers without ever coalescing into a coherent, Rortian vocabulary. The Bible may be a strong draught for others, but it fails to either camelize or elasticize her mind. And that, ultimately, is what she wants even more than to "fathom" the words or redescribe her life with them.

Using Vattimo's terms we might therefore conversationally embroider a bit further upon Dickinson's thought and see her "camel" as an emblem of strong metaphysics—the foundationalist tendencies one finds in one's heritage or one's own mind—and the process of elasticization as a version of the hermeneutics of weak thought. On the whole, poems like "Strong Draughts" fit comfortably into the Emersonian-Nietzschean tradition of literary pragmatism, for they are governed by the idea that other minds can be turned to the uses of life. The emphasis they often place on refreshment and stimulus in hermeneutic encounters puts them in sympathy with the Goethe quotation Nietzsche used to introduce his essay on the dangers of having too much or too little historical consciousness: "I hate everything that merely instructs me without augmenting or directly invigorating my activity" ("Uses" 59). Like the Emerson who wrote the "Ode Inscribed to W. H. Channing," however, she could not easily translate the activity of her own ongoing reflection into more directly invigorating discourses like religion or politics. In Emerson's words: "I cannot leave / My honied thought / For the priest's cant, / Or statesman's rant" (*Poems* 117). Because the strong draughts she received through reading and proposed through writing never became prescribed courses of action, she never played the Gramscian role of organic intellectual or attached herself to anything like a Habermasian project of emancipation.

Dickinson's conversations resulted in few sociopolitical commitments, but this does not diminish their theoretical value as forms either of critique or of self-creation. Many of the most famous and popular poems feature a skeptical, inquisitive "I" and aggressively redescribe God, prayer, and church: "Some keep the Sabbath going to church -" (Fr236C); "God is a distant-stately Lover -" (Fr615); "'Heaven' has different Signs - to me -" (Fr544); "God is indeed a jealous God -" (Fr1752). There are many more, and they all help us understand how Dickinson interpreted herself and her culture through hermeneutic engagements with Christianity. But to see the way she also relied on a Vattimo-style friendship criterion for a notion of truth as self-creative conversational event, it helps to look at another kind of conversational poem, one that more explicitly addresses the question of how to converse with strong vocabularies. It is all well and good to converse with the vocabularies of one's cultural heritage, but what if they are unyielding and saturated with absolutes?

In the following poem Dickinson stages a meeting in the grave between one person who has died for beauty and another who has died for truth. The two figures meet unexpectedly but recognize each other as kinsmen with much in common and a lot to discuss:

I died for Beauty - but was scarce
Adjusted in the Tomb
When One who died for Truth, was lain
In an adjoining Room -

He questioned softly "Why I failed"?
"For Beauty", I replied -
"And I - for Truth - Themself are One -
We Bretheren, are", He said -

And so, as Kinsmen, met a Night -
We talked between the Rooms -
Until the Moss had reached our lips -
And covered up - Our names -

(Fr448)

Dominated by reported speech and conversational vocabulary—"questioned,"
"replied," "said," "talked"—this poem narrates the formation of a conversational "we." (The pronouns are in the singular for the first seven lines and
the first-person plural for the rest of the poem.) The private conversation
raises for readers the strong metaphysical question of what it means to live
and die entirely "for" something such as truth or beauty and opens up several, mostly Romantic possibilities: dying in the cause of, in place of, or in
order to save. Yet the two corpses' retrospective summations imply a degree
of self-criticism that is only reinforced by the choice of the term "failed":
they pursued unreachable Ideals; they were consumed by their devotion to
(the metaphysical essences of) Beauty and Truth; they neglected their other
duties. There is a hint that both figures have failed in Christian terms as well,
for they have not, after all, died for God.

Despite all this, the unnamed interlocutors' equanimity and politesse suggest that their failures have not resulted in a particularly remorseful afterlife.
Rather than leading them to disappointment and suffering, their de-transcen-
dentalizing experiences have prepared them for a good conversation, and
their near-simultaneous deaths and removals from the life of the community
make them cultural "Bretheren" in an avant-garde of weakening hermeneutic experience. True to his principle, the devotee of Truth starts by asking for
a truth: Why has the speaker "failed"? Hearing her answer ("For Beauty"),
he concludes with an absolute-sounding, Keats-echoing claim that Truth and

Beauty "are One." But this gesture of strong metaphysics instigates rather than ends the conversation, for to all evidence the point is neither conceded nor contested by Beauty's advocate. And crucially, the Truth devotee questions "softly," suggesting that the kind of truth for which he died was not rigid or absolute: his gentle manner opens an interpretive rather than a logico-deductive conversational space. Now truth will be a shared event.

If we accept this scene as an emblem of Dickinson's recognition that she was often surrounded by devotees of Truth but was nonetheless capable of conversing with them, and if we emphasize how she learned to apply her heritage interpretively in a reader-oriented poetry of friendship and conversation, then we avoid the hypostatizing errors inherent in trying to decide which ideas or values from her cultural inheritance she accepted or rejected. Rather than seek to quantify influences or chart the way she transcended or submitted, we can look and listen for the ways she questioned, interpreted, and transformed, and join our thought where we will to the process.

If some of the situations and speakers we have seen so far point up the overly abstract nature of the Rortian model of vocabulary choice, and others synopsize the breadth and philosophical value of conversations with people and texts, then another group poses an even more radical question: What if the language of the other cannot become accessible as a "vocabulary"? What if we cannot connect with our conversation partners at all? Is edifying conversation still possible? The following poem represents a reasoned response to the pre-conversational experience of being emotionally affected, and perhaps edified, by languages one does not speak. Unable to converse in any of the usual ways, the speaker works instead with the associations triggered in her mind by others who remain irreducibly other, a South Wind and an Emigrant:

> A South Wind - has a pathos
> Of individual Voice -
> As One detect on Landings
> An Emigrant's address -
>
> A Hint of Ports - and Peoples -
> And much not understood -
> The fairer - for the farness -
> And for the foreignhood -
>
> *(Fr883)*

I note first how clearly this poem participates in Vattimo's and Rorty's general projects. The self-effacing speaker is eager to "detect" new voices and languages, which she then experiences as a call for interpretation: How to explain the pathos she feels in their presence? Yet the scene also defies both men's philosophical approaches: the speaker cannot really "interpret" the wind or the emigrant's foreign language, for she cannot recognize or reconstitute anything like their "vocabularies."

The poem invokes two settings: the speaker standing in the North and feeling the South Wind—but feeling it as a voice she hears—and listening, in the border zone of a ship's landing, to an emigrant amid a mixture of languages both known and unknown. Instead of seeing the wind and emigrant as pioneering, risk-taking adventurers, she projects onto them feelings of homelessness and nostalgia. Her own "pathos" thus emerges from her sympathy with their supposed exilic consciousness.

If, like the Rortian ironist, Dickinson's speaker here runs the solipsistic risks involved in monological conversation, then several details reflect the great sensitivity and humility with which she pursues her thinking. The word "Emigrant"—when "immigrant" would be more likely, given the setting—contextualizes the other as "leaving from" somewhere rather than "arriving here," and this brings that unspecified elsewhere along with its connotations of mysterious "Ports - and Peoples" into the center of her thought while deemphasizing her own perspective. Similarly, the phrase "much not understood" in place of what could easily have been "not much understood" emphasizes the excess or greatness of what is beyond the perceiving mind, not the paucity of what is in it, and thereby opens the speaker outward to potential edification. Lastly, the care she takes to be propositional rather than definitive is clear from the indefinite articles and singular nouns: "A South Wind," "a pathos," "An Emigrant's," "A Hint" are less categorical than *The* South Wind, *the* pathos, and so on. Her comments might well be true of other encounters with the South Wind or emigrants, but she respects the contingency of *this* one.

Feeling how incapable she is of translating and conversing (scientifically, through perception?) with the South Wind or (cross-culturally, through translation?) with the emigrant, the speaker finds herself with an angst and a theoretical problem logically prior to those of the Rortian ironist. Rather than being faced with vocabularies to accept or reject, words or sentences to interpret, or information to try to access, she must explain why she has been so affected by voices that are poignant but semantically incomprehensible. In a technique with which we are growing familiar, she does this by dramatizing the movement from prose or near-prose (the first six lines) to lyric (the last couplet). Readers may respond very differently to the sudden flurry of feathery "f" and "r" sounds in "The fairer - for the farness - / And for the foreignhood," but it is hard to translate them into anything like a vocabulary in the Rortian sense. On the contrary, they *feel* more like the voice of a lyric emigrant being overheard on a prose landing, as if the speaker were experimentally applying lessons learned and creating a mellow coda (no noisy "p," "b," "k," or "t" sounds here) that translates her exilic wistfulness and nostalgia. Instead of trying to speak *for* the emigrant and the wind, that is—for example, by guessing at their thoughts or transforming them into components of a *paysage moralisé*—the speaker speaks *like* them. Such "speaking like" has something in common with the role-playing ironist trying on vocabularies but also takes place as a self-othering, self-distancing event. The speaker's words may be governed by a philosophical question—Why do I feel this pathos?—but she voices her reply in a language that is foreign and irreducible to thetic prose.

Of course, unmistakably co-present with the striking sound effects in the final couplet is the clear thesis that the speech of wind and emigrant owes its beauty to being foreign and from far away. With the words "farness" and "foreignhood" the speaker isolates, or perhaps creates, two stable categories for the associations her experience has triggered. Although both words seem forcefully metaphysical and essentializing, drawn from the long philosophical tradition of identifying permanent attributes, these adjectives-made-nouns are not ordinary essences like redness or truthfulness. On the contrary, the "essence" of being far and foreign is, precisely, to be unknowable: they are self-weakening, anti-essentializing essentializations. In the poem, the connotations of these words include the very kinds of distance and otherness (from prose, from local geography and weather patterns, from known, comfortable routines of thinking and speaking) highlighted by the lyric performance. The fact that the speaker has chosen to work with this paradox suggests that she "lyricizes" her thesis in the last two lines not in order to "redefine" herself as an "essentially lyric being" but to borrow the affective power of wind and emigrant *without* being forced to make the liberal ironist's problematically strong philosophical claim to redescriptive ability, that is, without attributing vocabularies to them that she might apply, however tentatively, to herself.

For Rorty and Vattimo, a voice or language without a recognizable vocabulary, metaphorical system, thesis, or narrative would be of little interest in a philosophical conversation. But for Dickinson, to lyricize the tensions and movements among radically different language games—private conversations, metaphysical essences, the Bible, voices of wind and emigrant—is to recreate the conditions for seeing and thinking the kinds of pathos that she experienced among them.

Thus far we have seen Dickinson's intellectual and artistic status as an ironist and weak thinker reflected in many places: the "insufficient" lyric in its preliminary American phase; the even more slender and unfinished version of it that she preferred; the characteristically weak or childish voices she used; her general attitude of hermeneutic humility and distrust of strong metaphysics; her use of tropes and other lyric effects; her reader-oriented, conversationalist poetics; her unheroic, noncompetitive poetic stance toward other writers and thinkers; and her unintoxicated reading of the Bible. In what follows we will see both how Dickinson became aware of herself as a site of intellectual conflict torn or traversed by competing language games and how she responded, with great intensity, passion, and creativity, by developing a "variorum" poetics that scattered her voice into myriad personae and vocabularies—all in order to help her think.

2

Trying to Think with Emily Dickinson

Why not an "eleventh hour" in the life of the *mind* as well
as such an one in the life of the *soul* – grey haired sinners are
saved – simple maids may be *wise*, who knoweth?

EMILY DICKINSON to her brother Austin (1851)

The *poet* promises merely an entertaining *play* with ideas,
and yet for the understanding there enures as much as if the
promotion of its business had been his one intention.

KANT, *Critique of Judgement* (1790)

We'll build Alms-houses, and transcendental State prisons,
and scaffolds—we will blow out the sun, and the moon, and
encourage invention.

EMILY DICKINSON in *The Indicator* (February 1850)

IN 1870, during their first meeting, Emily Dickinson told Thomas Wentworth Higginson that "if I read a book [and] it makes my whole body so
cold no fire ever can warm me I know *that* is poetry. If I feel physically as
if the top of my head were taken off, I know *that* is poetry. These are the
only way I know it" (L342a). A few such memorable remarks about how
poetry makes one feel, along with hundreds of lyrics celebrating ecstasy, awe,
and exhilaration, have led many readers to privilege emotional and physical
responses to her poems as well. If we throw in Dickinson's famous opacity,
we can understand why many have concluded that her affective force does
not always depend on clarity of thought or even intelligibility. "Thank you
for not being angry with my impudent request for interpretations," wrote
Helen Hunt Jackson to Dickinson in 1876 after receiving a cryptic verse
(L444a), and more recently Margaret Peterson has argued that Dickinson's

most "impassioned" poems can become "a series of ecstatic assertions, an abandonment to excess verging on mental unbalance" (500). In what follows, however, I argue the opposite case and portray her not as a mystic but as a serious thinker. In my view Dickinson provides fewer ecstatic assertions than careful sequences of ideas and images, not so much "abandonment to excess" as thoughtful production of, and reaction to, extreme states of being. My goal is to show how dominant she found the category of thought, how committed she was to certain projects of thinking, and why she needed lyric poetry to address them.

Though any poem can broadly be said to reflect thought, and the word "thought" was regularly used in the nineteenth century to signify a piece of prose or poetry, Dickinson often took it as a theme. To the extent that one can generalize, her poems represent thinking as rapid, uncontrollable, or self-contesting and associate it with power, extreme inner experience, fantasy, madness, pleasure, logic, and suffering. Some celebrate it—"Best Things dwell out of Sight / The Pearl - the Just - Our Thought -" (Fr1012)—and others recognize its risks: "If wrecked upon the Shoal of Thought / How is it with the Sea? / The only Vessel that is shunned / Is safe - Simplicity -" (Fr1503B). One group draws attention to the specific problems involved in expressing thought or clothing it in language: "Your thoughts dont have words every day / They come a single time / Like signal esoteric sips / Of the communion Wine" (Fr1476). An analytical cluster considers the mind's basic powers, size, and shape—"The Brain - is wider than the Sky -" (Fr598); "The Brain has Corridors - surpassing / Material Place -" (Fr407)—and a related set describes the wildness and weirdness of thought: "The Brain, within it's Groove / Runs evenly - and true - / But let a Splinter swerve - / 'Twere easier for You - // To put a Current back - When Floods have slit the Hills -" (Fr563). Others posit thought as sufficient, or almost, to provide happiness: "It's thoughts - and just One Heart - / And Old Sunshine - about - / Make frugal - Ones - Content -" (Fr362); "To make a prairie it takes a clover and one bee, / One clover, and a bee, / And revery. / The revery alone will do, / If bees are few" (Fr1779). Myriad-minded Dickinson thought of many ways to think about thought.

That it was a consistent as well as kaleidoscopic topic becomes clear if we look at the classic distinction between mind and body. According to the S. P. Rosenbaum *Concordance to the Poems* (based on the 1955 Johnson edition), the word "thought" occurs a total of 69 times in the poems, "think" 43, and "thinking" 6. "Know" occurs a staggering 230 times, "knew" 80, "knowing" 13, "knows" 31, and "unknown" 34, putting forms of this verb in a virtual tie with "do" (170), "did" (150), and "does" (45) for fourth most common, after "to be," "to be able," and "to have." "Mind" is used 79 times, usually as a noun, "minds" 9, "brain" 26, and forms of "consciousness" 40. By contrast the verb "feel" occurs just 39 times, "felt" 35, "feels" 16, and "feeling" 8. "Body" occurs only 10 times and "bodies" just once. Such statistics are partial and decontextualized but nevertheless tempt us to cut the Gordian knot and declare that Dickinson's poetry is a whole lot more about mind and thought than about body and feeling.

When did Dickinson start thinking seriously about thinking? The following extract from an 1846 letter to Abiah Root, written less than two months after she had turned fifteen, carries *in nuce* many of her mature traits, not least of which is the desire to force the mind to take on subjects like Eternity and her own death:

> Does not Eternity appear dreadful to you. I often get thinking of it and it seems so dark to me that I almost wish there was no Eternity. To think that we must forever live and never cease to be. It seems as if Death which all so dread because it launches us upon an unknown world would be a releif to so endless a state of existense. I dont know why it is but it does not seem to me that I shall ever cease to live on earth – I cannot imagine with the farthest stretch of my imagination my own death scene – It does not seem to me that I shall ever close my eyes in death. I cannot realize that the grave will be my last home – that friends will weep over my coffin and that my name will be mentioned, as one who has ceased to be among the haunts of the living, and it will be wondered where my disembodied spirit has flown. I cannot realize that the friends I have seen pass from my sight in the prime of their days like dew before the sun will not again walk the streets and act their parts in the great drama of life, nor can I realize that when I again meet them it will be in another & a far different world from this. (L10)

The problem is that Dickinson cannot successfully "think" death and Eternity, but cannot "not think" them either; the difference here is the Kantian one between being able to conceive of death but not to present it adequately in an image, even with "the farthest stretch" of the imagination. As she struggles with this predicament she reveals a mind that sifts clichés—friends will pass "like dew before the sun"—but is also relentless and uncompromising: "I cannot imagine . . . I cannot realize . . . I cannot realize . . . nor can I realize. . . ." Her tenacious mind stretches, fails, realizes it fails, regroups, rewords, and reaches its limit again. In increasingly figural language, she describes each new failure without ever arbitrarily changing the subject or leaping into the safety of faith, platitude, or fixed position. As we will see, many later poems are similarly restless and resourceful attempts to supply imagery for the thoughts and experiences that defy the imagination.

While Dickinson did not read Kant directly, this letter suggests that she shared his basic attitude both toward the self-contesting mind and toward the links between certain sequences of thought and the experience of beauty or the sublime. In fact, her struggle with the idea of her own death exemplifies his description of the mind's negotiation with "aesthetic" ideas. By an "aesthetic idea," he writes, "I mean that representation of the imagination which induces much thought, yet without the possibility of any definite thought whatever, i.e., *concept*, being adequate to it, and which language, consequently, can never get quite on level terms with or render completely intelligible" (175–76). Later, many poems will make use of a basic scene in the theater of the mind that recurs in the *Critique of Judgement*, precisely the one Lyotard parlays into a description of the postmodern condition. This scene reappears whenever the faculty of reason finds something conceivable and rational—infinity, death, the very large, the very small—and then demands that the imagination represent it fully and adequately in an image. The way the imagination tries and fails to satisfy reason's demand for the unpresentable triggers a flood of associations and can lead to pleasure, pain, and the soaring sublime.

For Lyotard, "*modern aesthetics* is an aesthetic of the sublime, though a nostalgic one" because it highlights the unpresentable as something missing or lost and thus laments the impotence of the mind to produce or represent presence; postmodern aesthetics, by contrast, shifts the emphasis away from nostalgia and instead takes both pleasure and pain in the way reason defies and exceeds presentation (*Postmodern* 81). In these terms, Dickinson's frustrated letter to Root is profoundly "modern" because it gnashes its teeth at the failure of the imagination to equal the concept. Nonetheless, the seeds of a Lyotardian postmodern aesthetic are visible in the repetition and intensity of the contest between reason and imagination.[1]

Because the beautiful occurs when a satisfying image *is* found and harmony reigns throughout the mind's faculties, the very possibility of experiencing the wildness of the sublime—to which, as we will see further in chapter 6, Dickinson was attracted—depends on this process of the imagination repeatedly trying and *failing* to produce the image required by reason. In such a situation, as Lyotard notes, the "obligation to which the imagination is subjected by reason does not only leave the imagination terrified, but gives it the courage to force its barriers and attempt a 'presentation of the infinite'" (*Lessons* 151). As a teenager, Dickinson already had the courage of the terrified mind; later, writing hundreds of poems trying to present the unpresentable—of death, ecstasy, God, Nature, thought itself—or to render its absence palpable, she would take up Lyotard's neo-Kantian gauntlet: "it must be clear" he says, calling on would-be postmodern artists, "that it is our business not to supply reality but to invent allusions to the conceivable which cannot be presented" (*Postmodern* 81). Dickinson's lyrics record that she invented and analyzed allusions to the conceivable but unpresentable, and her lifelong commitment to such difficult projects of thinking has its early origins in her schooling.

In fact, while it may be possible to ascribe Dickinson's self-awareness about thinking, and its later emergence as a central force in her poetics, to special psycho-biographical conditions—for Suzanne Juhasz, her "move into the mind can best be understood as occasioned by her social and psychological situation as a woman who wanted to be a poet" (*Undiscovered* 12)—it is also important to see it as a logical outgrowth and application of the lessons she learned from a pedagogical culture that prized experiments and observation in all things, including thought. In January 1847 Dickinson wrote to Root that she was "much interested" in the Silliman's *Chemistry* she was studying, a book that opens with a quotation from Francis Bacon: "Man, 'as the priest and interpreter of nature,' seeks to extend his experience by experiment. Every experiment is but a question addressed to nature, asking for an increase of knowledge" (L20, 2). It was the kind of empiricist message that saturated Dickinson's education; she probably heard it defended three months later at an Amherst College senior declamation on the "defense of the empirical philosophy and the present age" (April 7, 1847; Leyda 1:118).

We will look more carefully at Dickinson's exposure to academic philosophy in the next chapter. For now it is important to emphasize how thoroughly her teachers and schoolbooks assumed that Bacon's inductive methods of experimenting on the physical world applied to analysis of the mind. Thomas Reid's landmark *Inquiry into the Human Mind: On the Principles of Common Sense* (1764) helped establish this widespread cultural assumption: "Wise men now agree, or ought to agree in this, that there is but one way to the knowledge of nature's works; the way of observation and experiment" (11). Whatever we know about the human body we owe "to anatomical dissection and observation," and therefore "it must be by an anatomy of the mind that we discover its powers and principles" (12). The crucial point is that "anatomizing" the mind does not mean performing exercises in logic, critiquing freestanding doctrines and beliefs, or hypothesizing. It means analyzing mental chemistry, the basic elements of which are ideas and perceptions.[2]

Today Dickinson's poems are often considered "experimental" in the sense that they are formally creative, playful, or transgressive. But as the best studies of Dickinsonian experimentalism usually suggest—for example, Cristanne Miller on Dickinson's experimental grammar and Paul Crumbley on her experiments with the physical substructures of written language—she usually had thoughtful intentions for her formal experiments.[3] Some of these came from Dickinson's Baconian culture, which generally encouraged her to discipline, observe, and expand her mind's abilities, and some from specific books that taught her the method of thought experiments.[4] Many of these, like her later poems, involve astronomy and great amplitudes. Felix Eberty's 1850 work *The Stars and the Earth, or, Thoughts upon Space, Time, and Eternity* is a short book from the Dickinson library that attempts to expand the reader's mind through guided mental experiments that involve vast times and distances. Eberty takes the fact, not then widely recognized, that light travels at a finite speed and spins out a series of impressive consequences: if there were observers very far in space, they would be able to see ancient history, and if those observers were to begin approaching the earth, they would receive a sped-up visual history. Retreating again, they would be able to observe events—including natural events such as lightning—in slow motion. Eberty's book is a sustained attempt to generate new and adequate images—"perfectly intelligible" perceptions of vast ideas, an experience of beauty in the Kantian sense—on the basis of strenuous rational exercise, and his conclusions are dramatic: "We have here a perfectly intelligible perception of the idea of the omniscience of God with relation to past events" (18).

Still more detailed and culturally influential were the experiments recommended by Isaac Watts in *On the Improvement of the Mind*. Dickinson knew this book well, for it was a cornerstone of Protestant educational culture of the day, a textbook at the Amherst Academy, and a required preliminary text for admission to Mary Lyon's Seminary. Watts encouraged her skeptical, tolerant, empirical, and eclectic epistemological attitudes while also teaching her how to experiment with her mind (147). He urged students to conduct severe mental exercises in order to bring themselves to the limits of their own understanding: "Spend a few thoughts sometimes on the puzzling inquiries concerning vacuums and atoms, the doctrine of infinites, indivisibles, and incommensurables in geometry," he advises, "wherein there appear some insolvable difficulties: do this on purpose to give you a more sensible impression of the poverty of your understanding, and the imperfection of your knowledge. This will teach you what a vain thing it is to fancy that you know all things, and will instruct you to think modestly of your present attainments, when every dust of the earth, and every inch of empty space, surmounts your understanding, and triumphs over your presumption" (8). Students who engage in self-abasing self-scrutiny learn to develop mental qualities and abilities such as intellectual modesty, acuity, flexibility, discrimination, capacity, and reverence for God.[5]

Watts's chapter 16, "Of Enlarging the Capacity of the Mind," describes three things that especially "go to make up that amplitude or capacity of mind which is one of the noblest characters belonging to the understanding" (144). The first is when the mind "is ready to take in great and sublime ideas without pain or difficulty"; the second when it "is free to receive new and strange ideas, upon just evidence, without great surprise or aversion"; and the last when it "is able to conceive or survey many ideas at once without confusion, and to form a true judgment derived from that extensive survey" (144–55).

In the first category Watts recommends teaching students about the "infinite divisibility of space or matter" and leading them to recognize that "there are bodies amazingly great or small, beyond their present imagination" (147). Like Eberty he draws on astronomy—how fast the earth moves while standing still, how vast the celestial distances!—but unlike the scientists also cites poetry as an important source of mental expansion: reading lyrics improves the mind by expanding, elasticizing, and toughening it. He especially recommends Milton, Dryden, and Pope, for their "sorts of writing have a natural tendency to enlarge the capacity of the mind, and make sublime ideas familiar to it" (148). Poetry often deals in "vast and sublime ideas," and even when the topic of a poem "doth not require such amazing and extensive thoughts, yet tropes and figures, which are some of the main powers and beauties of poesy, do so gloriously exalt the matter, as to give a sublime imagination its proper relish and delight" (148). For anyone seeking to think about or "realize" sublime and unrepresentable topics, passages like these encourage serious consideration of poetry in general. And in the way Watts assigns "tropes and figures" a prominent role in cognitively negotiating those topics, we can glimpse a key assumption supporting Dickinson's preference for the hermeneutic and psychotherapeutic functions of poetry.

In fact, from this perspective it is but one step from reception to production, from reading to writing, to reach the mixture of mental experimentalism and lyric language Dickinson pursued in many poems.[6] Watts's version of the process by which the mind gains "a greater amplitude of thought" resembles Eberty's and Kant's: the imagination grows exhausted from experimenting and eventually cedes primacy to the rational intellect. But instead of reason succeeding and forming perfectly intelligible ideas and images (à la Eberty) or failing and producing the soaring chaos of the sublime (à la Kant), Watts's post-experimental mind becomes devout. "Fancy, with all her images," becomes "fatigued and overwhelmed in following the planetary worlds through such immense stages, such astonishing journeys as these are, and resigns its place to the pure intellect, which learns by degrees to take in such ideas as these, and to adore its Creator with new and sublime devotion" (137). The way the adoration of God is affirmed without demonstration in the very last clause gives a good idea of how *On the Improvement of Mind* usually links faith to reason. To suspend the Christian message does little to alter most of the book, and in fact a skeptical reading is invited by the clashing exhortations to humility and self-doubt on the one hand and self-reliance and self-certainty on the other: "fix not your assent to any proposition in a firm and unalterable manner, till you have some firm and unalterable ground for it," counsels Watts, while repeatedly warning that a "dogmatist in religion is not a great way off from a bigot" (29, 14).[7] He also foresees the danger of getting trapped within a single, favorite discipline: the student must look "abroad into other provinces of the intellectual world" (124–25). The general impression one draws is that Watts's student readers had both the inspiration to read and think widely and the intellectual breathing room to pursue their own experiments.[8]

The second native "narrowness of mind" is its inability "to receive new and strange ideas" (150). And how do we overcome this inborn condition, asks editor Joseph Emerson, guiding the student reader? Why, by "travelling, reading, conversation, and philosophical experiments" (150). One goal of these activities is to increase one's exposure to startling scientific, especially astronomical, facts and ideas. Watts goes so far as to affirm the existence of other habitable worlds in the universe and postulates that they are already "replenished with intellectual beings, dwelling in bodies" (153). Meditating on mental experiments like this, the student's "understanding" learns to "stretch itself by degrees," and ultimately becomes open-minded in all branches of learning (153).

Trying to "realize" an adequate image of her own death scene and imagine "what it would be like" to be in a state of endless existence, Dickinson's letter to Abiah Root is formally, if not topically, the kind of experiment in self-stretching that Watts and his followers recommended for mental improvement. It makes the mind the site of resistance, study, and experiment, uses Watts-style premises, objectives, and procedures, and ultimately produces the proto-Kantian results of failure, dissatisfaction, and repetition.

In Dickinson's letter, however, what is not yet joined to the coiling and uncoiling mental activity is an associated and analyzed emotional experience; she does not worry over the ways the try of thought is affecting her as she is thinking and rethinking, and does not explicitly reach either Watts's idea that the process of mind enlargement is necessarily difficult or Kant's point that it is not the object but rather "the cast of the mind in appreciating it that we have to estimate *as sublime*" (*Judgement* 104).[9] Nor does she reach the point of Jean-Luc Nancy's finite thinker, who seeks resources to negotiate reason's failure from within the acceptance of the failure. Nor, despite the obvious fact that the dewdrop cultural clichés are not satisfying the demands of her intellect, does she pour energy into new figural language to meet the extraordinary demands of reason. She just keeps trying to think, or rather to *realize*, this recurring verb being the best one she has for expressing a complex desire to imagine fully and translate understandingly something unpresentable into conscious life. The difference Dickinson intends between "not realizing" and "realizing" is the difficult one between acknowledging conceptually that one is going to die and seeing or imagining unveiledly that one is going to *die*.

This early epistolary example of Dickinson thinking only sharpens the question: Why did she later decide that lyric poetry was the best language game in which to pursue these most difficult projects of thought? What became of her understanding of mental experimentation, poetic language, and the relationships between them? To answer this it is necessary to look at the way she linked thought and poetry in her only sustained professional literary conversation, her correspondence with T. W. Higginson. This will help us bring into view a thinking Dickinson, recognize and interpret many poems as negotiated transcriptions of difficult experiments and projects of thought, and point the way to interpreting and learning from them.

As literary history has recorded in italics, on April 15, 1862, Dickinson responded to Higginson's *Atlantic Monthly* essay "Letter to a Young Contributor" by writing to ask, "Are you too deeply occupied to say if my Verse is alive?" (L260). This question was abrupt but not as cryptic as it now sounds; she was asking for his opinion of four poems, each of which uses playful imagery to present cosmic or existential settings and questions: "Safe in their Alabaster Chambers -" (Fr124); "The nearest Dream recedes - unrealized -" (Fr304); "We play at Paste -" (Fr282); and "I'll tell you how the Sun rose -" (Fr204). The only one of these not featuring children prominently is "Safe in their Alabaster Chambers -," and it displays "meek" members of the resurrection safely sleeping.

Beneath these poems' thematic youthfulness and placid surfaces, however, the gears of thoughtful metaphors and complex lyric effects are grinding. The whirring "ee" and "r" sounds cycling through the first line of "The nearest dream recedes - unrealized -" aurally enact the poem's superimposed narratives of frustration: a boy chasing a bee and a mind reaching for heaven. All four poems mobilize parallel perspectives (children/adult, alive/dead, unaware/aware), and these multiple frames open the poems to many interpretations. Dickinson's alive-or-dead question for Higginson thus draws attention to a depth of thought that might easily be missed when a professional critic encounters the work of a new poet. Perhaps a second look, she hints, will reveal how much thinking has gone into the figures of "gem tactics," "steadfast honey," and the poems that carried them.

Dickinson also justified her question by explaining why she could not answer it: "The Mind is so near itself – it cannot see, distinctly – and I have none to ask –" (L260). When the mind encounters itself, reads its own writing, or thinks about its own thinking, it is so self-obtruding that it casts a shadow on its own light.[10] This is the main reason Dickinson wrote to Higginson, and her next three questions, asking whether he thought the verse "breathed," whether she had made "the mistake," and whether he would tell her "what is true," all follow from the same epistemological predicament (L260).[11]

It is an acute problem because, as becomes abundantly clear in the rest of the Higginson correspondence (seventy-two letters extant from 1862 to

1886), Dickinson often thought of writing as thought and, more specifically, as thought's response to troubling emotion. "I had a terror – since September – I could tell to none," she explains in April 1862, "and so I sing as the Boy does by the Burying Ground – because I am afraid –" (L261). Two months later she notes that when "a sudden light on Orchards, or a new fashion in the wind troubled my attention – I felt a palsy, here – the Verses just relieve –" (L265). Dickinson almost never describes or explains her writing in terms of her formal or stylistic choices, historical period, influence, audience, literary movement, appropriateness of theme, or any of the specific and technical difficulties she faces in shaping and sharing experience in literary language. This silence is one reason why critics have had difficulty pinpointing her ideas about her poetic composition; another is that she prized two things that are hard to reconcile: cognitive lucidity and intense emotional experience.

More than anything else, she seems startled by the way Higginson answered her second letter with comments on form: her "gait spasmodic," her style "uncontrolled" (L265). Shouldn't he have said what he thought of her thinking, or explained how he could find "spasmodic" the same writing she hoped had "told it clear" (L265)? He is the one who had introduced, in his "Letter to a Young Contributor," the two-step compositional metaphor of thought first, language second. "Labor . . . not in thought alone," he had exhorted potential poets, "but in utterance; clothe and reclothe your grand conception twenty times, until you find some phrase that with its grandeur shall be lucid also." In response, Dickinson picks up the trope but eschews the inflationary rhetoric of "grand conceptions" and phrases "with grandeur." She worries little about whether her poems manage to think or say anything grandly interesting, true, profound, or original. But if she is not self-deprecating on those counts, she does wonder whether she has made plain the distinctions that she sees: "While my thought is undressed – I can make the distinction, but when I put them in the Gown – they look alike, and numb" (L261). This response prioritizes the thinking over the wording and shifts the whole process to a lower social class, "weakening" or humbling it: to put a common "Gown" on undressed thought is much less pretentious and elitist than trying a series of dresses on a "grand conception."[12]

In August 1862 Dickinson continued the conversation by sending him two more poems and asking, "Are these more orderly?" Immediately following this question she provided a remarkable, if surreptitious, demonstration of orderliness in thought and language: a thirty-four-syllable series of perfect iambics, punctuated in alternating trimeter and tetrameter (6-8-6-8-6), expressing a thorough self-analysis. "I thank you for the truth. I had no monarch in my life, and cannot rule myself; and when I try to organize, my little force explodes" (L271). Followed by the provocative (and still iambic) comment "I think you called me 'Wayward,'" these lines are an invitation to conversation if ever there was one, a poetic performance in prose that both "rules" itself and explodes. Recalling the investment in intimate conversation we saw in the last chapter—in poems such as "He was my host -"—this whole sequence fairly begs to be taken up, responded to, respected, and understood.

This is especially true since the two poems included in this letter are strong statements of camelistic self-reliance based on the power of the mind.[13] In "Before I got my eye put out -" (Fr336) the speaker prefers the pleasures of the imagination to the beauties of physical eyesight, and in "I cannot dance opon my Toes -" (Fr381B) the speaker has never received formal ballet instruction but enjoys the ultra-private art of mental dancing. The first and last of the five stanzas show how easily the latter poem can be read as a comment on the Higginson-Dickinson relationship and an apologia, based on anonymity, self-reliance, and mental "glee," for her obstinacy as an autodidactic student: "I cannot dance opon my Toes - / No Man instructed me - / But oftentimes, among my mind, / A Glee possesseth me, . . . // Nor any know I know the Art / I mention - easy - Here - / Nor any Placard boast me - / It's full as Opera -."

Sometimes poetry was something Dickinson did rather than made. Casting herself as a sailor and Higginson as one of her tools, a compass, she wrote: "If I might bring you what I do – not so frequent to trouble you – and ask you if I told it clear – 'twould be control, to me – The Sailor cannot see the North – but knows the Needle can –" (L265). She also reported to him that "Two Editors of Journals came to my Father's House, this winter – and asked me for my Mind – and when I asked them 'Why,' they said I was penurious – and they, would use it for the World – I could not weigh myself – Myself – " (L261). Again, as these last two comments and many poems suggest, her recurring quandary is that because her mind may not satisfy its own demands or understand itself or its products, it needs the expanded hermeneutic powers that come with conversation. Higginson functions as a long-distance supplement to stabilize a mental economy that cannot achieve self-sufficiency; the "Ignorance out of sight" she clarified later that summer of 1862, "is my Preceptor's charge –" (L271).

Despite being anxiogenic, thought is a constant and valued theme in the correspondence. Along with Dickinson's disdainful complaint about how her own "Mother does not care for thought" (L261), perhaps her most famous remark comes in a question reported by Higginson to his wife: "How do most people live without any thoughts. There are many people in the world (you must have noticed them in the street) How do they live. How do they get strength to put on their clothes in the morning" (L342a). For Dickinson this was a serious question: life without thought is not life. Later she exclaimed: "How luscious is the dripping of February eaves! It makes our thinking Pink –" (L450). And she repeatedly referred to Higginson's writing as thought too: "I had read 'Childhood,'" she tells him, referring to his essay by that name, "with compunction that thought so fair – fall on foreign eyes –" (L449).[14] She opens one letter with the comment, "Your thought is so serious and captivating, that it leaves one stronger and weaker too, the Fine of Delight" (L458)—"Fine" meaning the price or penalty—and comments in another, "I recently found two Papers of your's that were unknown to me, and wondered anew at your withdrawing Thought so sought by others" (L488). She flattered him with the conceit that she had "thought that being a Poem one's self precluded the writing Poems, but perceive the Mistake. It seemed like going Home, to see your beautiful thought once more, now so long forbade it –" (L413). She then summed up their shared faith in the primacy of thought with this rhetorical question: "Is it Intellect that the Patriot means when he speaks of his 'Native Land'?" (L413). In 1869 she told him that to her a letter always feels "like immortality because it is the mind alone without corporeal friend"; while talking commits us to "accent" and "attitude," there is a "spectral power in thought that walks alone" (L330).

Perhaps most impressively, in the spring of 1876 Dickinson wrote to Higginson after reading two anonymous essays in *Scribner's Monthly*: "I inferred your touch in the Papers on Lowell and Emerson – It is delicate that each Mind is itself, like a distinct Bird –" (L457).[15] She had caught him out! In a twenty-four-year relationship marked by Dickinson's decorous diffidence, this confident interpretation of her friend's mental signature stands as proof of their intellectual kinship and her perspicacity. And finally, in the last month of her life, Dickinson wrote to tell him, "I have been very ill, Dear friend, since November, bereft of Book and Thought, by the doctor's reproof, but begin to roam in my Room now –" (L1042). She knew he would understand how important "Book and Thought" were to her.

It must be noted that this was not a one-way relationship. Higginson, for his part, also spoke of writing as thought and clearly understood and appreciated that thinking and solitude were essential to Dickinson's life.[16] At one point he tells this "dear friend" that he sometimes takes out her letters and verses, and when he feels their "strange power," it is hard to write to her (L330a). She enshrouds herself in such a "fiery mist" that he feels "timid lest what I *write*"—he italicizes *write* to suggest that he could do better face-to-face—"should be badly aimed & miss that fine edge of thought which you bear" (L330a). He continues: "It is hard [for me] to understand how you can live s[o alo]ne, with thoughts of such a [quali]ty coming up in you & even the companionship of your dog withdrawn. Yet it isolates one anywhere to think beyond a certain point or have such luminous flashes as come to you – so perhaps the place does not make much difference" (L330a). Critics have made much of the difficulties Higginson had in understanding Dickinson, but the truth is that they understood each other very well, not least because so much of their conversation was about thought and literary writing understood as thought.[17]

One group of poems shows Dickinson experimenting with a new generic shape for the lyric and using it to help push the "fine edge" of her thought "beyond a certain point." The express purpose of what I call her "try-to-think" poems is to force the mind to do something extremely difficult, often radically redescriptive. While much lyric poetry can generally be said to think through and express trauma, I nonetheless find these poems distinctive for the way they wrestle with Kantian aesthetic ideas, seeking to satisfy reason's insatiable demand for a complete image, narrative, or understanding of a difficult idea or experience. The try is usually sustained and serious, the verb "think" transitive, the goal of thinking explicitly stated, and the emphasis placed squarely on the willful movements of thought. The speaker in these poems usually tests and tries to transform her own mind using a wide variety of tools, and the resourcefulness of her consciousness makes virtually every poetic element interpretable as contributing to the overriding try.

As we will see in chapter 6, the 1882 "Of Death I try to think like this" (Fr1588) is exemplary for the way its thinking is written into the poem's fabric; deputized and fused in the try's service is a wide array of signifying strata including words, moods, figural elaborations, dashes, spaces, sound patterns, narratives, memories, and allusions. "The nearest Dream recedes - unrealized -" (Fr304B) is also a try-to-think poem, one of a large group trying to think immortality and eternity. With each word, mark, sound, image, and idea pressured so heavily, these poems reward close reading and can be understood as especially concentrated doses of Derridean-style bricolage. In the way they stage the mind attempting to satisfy, improve, or quiet itself, try-to-think poems sometimes also have a try-to-*believe* quality. In the 1863 "I think To Live - may be a Bliss," the word "may" should be emphasized in the first line; then the whole first stanza sets the terms for another thought-defying thinking:

> I think To Live - may be a Bliss
> To those who dare to try -
> Beyond my limit - to conceive -
> My lip - to testify -
> (Fr757)

In the rest of the poem the speaker tries to become, through the power of self-persuasive and self-transforming thought, one of the hypothesized "those" who live blissfully because they "dare to try" to conceive beyond her own "limit." Lastly, as these brief examples suggest, try-to-think poems are precisely sequenced, if difficult, thought experiments. Even as they represent conversations within isolated selves, they invite readers to (try to) repeat their steps and monitor the results.

The 1863 "I tried to think a lonelier Thing" (Fr570) exhibits all of these features. It is not the only poem in which Dickinson tried to understand that unique exposure of the self to infinity and emptiness that she often called loneliness, but it is an important one.[18] "Wherever Emily Dickinson's mental processes may have led," Albert Gelpi has written, "they began with an intolerable sense of emptiness which drove her to project as concrete evidence of her incompleteness the loss of childhood, father, mother, lover" (69). But those categories of concrete evidence are missing here, for the poem treats a case so extreme that it cannot be rendered intelligible or tolerable through traditional kinds of loss:

> I tried to think a lonelier Thing
> Than any I had seen -
> Some Polar Expiation - An Omen in the Bone
> Of Death's tremendous nearness -

I probed Retrieveless things
My Duplicate - to borrow -
A Haggard comfort springs

From the belief that Somewhere -
Within the Clutch of Thought -
There dwells one other Creature
Of Heavenly Love - forgot -

I plucked at our Partition -
As One should pry the Walls -
Between Himself - and Horror's Twin -
Within Opposing Cells -

I almost strove to clasp his Hand,
Such Luxury - it grew -
That as Myself - could pity Him -
Perhaps he - pitied me -

19] He - too - could pity me -

(Fr570)

One understands why the 1890s editions of Dickinson's poetry all passed this poem over, as did every other one until *Bolts of Melody* in 1945.[19] Despite its advertised attentiveness to the movements of the mind, it is hard to know how to interpret even its most basic gesture of trying to think. Is it, as the bold opening line suggests, a romanticized Wattsian exercise in mind enlargement, a proactive, virtuoso attempt to conceptualize an extreme human possibility? Or is it, as I have come to think, a more reactive attempt to use language, argument, and other mental tools to redescribe the painful conditions into which the poet has been thrown? I think the main purpose of this poem and many others is not to invent or define an extreme experience but to deal with it once it arrives, to knead it, battle it, alter it, realize it, or just survive it through thought.[20]

"I tried to think a lonelier Thing" poses a second problem: it does not give what it seems to promise: a full story of what and how "I tried to think." Although it begins in a reassuring past tense that makes us anticipate a clean resolution, we are ultimately deprived of critical distance. There is no dialectical click to end this uncompromising and uncomfortable poem, no final stanza beginning "Then loneliness despaired of me / and vanished into blue." This poem that begins so actively with a try ends in a painful stop-motion picture, a paralytic image of "almost" striving. Indeed the only thing still moving is thought itself, represented in this poem not as patient, observant, analytical, meditative, or argumentative but as creative, tenacious, and desperately involved.

The poem begins with a rapid series of thoughts (lines 1–6), then slows down with a tangential, almost conversational remark (lines 7–11), then ends with two evenly paced narrative stanzas (lines 12–19). Yet while the fast-slow-medium pacing rhythmically suggests balance and order, the intellectual and emotional atmosphere is uncertain and volatile throughout. Among other things, the speaker trying to think reaches for a glossary of nervous vocabulary: "tried to think," "probed," "borrow," "Haggard comfort," "Clutch," "plucked," "pry," "almost strove," "clasp," "Perhaps." There is no strong metaphysical confidence in that family of hesitant, grasping, uncertain terms.

What exactly does thought do when it "tries" to think? The poem's first line represents an attempt to will or define loneliness into the category of "thing," a hypostasizing gesture Dickinson uses to enable preliminary linguistic access to an otherwise unspeakable loneliness, roughly on the model of the assertive but mysterious "'Hope' is the thing with feathers -" (Fr314). The speaker then tries to find a clearer name for the "Thing" being thought, and we see right away both how important indexing can be in a serious try of thought and how much this particular lonely feeling defies nominative language. Constrained by reason to present it in an image, the mind provisionally generates two quiddities (lines 3–4), two tries, that is, at something more precise: the first is "Some Polar Expiation" and the second "An Omen in the Bone / of Death's tremendous nearness -." [21] These two molecules of intellection, so different yet suggestive—"drained" or "strangely abstracted" as David Porter would say—initially suspend the try of thought in doubtful parataxis.

How are they related, and how do they help the speaker think? First, "Some Polar Expiation" shows the mind leaping to a traditional kind of lonely undertaking, a cleansing process of soul-searching in which one divides, objectifies, despises, and ultimately rejects some part of the self. [22] This is not only more precise than thinking of a lonely thing; it is more purposeful, religious, moral, conventional, and self-directed as well, all of which suggests that specific cultural forces are pressuring the try of thought. Were it not for the frigid adjective "Polar," the idea of performing an expiation or atonement might actually seem consolatory, a painful but useful work. But by punning on polar expedition and exploration, the speaker emphasizes the unforgiving, epic, arctic, limits-of-the-civilized-and-natural-world connotations of the enterprise.[23]

In short, "Polar Expiation" expresses something like the feeling of being radically and painfully removed from one's natural surroundings, culture, and self. This second vision of the loneliest thing complements, improves upon, or perhaps replaces the first; and it is no longer retrospective and inward-looking but anticipatory: an "Omen in the Bone / Of Death's tremendous nearness -." This portent is felt rather than witnessed or imagined; suddenly death seems tremendously near in time (the speaker feels close to her death) and space (another dead soul or spirit is there, nearby). These feelings are self-alienating, too, but no longer lustrating. One does not willfully create omens for oneself in the way one examines, analyzes, and repents one's past acts. The omen of death "in the Bone" is received unexpectedly, from without, and remains to be interpreted.

The unlike options of expiation and omen might suggest that the poem is experimental in a playful sense, a game of how much loneliness would a lonely woman think if a lonely woman could think loneliness. Yet the care with which those two metaphorical clauses were chosen makes me think instead that the try of thought they represent is dead serious, an attempt to think a thought unspoken in surrounding cultural conversations. The reaching, creative motion of the mind is made evident by nonspecific articles: "*Some* Polar Expiation, "*An* Omen in the Bone." The reasonable, calculating, self-defining loneliness felt by a self undergoing "expiation" complements— or perhaps intensifies, if we think of them together—the unreasonable, incalculable, dispersive loneliness of a self thinking of death. Taken together, in fact, these tropes and figures for different extremes represent imagination's bold attempt to present hideous loneliness to reason, and amount to a basic set of loneliness-generating possibilities: the flash-glimpses of being coldly removed from one's past self (through expiation) or from one's present and future self (in death.)

Even as they name and hypostasize two of the most self-annihilating kinds of thought, the two phrases remain semantic placeholders, self-consciously inadequate way stations the speaker uses as she climbs toward the unreachable summit of a thought she can only try to think. And the deeper problem is that however brilliantly and succinctly she manages to bring a painful emotion into metaphorical language, she does not, for all that, palliate it. So that is what she tries to do next. Having put forth unstable but generative imagery, she surprisingly proceeds to reach into the world of the dead for a kindred spirit: "I probed Retrieveless things / My Duplicate - to borrow -." Since her duplicate qualifies only on the basis of also being "Of Heavenly Love - forgot -," the core idea is that somebody already dead has been, like her, rejected by God. The verb "probe" registers a tentative optimism—as it does, we will see, in the poem "Shall I take thee, the Poet said" (Fr1243)—for the speaker is neither "groping aimlessly" nor confidently "taking hold."

This makes it clear for the first time that the "lonelier" idea/feeling the speaker is trying to think is not just existential and inexplicable but derives from her catastrophically alienated ontological status. The idea that a rare and special loneliness was reserved for God's forgotten was a recurring thought for Dickinson,[24] one clearly expressed, for example, in this commiserating 1850 letter to Abiah Root:

> *You* have stood by the grave before; I have walked there sweet summer evenings and read the names on the stones, and wondered who would come and give me the same memorial; but I never have laid my friends there, and forgot that they too must die; this is my first affliction, and indeed 'tis hard to bear it. To those bereaved so often that home is no more here, and whose communion with friends is had only in prayers, there must be much to hope for, but when the unreconciled spirit has nothing left but God, that spirit is lone indeed. I don't think there will be any sunshine, or any singing-birds in the spring that's coming. (L39)[25]

In "I tried to think a lonelier Thing," the conative technique of borrowing one's "duplicate," or imagining a fellow "unreconciled spirit," is meant to mitigate the unique loneliness of the nonbeliever. The chief interest of this mental replication seems to be that it creates ex nihilo the smallest possible unit of imagined community. For some postmodern readers in a time of weak thought, this may represent a profoundly anti-consolatory—and perhaps therefore credible—form of consolation: a self thinking of another absent and possibly imaginary self, a copy-self or twin ontological orphan, has at least that chance of existence outside the self, of relationality with another. Strikingly absent from the speaker's fantasy are people from her own communities or characters from her reading; loneliness this extreme precludes the kinds of solace that might be found in Susan Gilbert Dickinson, Jane Eyre, or the prisoner of Chillon.

This leap into the radically unknown, anonymous, hypothetical, single other is not a full statement of method, but it is constructive. It serves as the founding premise for the rest of the try at thinking, and from it, somehow, a "Haggard comfort springs." This announcement interrupts the past-tense narration of what the speaker has felt and announces instead a general law, one that moves the poem into the thinking present and perhaps universalizes it. (Of course, in order to feel included and therefore relieved by the "Haggard comfort," a reader must also be "Of Heavenly Love - forgot -.") Yet the precise claim given lawlike properties is not easy to see:

> A Haggard comfort springs
>
> From the belief that Somewhere -
> Within the Clutch of Thought -
> There dwells one other Creature
> Of Heavenly Love - forgot -

The difficulty is that the phrase "Within the Clutch of Thought" is precariously ambiguous. It means reachable by thought, just within the power of thought, or else composed solely of thought, purely imaginary. The undecidability is important, painful to the speaker, and one can easily make the poem pivot upon it: since one cannot know that one's duplicate "dwells" somewhere, one must (try to) take it on faith. This is the difference between a Romantic misery-loves-company logic and the more desperately self-defeating awareness that one is fabricating one's own source of comfort.[26]

Negotiating those two possibilities, the last two stanzas of the poem are an uneasy endgame that relates the speaker's two attempts to do something constructive on the basis of the preceding thoughts: "I plucked at our Partition -." This Partition is the invisible, enigmatic, absolute line separating the speaker from her imagined duplicate: the line between life and death.[27] Crucially, it is "our" rather than "the" Partition, the collective pronoun revealing the obstinacy of the speaker's thought and signaling her determination not to relinquish the infinitesimal sense of community that she has captured or created. A "conversational we" has been formed, a communion of souls however imaginary or weak, and the Partition they share is thus both bridge and barrier between a live, thinking, trying consciousness and a hypothesized dead twin.

This poem is trying to realize, in the Dickinsonian sense discussed earlier, a terrifyingly solipsistic condition. The physical and visual activity of plucking at the Partition only makes us more aware of the impossibility of reaching across it. Like other Dickinson images of awkward, unnatural responses to intolerable conditions, it is extremely disconcerting and registers more failure than success. One thinks of the desperate bird in "Of Course - I prayed -" (Fr581) stamping her foot "on the Air" in protest to God's indifference. To feel something of the futility registered by the simile "As One should pry the Walls - / Between Himself - and Horror's Twin -," one need merely picture oneself thinking of one's own dead "duplicate" and plucking in the air (as opposed to more hopeful gestures like extending a hand).

It is no less unnerving if the speaker's actions are taken as a metaphor for movements of the mind; on the contrary, plucking would then join the series of probing retrieveless things and "borrowing" one's posited duplicate to form a trio of mental procedures desperate enough to be a symptomatology of unfathomably sickening loneliness. Indeed, the basic communicability of the poem's try hinges on the reader's willingness to identify with and follow a process of despairing thought well beyond where thinking would ever wish to go. While many readers may refuse, not recognizing or believing in this extreme loneliness, those who have come to trust Dickinson may go deeply into the experiment.

The result is a postmodern scene of two God-forsaken souls even more chilling than Beckett's *Godot*, in which, however bleak their circumstances, the two alienated characters at least share real conversation and a physical space. Since, in Dickinson's fantasy of estrangement, one person is alive and the other imaginary or dead, the job of the last stanza is to narrate the way the living speaker comes to accept and even enjoy being part of a carceral community stripped to the atomic minimum:

> I almost strove to clasp his Hand,
> Such Luxury - it grew -
> That as Myself - could pity Him -
> Perhaps he - pitied me -

The mirroring twins are connected only by a fantasy of mutual pity, but somehow this self-consciously pathetic vision results in a feeling of "Such

Luxury -." We see that it was the purpose of the original try of thought to produce this mental drama of a virtual community and make it credibly intelligible as a consolatory grace earned by thought alone. This feeling of luxury, this awe on the human trinket, would thus grow out of the confidence produced by the experimental force of thought itself; in fact, rereading the poem, I hear the implied but elided phrase "to think" in the middle of this last stanza: "Such Luxury - it grew [- *to think*] / That as Myself - could pity Him - / Perhaps he - pitied me -." That is what I think the poem is saying and the poet is thinking. Or at least trying to think, for despite the past tense, this is surely a fragile state and a momentary victory: How long can meditating on one's dead duplicate continue to console? Will this thought experiment not ultimately reinforce one's loneliness and return one, worse off, to the intolerable and ineffable loneliness one felt before trying to think it?

In this as in every other try-to-think poem, we do not know if Dickinson succeeded or even thought she succeeded in thinking what she tried to think. We know only that many of these were poems in which her speakers tried to help or save themselves by representing their own efforts to help or save themselves. Such trying, pragmatic poems invite us to join and repeat their thinking about and beyond thinking, but in the case of "I tried to think a lonelier Thing," we join, paradoxically, only at the risk of experiencing a loneliness we cannot sound.

If "I tried to think a lonelier Thing" is a Baconian thought experiment, a question put by the speaker to human nature and pursued in order to discover, express, and analyze extreme ontological and emotional conditions, then "Shall I take thee, the Poet said" analyzes the relationship between thinking and writing poetry. Unlike Poe's *Philosophy of Composition*, which reduces every stage of poetry writing to a rationalistic science, or Elizabeth Barrett Browning's *A Vision of Poets*, which does not address compositional questions at all, this poem portrays the process of word choice as the central paradox in the forward movement of thought and writing. Not only does it dramatize the poet's thinking about words and thought, but also it represents an excellent example—nearly a defense and illustration—of the variorum poetics for which she has become famous among postmoderns:

> Shall I take thee, the Poet said
> To the propounded word?
> Be stationed with the Candidates
> Till I have finer tried -

The Poet searched Philology
And was about to ring
For the suspended Candidate
There came unsummoned in -
That portion of the Vision
The Word applied to fill
Not unto nomination
The Cherubim reveal -

4 Till] *preceded by* <A>   4 finer] further • vainer   5 searched]
probed   6 was] just • when   8 There came] Advanced

(Fr1243)

Told in the past tense with a strong narrative line, this "try-to-think-of-a-single-word" poem has several features that lend it the feel of an epic or drama. It begins in medias res in the mental theater of a poet writing a poem at the climactic moment of choosing a single word. The opening image of a lone, authoritative, creative consciousness together with a single "word" naturally recalls the ur-scene of origins in Genesis: "In the beginning was the Word, and the Word was with God, and the Word was God," reads Dickinson's King James Version (1:1). In the poem there follows a suspenseful quest for a grail-word and, at the end, a deus ex machina in the form of a new "Vision." Since the poem self-reflexively describes the writing of one specific poem, it invites the interpretation of being the story of its own origins. Yet the ultra-specific encounter between a single word and a single poet also has a tremendous emblematic value: what is in play is not a poet, any poet, or poets as a group, but "the Poet," not a word, any word, or all words, but "the word." It is as if the speaker were using the writing of one poem and the choosing of one word to invoke, if not resolve, more abstract problems such as the passage from Idea to Matter, formlessness to form, chaos to order, spirit to body, uncertainty to certainty, plurality to unity, thinking to saying, secret to public.

Together these elements place the piece in a mythic, hero-based, conflict-driven register. Keeping this in mind, along with the word variants in the manuscript—few but very important—I will reinterpret and re-narrate the whole poem. My goal is to follow the acts of the speaker-poet who is trying to think and self-observe under difficult circumstances, that is, trying to find words for thought when the topic is itself "finding words for thought."

In generating an implied narrative and tone, I mean to join the speaker's thought, converse with it, and render explicit some of its underlying questions and sequences:

In the beginning were the Poet and the word. It was not clear to the Poet where the word had come from, but there it was, eager to be part of the poem She was creating. She considered the candidate-word carefully but, as had happened many times before, could not be sure that it was the best one. So, courteously, firmly, and without explaining why, She told it to wait with the other applicants while She thought things over. Then, to generate other nominees, She looked in reference books, etymological dictionaries, gazetteers, newspapers, history books, volumes of poetry, and many other places. She looked anywhere and everywhere, sometimes desperately rummaging, sometimes probing methodically in the places where She thought the best word might be, if in fact it existed. But the quest was fruitless, for no word proved better than the candidate she had been holding in suspension. Ready to give up, and not wanting to leave the poem unfinished, She reluctantly prepared to ring the bell.

Just then something unexpected and wonderful happened: the vision that had inspired and guided Her suddenly became clearer and brighter. Again, the Poet could not say how it happened, where the new vision came from, or why; She had not been fully conscious of it while sifting and comparing the words. Perhaps, She thought, the long process of seeking new word-nominees had changed Her thinking and somehow, imperceptibly, altered Her vision? But that did not seem exactly right, since the renewed vision arrived only after the word-seeking attempts had failed. But then why should failing to find the right word have produced a new vision, unless by demonstrating negatively that She had been trying either to express the ineffable or to find words that did not exist? In the end she felt that the new vision had not come from thinking at all. It seemed heaven-sent. She could testify to, but not explain, the miraculous fact that her vision had been suddenly transformed.

This interpretive embroidery raises several questions: Why does the "portion of the Vision" that comes "unsummoned in" turn out to be the one the candidate-word originally sought to fill?[28] And why did the "Vision" renew itself right when the poet was about to ring for the disappointing candidate?[29] Is it that the "Vision" dialectically adjusted itself to accommodate the word? Or is it rather that, unfertilized by the word, the Vision developed parthenogenetically and sprang full-grown into the Poet's mind? The speaker makes us very suspicious and eager for an answer, but absolutely refuses to decide whether poetic composition is a process of "discovery" or "invention," that is, whether or not the renewed vision came about as a direct result of trying to think. There is no *post hoc ergo propter hoc* fallacy: one searches for a word, and then the Vision does or does not come, and that is all one can say.

Why would a poet with Dickinson's experience—over twelve hundred poems by this point—write a poem about word choice without saying something more positive or constructive? The answer may lie in the play of the three agencies mediating the relationship of thought to writing in this poem: word, poet, and vision. The word, personified as a job-seeking candidate, has the ability to stay hidden or show up out of the blue, appearing before the Poet as something "propounded" from somewhere. The vision acts like one of the Homeric gods: it is peremptory yet inexplicably self-transforming; it comes and goes "unsummoned," flashes suddenly from absence to presence, and any laws it may obey are obscure. The mediating Poet has the power to search, probe for, take, reject, and suspend words, but is seemingly powerless over the vision, and does not even know how it is guiding her writing: she does not explicitly refer to it as she looks through philology for the word she needs. This Poet represents neither of the Godlike artists cherished by the Western tradition, the classical craftsman-wordsmith in rational control or the Romantic originator of unique self-expression. On the contrary: the Godlike artist evoked at the poem's outset gives way to a scrambling, dictionary-flipping, weak-thinking, postmodern variorum-consciousness standing passively and uneasily at the intersection between words and visions.

The poem's attention to two time frames helps clarify this ambiguous creative position. The first is on the order of a split second: the Poet is at one specific point, in one specific poem, choosing the next word. Since this process can take anything from no time (with no demand on the Poet's thought) to longer than a lifetime (an extravagant demand), the second temporality is longer and potentially infinite. The impression of writing as an ongoing, aleatory, and expectant activity like Nietzschean self-creation is reinforced by the poem's complete silence on such driving questions as how or why to begin or end a poem, how long it takes, or what was wrong with the suspended candidate in the first place. "Shall I take thee" thus represents a defiant test case for Barbara Herrnstein Smith's taxonomies of poetic closure: at the start of the poem, the "poem within the poem" is already under way; at the end, the rest of it remains to be written. Nor can we be sure what kind of identity or difference there is between the "frame" and the "embedded" writing.

Thinking and creating in the extremes of the manuscript's times and spaces, dependent on the fickle divinity vision, the kind of Poet profiled here will sometimes find herself halfheartedly settling for the least unpromising term.[30] When we read that the "propounded"[31] word is "stationed" with other "Candidates," we cannot help but look to the manuscript page, and there they are, all equally (non)present and (un)authoritative, complementary, competitive, and metrically equivalent: the candidates for *this* poem, the one we are reading, not the one we are reading about.

"Shall I take thee" is thus itself a thought propounded, another lyrical description of thinking about thinking, and its close attention to word choice raises the kind of question central to the next three chapters: Where does Dickinson get her vocabulary, and what does she do with it? Indeed, why does the Poet turn to "Philology"? Is it an accident that this poem is so Latinate, polysyllabic, erudite, and past-participled? The uses Dickinson made of the word "philology" in other poems suggest that it synecdochizes distractingly inessential information, and here too it seems impotent. As the variants make clear, the Poet can *probe* for words (that is, methodically seek and analyze them), or *search* for them (that is, rely on random coursing through sources), or even try "finer" methods, but none of these procedures is given the upper hand, and none grants any more direct contact with the "Vision" than does the speech flung at the heavens in "Prayer is the little implement."

Like disappointment in the limitations of prose and rational thought, then, disappointment in philology seems to be another necessary initiating condition for Dickinson's poetry. This poem's speaker makes it clear that even though what she needs only seems to come "unsummoned," her habitual instinct and first recourse is hermeneutic: to *read*, to search her linguistic heritage. And although she can offer no reasoned argument why this might produce or enhance the visions that visit her, as a Baconian thinker, observer, and experimenter she can testify to the patterns that have emerged in her consciousness over years of writing. So she will turn to "philology" to help with this poem, and the next one too, and trust that somehow, each time, her vision will be mysteriously altered. Such a consistent wager on hermeneutics, on the power of philology to produce miraculous redescription, encourages Dickinson's readers to try to understand each of its three phases: the search for the contexts and manners in which a poet acquires words and ideas; the disappointment in the existing vocabulary to express or reshape one's vision; and the poems that result from trying to think in these conditions.

3

Dickinson and Philosophy

I must analyse, / Confront, and question . . .

ELIZABETH BARRETT BROWNING, *Aurora Leigh* (1856)

I heard long since at school that Diogenes went to sea in a tub.
Though I did not believe it, it is credible now.

EMILY DICKINSON to Elizabeth Carmichael (1884?)

A GREAT MANY of Emily Dickinson's nearly two thousand poems and
one thousand letters can be interpreted as philosophical fragments in
the early-nineteenth-century Athenaeum tradition of German Romanticism.
That was a time, Philippe Lacoue-Labarthe and Jean-Luc Nancy remind us
in *The Literary Absolute*, when the very idea and destiny of literature was
linked to that of the short philosophical text, when "the union of poetry and
philosophy" that had been "postulated and called for" since Plato and Aristotle was realized with new intensity (13). Nancy and Lacoue-Labarthe are
mainly concerned with figures such as the Schlegels, Novalis, and Schelling,
but much of Dickinson's writing likewise takes place as both a philosophical
and a poetic act. Each lyric can be read as carefully closed upon itself and
delimited from the others and the world—like the miniature, self-enclosed
"hedgehog" work of art Friedrich Schlegel described in Athenaeum frag-
ment 206—and each also converses with a wider cultural and intellectual
heritage.

Academic philosophy was an important part of Dickinson's inheritance.
She met with it in textbooks, sermons, poetry, fiction, literary journals, news-
papers, and conversation. There were hybrid literary models such as Martin
Tupper's ultra-popular *Proverbial Philosophy* or Carlyle's *Sartor Resartus*
and quasi-philosophical commentary strewn across the cultural landscape.
"Thought may be first written in an unintelligible jargon," opined Edwin

Whipple in an 1859 book of literary criticism from the Dickinson library, "in Benthamese or Kantese, for instance; but every Bentham finds his Dumont, and every Kant his Cousin" (11). Period fiction abounds in snapshots of philosophical arguments and positions, usually accompanied by entailments for faith or politics. To take but one example of a book Dickinson read carefully and enjoyed in February 1849: *Picciola: The Prisoner of Fenestrella; or, Captivity Captive* opens with the Count de Charney having "set aside the doctrine of innate ideas, and the revelation of theologians, as well as the opinions of Leibnitz [sic], Lock [sic], and Kant" (Saintine 8). He resigns himself instead to the "grossest pantheism" and "unscrupulously" denies God, his brain inspired with "the conclusion that the world is a conglomeration of insensate matter, and CHANCE the lord of all" (8). The plot unfolds in parallels between his gradual release from physical and from philosophico-spiritual imprisonments.[1] By the end he has learned, through careful observation of a flower and conversation with a friend, that there is a contradiction in Locke "since he rejected the doctrine of innate ideas, and seemed to admit the possibility of intuitive knowledge" (217). De Charney's heart is "purified" and, in his "expanded mind," "mild and consolatory ideas" now succeed one another in "gentle gradation" (226). Dickinson called this book a "wondrous, new companion," and the fact that her cousin William Cowper Dickinson sent it to her suggests that he understood and encouraged her philosophical leanings (L27).

So many philosophical controversies, personalities, and doctrinal positions were summarized, fictionalized, and otherwise retailed within Dickinson's circumference that a critic cannot hope to trace them all. This is especially true since the decade separating the end of her formal schooling and the beginning of her writing poetry—from the late 1840s to the late 1850s—was a time in which America exploded with writing, and Dickinson read and thought constantly. Yet, since her poetic bricolage depended on the acquisition and comparison of disciplines and discourses, the time she spent studying, conversing, and reading in her teens and twenties was an important prolegomenon, and we would like to know as much as we can. In this chapter I examine her exposure to philosophical givens and describe some of the ways she conversed and created with them. I do so not in order to suggest that they are the "origin" or "cause" of the open poetics, conversational hermeneutics, try-to-think poems, or other signature traits we have seen, but to say something about how Dickinson's thinking and experimental poetics took shape conversationally.

. . .

It turns out not to be easy to summarize Dickinson's "philosophical givens." For one thing, the dates are no accident in the title of Bruce Kuklick's book *The Rise of American Philosophy: Cambridge, Massachusetts, 1860–1930.* Historians of American philosophy move quite briskly through the early part of the nineteenth century, for most think Emerson was right when he said in "The American Scholar" in 1837 that the country's "sluggard intellect" had thus far deserved credit for nothing more than "exertions of mechanical skill" (53). Today the story almost always goes that, dating back to before the Revolution—to John Witherspoon's introduction of the subject to the College of New Jersey in 1768—American philosophy was a weak and sub- missive handmaiden to religious orthodoxy. Instead of being a sign of philo- sophical vitality, the textbooks on "mental" and "moral" philosophy that flew off the presses starting in the 1820s were derivative echo chambers shot through with associationism, faculty psychology, Locke's empiricism and materialism, and the Scottish Common Sense philosophy of Thomas Reid, Dugald Stewart, and Thomas Brown. "Though the Scottish texts furnished the models and inspiration for the new American academic orthodoxy," sum- marizes Herbert Schneider in his classic book on the history of American philosophy, "a flood of American texts appeared, all on the same general pattern" (209). "Between 1827 and 1860 the number of textbooks on mental philosophy proliferated as quickly as did the colleges," confirms Rand Evans (43). Indeed, for two generations after 1810, complains Harvey Townsend, "there were few contributions to philosophical literature, but innumerable textbooks, outlines, and commentaries" (101). Terence Martin decides that this unthreatening "philosophy of containment" and all its "furniture of the mind" was simply something "Americans and America lived through" (11), and Schneider pointedly suspects that the Scottish Common Sense philoso- phy dominating American schools was introduced in order to make "reason a moral sedative," that it was "administered in our colleges in excessive doses by the clergy in the hope that it would be an antidote to the powerful stimu- lants of the experimental sciences" (217). He finds the "literature of Scottish common sense in America" to be "dull" and "pedantic," nothing more than a meretricious attempt to put "antiquated dogmas" into Common Sense gift wrap and Common Sense itself into "the academic garb of science" (217).

Contemporary thinkers now wonder how any of this so-called thinking could ever have been important or compelling. Nobody even earned a phi- losophy Ph.D. in an American institution until Charles Fraser MacLean in

1866 at Yale. There had not been a truly original thinker in the country since Jonathan Edwards, and would not be another—unless you resort to counting Emerson—until the age of Peirce, Royce, Dewey, and Santayana. Nothing significant happened in American philosophy until the Transcendentalists and the St. Louis Hegelians started seriously transplanting German and French ideas in the 1830s, and (although they were interesting) their impact in the academy was virtually nil. Naturally, one can assume that at ultraconservative colleges like Amherst during Dickinson's lifetime it was *absolutely* nil.

This kind of talk makes it very difficult to recover and understand Emily Dickinson's philosophical training. On the one hand, few historians or philosophers today waste their time studying the "innumerable" books of the first half of the nineteenth century, and on the other, literary critics who have studied Dickinson's poems of mental experience or written her into her culture have avoided her readings in philosophy.[2] On historical grounds alone the subject deserves to be integrated into the critical conversation on Dickinson. As we will see, it also shows par excellence how she wove a strong metaphysical discourse into a hermeneutically humble poetics of weak and conversational thought.

The story about fetid American philosophy is sometimes told as a backdrop to the (more heroic) hybrid philosophico-religio-literary one about the origins of American Transcendentalism. German Idealism began crossing the Atlantic in the 1810s–20s, this one goes, just in time to help a generation of young, ambitious Americans like Channing, Emerson, and Parker break out of the Lockean materialist philosophy in which they and their spirituality had long been confined. (*The Cambridge History of American Literature* relates this with a chapter titled "The Assault on Locke.") The metaphysics of Kant and his speculative followers such as Fichte and Schiller were interpreted, distorted, and funneled through texts and translations by Madame de Staël, Coleridge, Victor Cousin, James Marsh, and Thomas Carlyle in such a way as to provide a new intellectual basis for combining rational inquiry into nature, God, and life with high spiritual feeling. By the end of the nineteenth century, Kant, Hegel, and the rest of German metaphysics had earned a solid place in the American academy and the long-lingering prestige of British empiricism and the Scottish Enlightenment had been erased, with the Scotsman James McCosh at Princeton (president from 1868 to 1888) being the last dinosaur holdout.[3]

Dickinson's philosophical background is complicated because it recapitulates much of the convulsive intellectual experience of nineteenth-century New England. Exposed first and robustly to the principles of Scottish Common Sense and British empiricism, she was well positioned geographically, intellectually, and temperamentally to register the liberating speculative energies gathered and released by Transcendentalism as well. Thus, although many poems reflect tensions and mixtures between different philosophical vocabularies, in this chapter I look first at Dickinson's exposure to mental and moral philosophy before moving at the end of the chapter to a consideration of how her outlook might have been affected by the more German-inspired metaphysics.

Within Dickinson criticism there is the added problem that the first direct answer to the question of Dickinson and philosophy was also one of the most authoritative, influential, and negative: the "'Mental Philosophy' recited by a girl of fifteen from Upham's manual cannot be taken seriously." So wrote Stephen Whicher in his 1938 biography (47), and Dickinson biographers and critics have followed his lead so unanimously that it is necessary to examine in detail why he thought that.[4] His main assumptions seem to have been that philosophy was too difficult, too esoteric, and simply not intended for students that young or that female.

In nineteenth-century American universities and colleges, the disciplines of mental (or intellectual) and moral philosophy (the categories are Scottish) were routinely taught by the president, always also a clergyman, often only to the senior class as the capstone or *summum* of their education.[5] Even when it was not taught by the president, the prestige of the discipline conferred on its professors an elevated status both in their institutions and in the communities where they often also preached: in the 1840s Henry Boynton Smith turned down a professorship in rhetoric at Amherst, but he could not refuse a subsequent offer in mental and moral philosophy (Dwight 799). It was therefore a significant symbolic shift—one lengthily lamented by William Tyler in his history of the college—when Amherst president Heman Humphrey stopped teaching it in the mid 1830s.[6] Later presidents resumed the practice.

As acidly noted by Schneider, the main reason the disciplines of mental and moral philosophy were seen as so important was that they gave rational support to Christianity. The "mental" science of thinking preceded and grounded the "moral," and this was an especially important nexus at Christian colleges like Amherst, where the majority of graduates became preachers or missionaries. As Nathan Welby Fiske, Professor of Mental and Moral Philosophy at Amherst from 1836 to 1847, summarizes in his lecture notes:

"*Natural* philosophy you begin with; then mental; then moral; last moral, here higher responsibilities. Ignorance *here* not safe. Educated men that *not only do right,* but rooted in *principles.*"[7] At Amherst, educated men did right because their Christianity was rooted in Lockean and Scottish doctrines.

The following chart of senior-year requirements for Amherst's academic year 1862–63 shows the relative importance of mental and moral philosophy. (There are a total of 522 Dickinson poems extant from the years 1862 and 1863.) The numbers refer to "exercises," three required each weekday and two over the weekend:

Senior Year

Mental and Moral Philosophy	204
Geology	57
Constitutional Law	54
History	58
Butler's Analogy	48
Rhetoric	39
Elective Studies	36
Mineralogy	24
Natural Theology	18
Political Science	12
Zoölogy	11
Bible Lectures	9
	570

That is a tremendous amount of mental and moral philosophy, and one can understand why historians such as George Paul Schmidt, Martin, and Kuklick portray it as something like a nationalized ideological indoctrination.[8] "Custodian of the truths essential to civilization, the philosopher-president conveyed them to young men who would assume leadership on the East Coast," writes Kuklick (*History* 73). By the same token, since it was meant for seniors at all-male Christian colleges, one can easily assume that the discipline was too imposing, masculinist (recall Whicher's "girl" of fifteen), and abstruse to be meaningful for female teenagers interested in poetry. Inaccessible in almost every way, it comes across as nearly a pure form of Vattimo's domineering metaphysics, a promulgator from on high of precisely the kind of rigid "doctrines" Dickinson disliked.

Such an impression is only reinforced by the detailed posthumous assessment Tyler gives of Fiske's teaching style:

> As a general fact, he was liked by Juniors more than by Sophomores, and by Seniors better than either; and individual students, not exactly loved, perhaps, but honored and valued him just about in proportion to their love of learning, truth and holiness. The learning of Prof. Fiske was exact rather than comprehensive. He was too clear, discriminating and positive in his opinions both in theology and philosophy, to be a universal reader or even a patient and impartial student of either of these departments. But what he did know he knew thoroughly— what he believed he believed with all his mind and might—what he loved he loved with all his heart, and therefore could teach with rare skill and power. Faith in the providence of God and in the gospel of Christ was the controlling principle of his life. To please and honor God, his Maker, Redeemer and Sanctifier, was the chief end of every labor. (296)

Above and beyond the cultural misfit of gender, age, and scholastic preparation, it is all too tempting to assume that Dickinson's creative intellectual personality and restless spirituality differed so much from Fiske's unimaginative exactness,[9] self-certitude, and sanctimoniousness—Edward Hitchcock Jr. recalled him as "repulsion inspiring"—that she could have learned but little from him or his mental-moralizing successors at the college (Leyda 1:xlvi).

Such a conclusion oversimplifies the way the austere discipline actually presented itself—as part of the college, the town community, her own schooling, and the culture of New England. To appreciate its embeddedness in these fabrics, it helps to begin with a list of the Amherst professors of mental and moral philosophy, the years they taught, and a few details of their relationships with Dickinson and her family.

1835–36. Edwards Park, Professor of Mental and Moral Philosophy. One of the boldest and most liberal Protestant theologians throughout the 1840s and 1850s, Park maintained strong ties to Amherst and returned frequently. Dickinson reacted enthusiastically to a sermon he delivered in Amherst in November 1853: "We had such a splendid sermon from that Prof Park – I never heard anything like it, and dont expect to again . . ." (L142).

1836–1847. Nathan Welby Fiske, Professor of Intellectual and Moral Philosophy. Fiske's daughters Helen (the future Helen Hunt Jackson) and Ann were the same ages as Emily and Lavinia Dickinson, respectively, and Hitchcock considered Mrs. Fiske "totally different from the Professor" (Leyda 1:xlvi). Ann and Lavinia were extremely close as children, and as adults Helen and Emily grew very close too, mainly through correspondence. (In an 1886 letter to Higginson following Jackson's death, Dickinson quotes from Heman Humphrey's 1848 *Tribute to the Memory of Rev. Nathan W. Fiske* [L1042].) The Fiske materials in Amherst's Frost Library are an important aid to understanding how mental and moral philosophy was taught at Amherst. They include detailed lecture notes and a book of questions that he used to organize his course, "published at the request of the senior class" in 1842 by Amherst publishers J. S. & C. Adams, and show that his teaching was based mainly on Reid, Stewart, Upham, and Brown.[10] In an 1850 review of Humphrey's *Memoir of Nathan W. Fiske*, Samuel Harris sums up Fiske's philosophical position as a Common Sense, empiricist hardliner:

> Prof. F. belonged to the school of the Scotch philosophers. Having a mind remarkably discriminating, capable of the keenest analysis and of the most concentrated attention, he could not fail to be eminent in his department. He was intensely Baconian, building his philosophy on the most rigid induction of facts. With that class of speculatists who, during his active life, began to attract attention in this country, of whom we may select as the representative, R. W. Emerson—that Endymion of philosophy, beautiful dreamer courted by moonbeams—with these he had no sympathy, we may almost say, no patience. As objects of a similar feeling, he seems to have grouped together the peculiar views of the Arminians and of Coleridge, the various forms of what is loosely called transcendental philosophy, and all the speculations which are wont to stigmatize the results of induction as "warehouse collections of mere physical facts." (75)

1847–1850. Henry Boynton Smith, Professor of Mental and Moral Philosophy. "Professor. Smith. preached here last Sabbath & such sermons I never heard in my life. We were all charmed with him & dreaded to have him close" (Emily to Austin Dickinson, February 17, 1848, L22). Smith studied in Halle with Hermann Ulrici and Friedrich Tholuck, "whose friendship for him," notes Timothy Dwight in a *New Englander* review of his wife's 1881 memoir *Henry Boynton Smith: His Life and Work*, "became very strong and continued until the close of their lives" (796). He then studied in Berlin under Johann Neander and Ernst Wilhelm Hengstenberg before coming to Amherst. He contributed articles on German philosophy—Kant, Hegel, and others—to the *New American Cyclopaedia*, edited by George Ripley and Charles Anderson Dana, and published a series of books articulating a Christocentric theology: *The Relations of Faith and Philosophy* (1849), *The Nature and Worth of the Science of Church History* (1851), and *The Idea of Christian Theology as a System* (1857), among others. Walter Conser describes Smith as one of America's important antebellum practitioners of "mediational theology," that is, thinkers who drew from German theology to uphold the unity of religion and science.

1850–1858. Joseph Haven, chairman and Professor of Intellectual and Moral Philosophy. In 1858 Haven published the widely used textbook *Mental Philosophy* (figure 1) and is ranked by Schneider second only to McCosh as the "most persistent exponent of the Scottish tradition" in America (550). To look through Jay Leyda's *Years and Hours of Emily Dickinson* is to see this Common Sense philosopher regularly visiting the Dickinsons, chatting with Lavinia, throwing large parties, and holding lectures to which the Dickinson children were invited. In June 1852 Emily credited him with helping Amherst grow "lively." In 1853 he came to tea and served with Emily's mother as one of the three Fine Arts Committee members for Amherst's Fourth Cattle Show. In July 1856 he conducted the wedding ceremony for Austin Dickinson and Susan Gilbert. In 1858 Emily sent a note to Joseph's wife, Mary, asking to borrow two De Quincey volumes that had been checked out of the college library. In an 1859 letter to Mary, Emily remarks that the Dickinson family has "hardly recovered laughing from Mr Haven's jolly one," a joke he must have sent in a letter (L200). After Haven accepted the position at Congregational Seminary in Chicago in July 1858, Emily kept up, through Mary, a warm correspondence with the family.

1854–1876. William Stearns, Professor of Moral Philosophy and Christian Theology and president (1854–1876). Emily and Austin knew Stearns's son Frazar, an Amherst College student. His death in the Civil War struck them both deeply and occasioned the poem "It dont sound so terrible - quite - as it did -" (Fr384).

1. *Advertisements for books, including Dickinson family friend and Amherst College professor Joseph Haven's* Mental Philosophy. *From* Annual of Scientific Discovery; or, Year-book of Facts in Science and Art for 1858, *ed. David Wells (Boston: Gould & Lincoln, 1858).*

1858–1890. Julius Hawley Seelye, Professor of Mental and Moral Philosophy (1858–1890) and president (1876–1890). Seelye was an 1849 graduate of Amherst and a close friend of Austin his entire life; like Smith he studied philosophy at Halle (1852–53). In his classes he used two nationally prominent books written by his uncle Laurens P. Hickock that he helped revise and edit: *A System of Moral Science* (1853) and *Empirical Psychology; or, The Human Mind as Given in Consciousness* (1854). Hickock himself moved to Amherst in 1868 and enjoyed a vigorous retirement until his death in 1888. Dickinson saw Seelye preach in Amherst's First Church on February 6, 1858 (on the topic of "Predestination"), after which she wrote the letter to the Havens in which she famously said, "I do not respect 'doctrines,' and did not listen to him, so I can neither praise, nor blame" (L200). The comment speaks both to her anti-metaphysical attitude and to her loyalty to the recently departed Haven. Leyda reports that Seelye's daughters counted a total of seventy-five letters from Emily Dickinson before they burned them.

So much "small-town" contact with the Amherst philosophy faculty vitiates the conclusion that Dickinson was daunted by the elite status of either the discipline or its local exponents. But as philosophico-intellectual mediators, the Amherst students were surely at least as inspirational and effective. Between 1845 and 1862 the college graduated a total of 711, just under 40 per year, and the Dickinson family had relationships with a significant percentage of them.[11] Some were family friends, some worked in Edward Dickinson's law firm, some worked at the Amherst Academy after their graduation, where they interacted with the Dickinson children and their friends. Mental and moral philosophy dominated their last year of study, and the students' minds and conversation naturally included it.[12] It is no surprise to see Emily Dickinson's cousin William Cowper Dickinson borrowing Upham from her family library three years after his graduation; the subject was meant to outlast the classroom. In June 1849 Austin himself gave a public dissertation titled "Mind Developed in Action."

Such events were in the nature of things, for the New England of the 1830s and 1840s in which Emily's generation was raised was extremely attuned to minds and mental process. One can even speak of an obsession with it that includes but transcends the Baconian mental experimentalism examined in chapter 2.[13] The Transcendentalists had done much to spur speculative thinking about thinking, most emblematically, perhaps, in the way Emerson celebrated "Man Thinking" in "The American Scholar." Interest was also raised by ongoing attempts at refuting or reconciling such forces as Locke, the Scots, the Transcendentalists, and German theologians and philosophers. Other developments included publications such as Sampson Reed's influential 1826 work *The Growth of the Mind* (which inspiringly replaced the passive, combinatory, Lockean model of the mind with an organic and developmental one) and the rise of phrenology, physiology of the mind, and mesmerism.

A key point of contention was the unity between Christianity and Scottish Enlightenment philosophy. In Dickinson's lifetime this bond came under pressure from liberalizing thinkers of many kinds, but throughout much of the century it remained cherished and championed in Amherst by leading figures such as Fiske, Smith, Haven, Stearns, and Seelye. Historians of American intellectual history generally consider the first explosive fracture in the Scot-Christian coalition to be the dissent published in 1829 (the year before Dickinson's birth) by James Marsh in his "Preliminary Essay" to Coleridge's *Aids to Reflection*. Marsh audaciously argued that American Christianity had in fact been *perverted* all along by British empiricist and Scottish Common Sense philosophy:

> It is our peculiar misfortune in this country that, while the philosophy of Locke and the Scottish writers has been received in full faith, as the only rational system, and its leading principles especially passed off as unquestionable, the strong attachment to religion, and the fondness for speculation, by both of which we are strongly characterized, have led us to combine and associate these principles, such as they are, with our religious interests and opinions, so variously and so intimately, that by most persons they are considered as necessary parts of the same system; and from being so long contemplated together, the rejection of one seems impossible without doing violence to the other. (quoted in Good vi)

As James Good notes, Marsh's writings were a "watershed in the history of American thought" and a decisive step "toward the emancipation of American philosophy from its complete subordination to theology" (vi). Even basic vocabulary was destabilized: "In the years following Marsh's edition of Coleridge," notes *The Cambridge History of American Literature* on the publication of *Aids to Reflection*, "people rushed to apply the [new] distinction between the Reason and the Understanding to every knotty problem that had perplexed them" (2:355).[14] Upham, for example, suddenly mentions Kant and Coleridge, specifically in order to refute their unwarranted use of the word "reason" (135).[15] And throughout the 1840s, Amherst's Fiske sought to destroy the heresy by asking his students a series of leading questions:

> State the distinction famous as having been made by Coleridge between
> *The Reason* and *The Understanding*.
> Is it anything more than a discrimination between two varieties of
> judgment?
> How important is such a distinction? (42)

"Not very" was the only correct answer.

Publications on subjects such as psychology, physiology, and mesmerism also spurred interest in the mind, as one sees in the writings of Poe or Hawthorne, and starting in the early 1830s Lorenzo and Niles Fowler brought national prominence to phrenology. Its mixture of brain, mind, and self-improvement ultimately won converts, including Horace Greeley, Henry Ward Beecher, and Walt Whitman. (The beleaguered Fiske also responds to mesmerism and phrenology [65–66].) Perry Miller in *The Life of the Mind in America: From the Revolution to the Civil War* even finds great intellectuality in the camp revivalism of the period.

In fact, the long tradition of writing about "the New England" and "the American" minds that culminates in Miller existed as a branch of the antebellum search for national identities in culture and politics. Local instances of mind-mania during the time when Dickinson was finishing her formal education include the lecture "Mental Culture as the True Local Policy of New England," given in Northampton on August 9, 1848, by Rufus Choate and covered by Samuel Bowles for the *Republican* (Leyda 1:150). On April 7, 1850, Edwin Whipple addressed a lecture to the Amherst Literary Societies with the title "The American Mind." On February 18, 1852, Emily wrote to inform Austin that there were "a good many lectures here now, before the Lyceum," and five days later the topic was "Is the reading of fictitious works beneficial to the human mind?" (Leyda 1:237).

Three further examples will help illustrate how imbued Dickinson's circle was with the specific language of mental philosophy. When her good friend George Gould, editor of the Amherst College student paper *The Indicator*, jestingly described her 1850 prose poem–Valentine epistle, he demonstrated easy familiarity with the discipline: "Now this is, after all, a very ingenious affair. If it is not *true*, it is at any rate philosophical. It displays clearly an inductive faith; a kind of analytic spirit, identifying each independent truth, and fixing it as a primary essence, which the author had known, and felt" (Leyda 1:169). Induction, analysis, verification of independent truths grounded in individual experience and thought: this synopsis of mental philosophy's prevailing combination of empiricism and Common Sense cannot be confused with speculative or Idealist theories trading in hypotheses, a priori foundations for rational thought, or intuitions of the divine mind. In a more serious vein, albeit with a subterranean try at humor, Austin relies on the language of mental faculties in a letter he wrote in December 1850 to Susan Gilbert after learning from her of a "crisis in our sentiments." Intermittently capitalizing abstract nouns (a habit his sister would make famous), he describes himself being visited by his depressing "old companion Reflection," with "memory, officious to remind of all done amiss in the Past—with Imagination, ready to predict the Future" (Leyda 1:185). And Emily herself showed how comfortable she was with the going platitudes about the improvement of one's mental faculties. "You are reading Arabian Nights," she faux-moralized to her brother the day after she turned seventeen. "I hope you have derived much benefit from their perusal & presume your powers of imagining will vastly increase thereby. But I must give you a word of advice too. Cultivate your other powers in proportion as you allow Imagination to. Am not I a very wise *young lady?*" (December 1847, L19). As both of them knew, the faculty of combining ideas (imagination) had to be developed *proportionally* with reason, memory, judgment, and other mental powers. Otherwise, as Watts had informed their whole generation, "where the genius is bright, and the imagination vivid, the power of memory may be too much neglected, and lose its improvement" (Watts, *Improvement* 167).[16]

This brings us to Dickinson's education. Along with her sister Lavinia, she entered Amherst Academy for the fall term beginning in September 1840. She attended until spring 1847, then studied at Mary Lyon's Female Seminary (now Mount Holyoke College) in South Hadley from fall 1847 to spring 1848. Richard Sewall comments that if "ever there was a blossoming period in her life, full and joyous, the years at the Academy—seven in all, with a few terms out for illness—were it" (337). Among the textbooks we would expect—algebra, geography, arithmetic, grammar, Latin—there were also many related to philosophy, a broad term then evolving from "natural" philosophy to the more mental, intellectual, and moral kinds. Among the academy's books were Francis Grund's *Natural Philosophy*, Levi Hedge's *Logick*, Lord Kames's *Elements of Criticism*, Upham's *Intellectual Philoso-*

phy, Watts's *Improvement of the Mind*, John Abercrombie on the *Intellectual Powers*, and Francis Wayland's *Moral Science*. Dickinson's family library also contained a number of standard philosophy books, including Locke and Thomas Brown.[17]

As the book list suggests, the schools took the subject seriously. In 1841 a letter to the *Northampton Courier* praised the quality of the Amherst Academy student recitations in two subjects: botany and "Intellectual and Moral Philosophy" (Leyda 1:71).[18] And in 1845, at the age of fourteen, Dickinson also spoke enthusiastically about it, putting it first in a breathless description of her school subjects: "We have a very fine school," she wrote in a lengthy letter to Root. "I have four studies. They are Mental Philosophy, Geology, Latin, and Botany" (L6). As the Root letters show so well, the experience of witnessing her friends die or undergo religious conversions had brought forth the deepest questions in her mind, and she had already begun thinking about them in a disciplined way.

Many of the school's textbooks include exhortations to the kind of mental Baconism we saw in the last chapter. In his introduction to Abercrombie, Jacob Abbott encourages students to write out "additional illustrations of the principles brought to view,—illustrations furnished either by the experience or observation of the pupil, or by what he has read in books." Writing such exercises,

> especially if they are derived from your own experience, will have another most powerful effect. They will turn your attention within, and accustom you to watch the operations and study the laws of your own minds. Many pupils do not seem to understand that it is the powers and movements of the immaterial principle within their own bosoms, which are the objects of investigation in such a science. . . . A perfect system of Metaphysical Philosophy might be written, with all its illustrations drawn from the thoughts and feelings of any single pupil in the class. (23–24)

There is every reason to believe that Dickinson shared the assumptions about the value of mental philosophy that caused so many books to be published and led so many educators to include them in school curricula.

If Whicher underestimates Dickinson's willingness and ability to study mental philosophy, then he also does little justice to the philosophers themselves, who did what they could to tailor their products to teenagers. The full title of the Amherst Academy's Upham text reads *Elements of Mental Philosophy, Abridged and Designed as a Text-Book for Academies and High Schools.*[19] In fact, many of the philosophy books available to Dickinson and her peers were adapted—not to the detriment of lucidity—from more prolix works, and are not impenetrably technical treatises.[20] Their basic distinctions and arguments are illustrated with examples from everyday life and lie well within the grasp of an eager and able student. Most combine the materialist philosophy of Locke with the Scottish Common Sense philosophy of Thomas Reid;[21] and to the extent that Scottish ideas were widely understood to uphold their faith, churchgoing students (an overwhelming majority) would have been prepared for them.[22] In another negative description of the way collegiate philosophy was taught, Kuklick reveals a further reason why these books had to be clear and comprehensible: "The philosophers at these colleges provided their pupils with a moral sense of their place in the world. The endeavor was socially justified but intellectually thin because the first responsibility of academics was not understanding the cosmos but coaching schoolboys in provincial academies" (Kuklick, *History* 58).

Fiske, coach par excellence, asks in his lecture notes, "Why is it that most persons need to cultivate especially the habit of looking into their own minds?" His answer is limpidity itself: "Because the very circumstances of life tend to promote habits of attention to external objects, & hinder *reflection*— constant outward changes *turn us off* from *looking within*" (box 2, folder 3). Besides validating the solitary, self-reliant, and thoughtful practices that Dickinson would eventually and sometimes devilishly make her own, this discipline promised an epistemological holy grail: a "method of readily reading the lessons from our own inward experience." So, at least, wrote Laurens Hickock, author of the popular textbook used at Amherst College by family friend Joseph Haven (*Empirical* 17).[23] And although the habit is hard to acquire, investigating one's own "mental facts" is not a chore. On the contrary, it is fun:

> The organs of sense must be shut up, and the material world shut out, and the mind for the time shut in upon itself, and made to become familiar with its own action. The man must learn to commune with himself; to study himself; to know himself; to live amid the phenomena of his own spiritual being. When this habit of intro-spection has been gained, the investigation of mental facts becomes not only possible, but facile and delightful. (17)

If the question is raised about the value, in no-nonsense, ultra-pragmatic nineteenth-century America, of forcing youth to shut up their organs of sense in order to pursue "metaphysical inquiries," then the pedagogues' first answer would be that turning the mind away from the "external and visible creation" and back upon itself increases one's "power of attention and abstraction," a skill of "great value in all the pursuits and occupations of life" (14). There is also the obvious benefit to mental athleticism and stamina. "Metaphysical studies are intended as a sort of intellectual gymnastics," says Abercrombie, very suggestively if one thinks of Dickinson's poetry. They should be neither too easy nor too difficult but nearly equal to the powers of the pupil, "so as to call them into active and vigorous exercise" (16). Most of all, however, young people needed metaphysics for the moral reasons that later philosophers so disparage. A "close connection exists between our intellectual habits and our moral feelings," asserts Abercrombie before adding, in an argument tested by many Dickinson poems, that while we have "little immediate voluntary power over our moral emotions," we *do* control "the intellectual processes with which these are associated." Thus "we can direct the mind to truths, and we can cherish trains of thought, which are calculated to produce correct moral feelings; and we can avoid or banish mental images or trains of thought, which have an opposite tendency. This is the power over the succession of our thoughts, the due exercise of which forms so important a feature of a well-regulated mind: its influence upon us as moral beings is of still higher and more vital importance" (234).

Asking how much and what kind of "power over the succession of our thoughts" we really have is a good way to begin understanding the importance of mental philosophy to Dickinson.[24] Books in the tradition of Scottish Common Sense philosophy rely on the model of a sound, healthy, or "well-regulated" mind that reflexively generates and accepts basic concepts. Upham, for example, argues that the ideas of "personal identity" and "Self-existence" "flow out . . . from the mind itself; not resulting from any prolonged and laborious process, but freely and spontaneously suggested by it. . . . We cannot look, or touch, or breathe, or move, or think without them. These are products of our mental nature too essential and important to be withheld" (126). The model holds true for moral philosophy: there are "First Truths" or "primary articles of moral belief," says Abercrombie, that "arise by a natural and obvious chain of sequence, in the moral conviction of every sound understanding." To demonstrate them does not require "any process of reasoning, properly so called," because the conviction "forces itself upon every regulated mind" (42). Similarly, the "*Moral Principle*, or *Conscience*," is, "in every mind in a state of moral health," the "supreme and regulating principle, preserving among the moving powers a certain harmony, to each other, and to the principles of moral rectitude" (53). The harmony guaranteed by the healthy conscience—the "due exercise of which forms so important a feature of a well-regulated mind"—is evidenced in the control one has over the "succession" of one's thoughts (234).

It was easy for many thinkers to point out that thoughts "succeed" one another in time, and Upham was still sounding a common note when he said that there were patterns to the way they do—"our thoughts and feelings, under certain circumstances, appear together and keep each other company"—and even when he added that these processes of "association" were governed by observable laws: "circumstances under which the regular consecution of mental states . . . occurs" (152–53). But it was not at all easy to identify those general laws or taxonomize the rules by which certain ideas, in certain circumstances, provoke, inspire, attract, or otherwise lead to— these verbs convey the problem—certain others, nor to understand the role of human volition in the process. Thus mental philosophers spent much of their time observing and analyzing the logic of "association," the sequences of events external and internal to the mind, and identifying patterns and causal structures among them.

Modern associational analysis began with Locke. In the fourth edition of *An Essay Concerning Human Understanding* he added the chapter "Of the Association of Ideas" in order to explain why most reasonable people exhibit some "madness" or strange beliefs; his answer was that the hazards of their experience had caused them to form strong but irrational associations among certain ideas. Developed more systematically by John Hartley and others, associationist theses fit the mechanistic models of mind used in Scots-derived textbooks, and the dangerously nihilistic conclusions Hume reached with them made their study important. Hume had limited himself to three basic categories, originating in Aristotle, of how thoughts become associated with one another: contiguity in time or space, contrast, and resemblance. Many authors add more: Upham submits "cause and effect," and Catherine Beecher, in a chapter titled "Association" in her 1831 *Elements of Mental and Moral Philosophy: Founded Upon Experience, Reason, and the Bible*, nominates four other ways in which ideas become joined: strong emotional attachment (as one remembers a friend on the anniversary of her death);

continued or repeated acts of attention (as one interassociates all the details of a painting one has studied carefully); recent association (as one remembers a line of poetry right after it is spoken but not the next day); and few or many associations (as when one has heard a tune sung by only one person, person and song are connected until other instances come to confuse them) (42–9).

Widespread uncertainty over the nature and variety of associative principles is a key reason why Rand Evans defines "orthodox" Scottish thought as Thomas Reid, Dugald Stewart, and nobody else. Starting in the 1820s, Thomas Brown tried to improve upon these two precursors by extending and better integrating associationism into Common Sense philosophy, going so far as to try a new vocabulary of "suggestion" in place of "association" and adding a category of processes that *strengthen* connections between ideas (45).[25] In his *Elements*, Stewart shrugged his shoulders and took the simplest route: it is not necessary to try to "specify those principles of association" omitted by Hume, for "it does not seem . . . that the problem admits of a satisfactory solution; for there is no possible relation among the objects of our knowledge, which may not serve to connect them together in the mind" (161). Levi Hedge followed another common approach in his *Elements of Logick*, the textbook used at the Amherst Academy. He argued that certain ideas *tend to attract* others. "By the association of ideas is understood that connexion among the thoughts, affections, and operations of the mind, by which one has a tendency to introduce another" (25). But where Hedge and others spoke of the "tendencies" of some thoughts to summon forth others, Brown denied that ideas have any inherent, natural powers of attraction. He preferred to say that all connections are mind-dependent relationships among mental states.[26] "Our various feelings, similar or dissimilar, kindred or discordant, are all mere states of the mind; and there is nothing, in any one state of the mind, considered in itself, which necessarily involves the succession of any other state of mind" (267).

This is enough to suggest that during the years of Dickinson's education and beyond, associationism represented both a widely accepted vocabulary and logic for mental experience as well as a contested philosophical site with unresolved questions. For Dickinson, the associationist vocabulary was often linked to descriptions of extreme experiences like madness and the sublime,[27] for she saw that if one could not testify to "harmony" among the moving powers of one's mind, then the textbook doctrines all but required a (dangerous but exciting) self-diagnosis of "unregulated." Upham, who in 1840 produced one of America's first books on mental illness, and whose

Mental Philosophy—the book William Cowper Dickinson borrowed from Emily's family library—includes a lengthy treatment of the topic, says explicitly that when the mind's "law of association" becomes "disordered," then various forms of "mental alienation" can occur, including lightheadedness ("demence") or "dissociation" (250).[28] In fact, he redescribes persons whose main disorder is "a deficiency of the ordinary power over associated ideas" as "flighty," "hair-brained," and "a little cracked," (250) this last term of course being cognate with the one Higginson famously used in his own description of Dickinson: "my partially cracked poetess from Amherst" (L481).[29]

Thus the epistemological issues discussed in the last chapter—Dickinson's worries that she could not clearly see her own mind or "realize" what she was trying to think—represent only a few of many that play out in poems on problematic mental experience.[30] All of her minds and brains going off track, exiting the skull, getting splintered, feeling funerals, staggering, getting tipsy, visiting the house of Awe, recovering after horror, and finding themselves otherwise "unregulated" can thus be taken as more, and other, than figurative testimonials of personal experience, fantasies, or indirect criticisms of patriarchy or theocracy: they are also exercises designed to explore the explanatory and descriptive limits of evolving theoretical vocabularies.[31] Dickinson's attention to sequences of ideas and her recurring rhetoric of cogs, grooves, belts, and planks for mental functions reflect her thoroughgoing familiarity with associationist and mechanistic philosophies of mind, just as all the snapping, breaking, splintering, and leave-taking reveal her dissatisfaction with them. As a poet and thinker she was perhaps more "cerebral" or "introspective" than many of her educated peers, but if so the difference does not compare with her unique willingness, seemingly a necessity, to use lyric poetry on her own terms for mental analysis and experimentation. If, as we have seen, "trying-to-think" poems were a lyric subgenre she developed to respond to what most resisted her thought, then a set of related poems helped her explore the limits of mental and moral philosophy.

Many experiment explicitly with the basic philosophical problem of consecution or thought association:

> The Brain, within it's Groove
> Runs evenly - and true -
> But let a Splinter swerve -
> 'Twere easier for you -

To put a Current back -
When Floods have slit the Hills -
And scooped a Turnpike for Themselves -
And trodden out the Mills -

5 a Current] the Waters   8 trodden out] blotted out - shoved
away -

(Fr563)

Here we find several of the famous Dickinson "aftermath" questions: How and why is linear thought disrupted, and what happens to thinking when it is? What vocabulary is appropriate to describe the subsequent disordered state of mind? Can a "flooded" mind reimpose order upon itself? The poem invites more than one redescription, for it responds in both experimental and logical terms. As an experiment to test the descriptive power of mechanistic models of the mind, the poem's lab directions are: "Let thought be running normally, then let an event deflect it, then carefully observe, analyze, and describe the results." And as a syllogism: "If your thought is running smoothly, and if it is then traumatized, then you will not be able to restore order." That this is proposed as a general analysis rather than merely a troped presentation of subjective experience is clear from the fact that it speaks of "The" (not "my") Brain and of the current of thought that "you" (not "I") cannot restore.

It is instructive to compare Dickinson's lyric analysis with the philosophy of the day. Dugald Stewart, in a section of his *Elements of the Philosophy of the Human Mind* titled "Of the power which the mind has over the train of its thoughts," uses the strikingly similar figural language of "currents" of thought being "diverted" into a new "channel":

> By means of the association of ideas, a constant current of thoughts, if I may use the expression, is made to pass through the mind while we are awake. Sometimes the current is interrupted, and the thoughts diverted into a new channel, in consequence of the ideas suggested by other men, or of the objects of perception with which we are surrounded. So completely, however, is the mind, in this particular, subjected to physical laws, that . . . we cannot, by an effort of our will, call up any one thought. . . . the train of our ideas depends on causes which operate in a manner inexplicable by us. (165)

Stewart's example of "interrupted" thought is innocuous, though, along the lines of a turn in conversation or a knock on the door, and he simply declares the associative logic "inexplicable." His ensuing discussion describes how to gain *indirect* control over one's own associative processes through habitual strategies of mental improvement such as memorization and repetition. But a less sanguine Dickinson wonders about truly dangerous events, not Stewart's shifting "ideas" in "the mind" but *splinters* in the *brain*.

Dickinson's painful image of a splinter was not manufactured by Locke, Reid, Stewart, Brown & Company, and it is hard—I think by design—to interpret it back into mechanistic or Common Sense philosophical vocabularies of the mind.[32] Calculatedly placed into the smooth current of iambics as part of the experiment, it serves two functions: it represents in a vivid figure a radical event in thought—something going horribly wrong—and it performs that event in the flow of the poem by lodging a disruptive and disorienting splinter in the reader's brain. Both effects are achieved by the rubbing of different descriptive languages against each other: the arresting figure is taken from a medico-physiologico-phrenological vocabulary and injected into the associationist account of the mind. "When the brain is irritated by a splinter, convulsions are produced, which cease as soon as it is withdrawn," writes phrenologist Franz Gall (2:57). In the section of a book on head injuries devoted to the brain, surgeon François Quesnay cautions that sometimes patients die owing to "the effect of a hidden internal cause, a splinter, for example, or an abscess in the substance of the brain, or a suppuration."[33]

Contemporaries of Dickinson who were bringing together vocabularies of mind and brain include Thomas Brown, who spoke explicitly of his own "physiological view of the mind," and phrenologists like the Fowlers who had long been arguing that neither physiology nor philosophical introspection could alone explain the workings of the mind. In the preface to his 1855 work *The Senses and the Intellect*, Scottish philosopher Alexander Bain also speaks of discarding the language of "faculties," committing fully to associationism, and thereby uniting philosophy and physiology, mind and brain: "Conceiving that the time has now come when many of the striking discoveries of Physiologists relative to the nervous system should find a recognized place in the Science of Mind, I have devoted a separate chapter to the Physiology of the Brain and Nerves. . . . In treating of the Intellect, the subdivision into faculties is abandoned. The exposition proceeds entirely on the Laws of Association, which are exemplified with minute detail, and followed out into a variety of applications" (iv). The splinter in Dickinson's poem is thus a kind of contact or crisis point between paradigmatic discourses fitfully trying to cohere. ("How far," Fiske asked his Amherst students in the 1840s, "does the consideration of the brain and nerves belong to mental philosophy?" [17].) If the problem is that, once off track, thought cannot remechanize itself or reason its way back to the true Groove, then one source of the theoretical intractability is that the mind cannot find a single vocabulary to describe and unite the three phases of trauma (before, during, and after). Bain's efforts notwithstanding, associationism did not explain things very well on the level of brain science, and physiologists and phrenologists did not really speak to the philosophical questions of the patterns in imaginative or reasoned thought.

Thus Dickinson's speaker in "The Brain, within it's Groove" is another Rortian ironist who struggles between vocabularies and avails herself of tropological redescription. In this case she adopts verbs of human industry to describe how thought exceeds itself, the "turnpikes" and "hills" recalling the phrenological and anatomical images of brains that Dickinson knew (figure 2). By repeating with destructive power the very constructive activities that first inscribed them on the mental landscape—scooping turnpikes

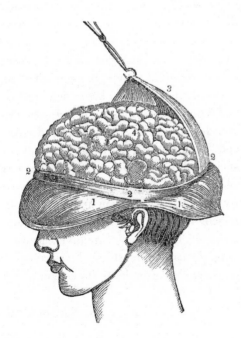

2. *A view of the brain from Cutter's* Treatise on Anatomy, Physiology, and Hygiene *(1852). "When Floods have slit the Hills - / And scooped a Turnpike for Themselves -"* (Fr563).

and slitting hills—thought overwhelms its own works, physical space, and substance. This includes both philosophical categories (memories, ideas, reasons, projects, associations) and physiological ones (gray matter and cranial fluid). These mental "Floods" are simultaneously natural, religious, and technological images: they can be produced by an indifferent nature, an angry God, or a miscalculating human engineer. As with examples we have seen in earlier chapters—for instance, the "implement"/"Apparatus" metaphors in "Prayer is the little implement" and the "elastic"/"Camel" options in "Strong Draughts of Their Refreshing Minds"—the ironist speaker again shares out, through tropes, the "incommensurable discourse" problem in new permutations: at any point the reader can opt into or vary this mind-brain experiment by choosing among the various meanings introduced by the "Flood" metaphors.

And one can watch the speaker/poet struggle with precisely how to generate and circumscribe descriptive possibilities, too, for the poem's variants again record the pluralizing forward edges of her thought process. For "a Current," there is "the Waters" and for "trodden out" there are the two choices of "blotted out" and "shoved away." It is worth pausing to consider them, for they chart possible responses to the question of *what form thought takes* once it has broken through its own limits. Can thought, in its usual pretraumatic state, be described—à la Stewart, and long before William James's "stream of consciousness"—as a "Current," with its connotations of steadiness, teleology, and linearity? This would maintain the contrast with posttraumatic, destructive "floods" in the mind. Or was thought, all along and in all of its pre-, during, and posttraumatic states, better described by "waters," a word with value neutrality, ateleology, nonlinearity, and very different biblical suggestions (of primordial chaos)? Dickinson did not decide.

The options "shoved away" and "trodden out" translate a rough physicality—pushing hands and stomping feet—as if the immaterial mind had lost its temper and allowed the physiological brain to supersede it. And "blotted out" reaches for still another way to register both brain and mind; it signals the physical effacement of a memory being splintered, convulsed, and eliminated, but it also captures the purely conceptual disruption of sequential thought as linear mental writing: ink can be transformed into coherent thought through writing, but can also spill over on itself, flood, and return itself to senseless blackness.

A companion poem seeks another way to describe the mind's response to trauma:

I felt a Cleaving in my Mind -
As if my Brain had split -
I tried to match it - Seam by Seam -
But could not make them fit -

The thought behind, I strove to join
Unto the thought before -
But Sequence ravelled out of Sound -
Like Balls - opon a Floor -

5 strove] tried   7 Sound -] reach -

(Fr867B)

As in poems like "I felt a Funeral, in my Brain," this one uses the verb "feel" in the preterit to set up a passive "I" thinker as both past site and present repetition of an unexpected, unprovoked, and divisive mental event. Again it is a problem of how to negotiate the irreconcilable vocabularies of "Mind" and "Brain"—both words are introduced in the first two lines. Here the term between is "thought," treated as a countable noun like "idea." But unlike much metaphysical philosophy, this poem assigns both physical and conceptual properties to thoughts.

The lyric "I," which has a clear relation neither to the whole nor to either half of the split brain, first seeks to bring order to discordant thought the way a seamstress matches fabrics or aligns seams. Despite the violence of a "Cleaving," the domestic image is philosophically heartening, for it is visualizable: two halves of a brain, or two thoughts, next to each other and needing to be sewn together. But the second stanza introduces the words "before" and "behind" with deliberate ambiguity to mark either relative time or place (perhaps both). If the results of the brain-cleaving can be understood as pieces of fabric, then it is a problem of space and material substance: thoughts coexisting in the mind must be integrated or synthesized. But if the thoughts occur at different times, then this raises complicated associationist questions of memory and causality: Did the former thought *cause* or *attract* the latter? Does the presence of the second thought in the mind distort the memory of the former? The ambiguity of "before" and "behind" opens up the ambiguity of the "Cleaving" event itself.

Upham solves this kind of problem by denying simultaneous co-presence entirely: "When it is said that our thoughts are brought together; that they are placed side by side, and the like, probably nothing more can be meant than this, that they are immediately successive to each other" (140). Thomas Brown, whose four volumes of lectures are dedicated to analyzing the mind in its successions and compound presence, nonetheless clings to a principle of irrefragable mental "unity" and rejects the very thought—the co-presence of incompatible thoughts or mental states—that Dickinson's poem is trying to think: "To suppose the mind to exist in two different states, in the same moment, is a manifest absurdity" (295). For Upham too it is "impossible, in the nature of things," that a person should "have a notion of himself as a twofold or divided person" (127).

Yet Dickinson's (absurd and impossible) speaker describes thought dividing and pluralizing across both time and space and producing a crisis of infinite associations. The second stanza recounts the failure of the mind to piece them all together through an extension of the seamstress simile: "But Sequence ravelled out of Sound / Like Balls - upon a Floor -." As thread, yarn figures both the linearity and temporality of thought (its consecution), and as balls it figures unitary and discrete aspects such as individual ideas or images. The vanishing hum of thoughts unsewn is thus like balls of yarn dropped from one's lap to the floor: discrete sounds, then a blur, and then silence. Although thought achieves a kind of quietude by the end of the poem, it is—as with the case of mental turnpikes being flooded—visually disconcerting to think of the mind as a floor with mixed-up strands of thought rolling all over like escaping balls of yarn. Sharon Cameron's comment that Dickinson usually manages to "create the fiction of disorientation while rescuing the reader from the fact of it" is true here only in the compromised sense that we are invited to watch the failure of our own thought (*Lyric* 49).

Another try-to-think narration of how reason fails to satisfy its own demands, this poem joins the neo-Kantian group emphasizing *repeated* attempt and failure: "I tried to match . . . But could not"; "I strove to join . . . But. . . ."[34] In the first stanza the speaker tries to conceive of, and integrate, the two thoughts as co-present; in the second she adds the idea of succession, but the result is still a failure. The reader can hardly ignore that these two very different stanzas are themselves examples of a "thought before" and a "thought behind," that is, two separate events in lyric space and time. Because they are incompatible tries at thinking the same event, the reader is enjoined to repeat the speaker's experience, to try to match the two stanzas seam by seam, to make them fit. The challenge is difficult because each stanza separately narrates a different failure to do exactly that: "I strove to make the two stanzas commensurable and co-present," readers may think after thinking for a while, "but could not make them fit."

There exist more mild-mannered siblings in this post-associationist family of mental poems. The little-studied "A Thought went up my mind today -," for example, represents the disorderliness of memory and thought association quite peacefully, with no catastrophe, no loss of mental identity, and no conversationally provocative reference to "you" the reader. Rather there is casual self-observation and description:

> A Thought went up my mind today -
> That I have had before -
> But did not finish - some way back -
> I could not fix the Year -
>
> Nor Where it went - nor why it came
> The second time to me -
> Nor definitely, what it was -
> Have I the Art to say -
>
> But somewhere - in my soul - I know -
> I've met the Thing before -
> It just reminded me - 'twas all -
> And came my way no more -
>
> *(Fr731)*

This testimonial narrative depicts thought as coming and going, forming and unforming, obeying unknown temporal laws and following an unpredictable, erratic orbit. One might paraphrase by saying that thought behaves like a bee or a comet, except for the remarkable fact that this poem has committed to representing thought without precise imagery of any kind. Thought just has movements and directions: up and down, this way and that. Here we are very far from cleavings, splinters, balls of yarn, pieces of fabric, italic seeds, or any of the other aggressive and complicated tropes Dickinson tried for thinking. Nor is there a single polysyllabic Latinism, expensive piece of philology, or fracture in syntax or meter. The poem is unworried and unhurried, sailing along in everyday words and ballad stanza.

And yet it has a philosophical edge, too. It employs the argument

Nietzsche turns against the "superstitions of logicians" in *Beyond Good and Evil*: A thought comes "when 'it' wishes, and not when 'I' wish," so it is "a *perversion* of the facts of the case to say that the subject 'I' is the condition of the predicate 'think'" (24). And it quietly but efficiently establishes a terrible set of problems for associationist philosophers: What can one know about a thought one started but did not finish thinking, a "half-formed" thought that one does not now understand and can barely recognize as having seen before? To what laws does such a mutant obey? Does it *count* as a "thought"? Was it one's own thought, then or now?

The questions are endless because the speaker has invoked a situation of almost total ignorance: she does not know what the half-formed thought was, when it came the first time, why it left, where it went, or why it came back. (An important companion poem is "This is a Blossom of the Brain –" [Fr1112].) Her only positive claim to knowledge is that she has previously "met" the "Thing." That last term, as we saw in "I tried to think a lonelier Thing," is a deliberately vague, all-purpose, preliminary one for the most intractable objects of cognition, that is, what one is beginning to try to think. It is therefore telling that it occurs here in the last stanza. On the opposite end of the spectrum from the poems on psychological trauma, "A Thought went up my mind today –" thus represents the sort of mental ephemera that both demand and resist analysis. Only a poet trained and invested in describing her own mental facts could have written it.

As a group, the poems of mental experience neither directly critique existing versions of the laws of association nor try to refine definitions of philosophical terms such as conscious states, ideas, or sensations. But they are skeptical about the artificial reconstructions and additive logic used in the textbooks to describe and explain mental processes and, on the whole, anticipate Bergson's points that associationists have little ability to predict why, in the presence of one thought, the mind remembers or produces another, or to explain the processes by which the self supposedly adds or combines simple psychic states to form complex ones.[35] Perhaps most fundamentally, the poems lack the basic faith of many philosophers in such things as the "unity" of mental states or the isolable independence of ideas and percepts. Such data may make it possible to isolate a "train of thoughts" to analyze, but what if they are just convenient hypotheses? The way Dickinson isolates and examines difficult limit cases and introduces new vocabularies and tropes shows that she was searching for richer descriptions of her mind's activity.

• • •

Because Dickinson's philosophical attitudes often transcended association-ism, Common Sense, and empiricism, to understand how her poetry took part in the philosophical culture of the day it also helps to examine what one might call in shorthand her neo-Kantianism. For every poem that features a passive, substantial, Lockean subject and mind responding (at least at first) mechanistically according to its susceptibilities, there is one with a more ac-tive, shaping, and usually frustrated Kantian subject peering at and into the supersensible.[36]

And where, one might wonder, did Dickinson acquire Kantian perspectives, and how might they have enabled her to apply interpretively the sequences she had learned from mental and moral philosophy? In her time Germany originated all the main challenges to the textbooks' Lockean-Scottish philos-ophy, and thus her speculative and neo-Kantian attitudes have roots in her, Amherst's, and New England's reception of German thought and culture. "I don't go to school this winter," she wrote to Root in January 1846, "except to a recitation in German. Mr. C[oleman] has a very large class, and father thought I might never have another opportunity to study it. It takes about an hour and a half to recite" (L9).

Twenty years earlier the idea of a teenager anywhere in America joining a large class in German would have been both unthinkable and unrealizable. When Carl Follen first began teaching the language at Harvard in 1825—as an elective to very few students—German books were scarce across New England and interest was very low.[37] By the mid-1840s, however, German language, literature, and philosophy had swept into Cambridge and extended westward to Amherst with a force strong enough to persuade Edward Dick-inson to risk sending Emily, otherwise too frail to attend school, to classes in the subject.[38] The teacher, the Reverend Lyman Coleman, was the first teacher of German at Amherst College, where he also taught Greek, and the father of Emily's and Lavinia's close friend Eliza.[39] In 1851 Lavinia noted in her diary that she had just finished reading Carlyle's *Life of Schiller* (Leyda 1:192). Expatiating upon the fact that one of the "most alluring" objects of Schiller's attention was the philosophy of Kant, Carlyle goes on to describe the debates over Kant in the early nineteenth century: "The transcendental system of the Königsberg Professor had, for the last ten years, been spreading over Germany, which it had now filled with the most violent contentions. The powers and accomplishments of Kant were universally acknowledged" (169). Every thinking person—except Goethe, who brilliantly held aloof—was forced to take sides. "Let us not forget," exhorts Carlyle as he defends

Schiller for being poetically inspired by Kant, "that many things are true which cannot be demonstrated by the rules of Watts' *Logic*" (177).[40] Language like this could not have been better calculated to attract the eyes of the Watts-educated Dickinson children.

The odds are very good that Lavinia's older sister Emily read this too, or heard a similar story, and not just because she fraternized with Amherst students, read most of what Lavinia read, and kept a picture of Carlyle on her wall throughout her adult life. By the 1850s, before Dickinson began writing poetry seriously, German literature and philosophy had become prominent in American life.[41] The prefatory biography to Dickinson's edition of Thomas Brown's *Lectures* points out that Brown wrote an important review of the philosophy of Kant; he also learned German and "dipped deeply into the German philosophy" (12, 13). As noted earlier, almost all the Amherst College philosophy faculty had studied German, been trained in Germany, or responded vigorously to German thought. Daniel Breazeale notes that Laurens Hickock's 1849 *Rational Psychology* was a Kantian exposition that "was surely instrumental in acquainting American readers with the details of Kant's theoretical philosophy" (230).

Again, while individual sources are hard to trace exhaustively, the broad strokes can be drawn, starting with the historical link between Dickinson's German recitations and the publication, thirty years earlier, of Germaine de Staël's *De l'Allemagne*. This book appeared in English as *On Germany* in 1814 in New York, and in a sudden and comprehensive way brought German literature, philosophy, religion, and manners into the rest of Europe and America. Recent scholarship has shown that de Staël's importance and influence cannot be overstated. "The keen interest," explains Kurt Mueller-Vollmer,

> among intellectuals and the general reading public in Staël's *On Germany* began in 1814 and reached a peak in the 1820s and again in the 1830s, culminating in the early 1840s in the Transcendentalists' exhortation of a specific canon of German works of literature, philosophy, and theology. Practically all the Transcendentalists received their initiation to things German—literature and thought—through *On Germany*. This includes Ralph Waldo Emerson, Margaret Fuller, James Freeman Clarke, and Charles Timothy Brooks, as well as George H. Calvert, George Ripley, John S. Dwight, Theodore Parker and Henry W. Longfellow. (150)

To that impressive list one can add George Ticknor, Joseph Cogswell, Edward Everett, Moses Stuart, Alex Everett, James Marsh, and George Bancroft, all of whom, notes Henry Pochmann, "were incited by her book either to undertake the study of the German language and literature or to pursue more vigorously such studies as they had already initiated" (552). Mueller-Vollmer speculates that what attracted the Transcendentalists to de Staël was her idea that German literature and metaphysics grew out of the Protestant spirit; it was a book that helped them "discover their own spirituality and develop their aesthetic program as it moved them to articulate a literary discourse of their own" (151). He also notes how James Mackintosh's reception of *On Germany* in the *Edinburgh Review* helped shape the American reception of German philosophy. Regardless of the thinkers de Staël discusses, according to Mackintosh, they always tend to "consider thought, not as the product of objects, or as one of the classes of phenomena, but as an agent which exhibits the appearance of the outward world, and which regulates those operations which it seems only to represent"; this "search for the hidden power of the human mind," concludes Mueller-Vollmer, is precisely what would "motivate and guide the New England transcendentalists' reading of Kantian and post-Kantian idealist philosophy" (145). Dickinson's attraction to Emerson and Transcendentalism, her commitment to a new poetics, her various emphases on the mind as an active, dangerous, and powerful experimental agent, and her idiosyncratic departure from religious orthodoxy share this lineage.

Frederic Henry Hedge's 1833 review of Marsh's edition of *Aids to Reflection* describes the "Preliminary Essay" as "the vindication of German metaphysics" and "the *first word* . . . which any American had uttered in respectful recognition of the claims of Transcendentalism" (Good vi).[42] Into the breach between Christianity and Scottish thought poured thinkers ready to try redescribing their spiritualism on more intuitive, speculative, or Idealist grounds.[43] "By the 1840s," summarizes Kuklick "as various German doctrines acquired a public, collegiate thinkers were required not merely to disparage Hume's empiricism but also to fight post-Kantianism, which was often stigmatized as pantheism, the position that God was the universe" (Kuklick, *History* 70).[44] Rand Evans describes this squeezed situation in American colleges as conflicted and heterogeneous:

> By the 1840s, the homogeneity of British thought, whether that of Locke or Stewart, had largely disappeared in many of the American colleges. An English observer of the American philosophical scene in

the 1840s described the influences on American textbooks as being Anglo-Scottish and Franco-German. By Anglo-Scottish he meant the Locke-Reid-Stewart-Brown influence and by Franco-German, the influence of Kant and the post-Kantians, such as Schelling, Fichte, and Hegel, through the interpretations of the French eclectics, such as Victor Cousin, and the English poet and philosopher Samuel Taylor Coleridge. (44)

By the 1840s Sir William Hamilton had become known for his attempts to combine Reid and Kant, and many American thinkers, notably Emerson, were also inspired by Victor Cousin's eclectic and combinatory approach to intellectual history and his willingness to unite empiricism, Scottish Common Sense, and German metaphysics.[45]

In the Frost Library in Amherst there is a notebook recording the "Names of Students in Amherst Academy" from the fall term 1846 to winter 1847–48; it also contains handwritten notes titled "An Abstract of Cousin's Lectures introductory to his History of Philosophy." Cousin's presence there suggests not only that Dickinson was perhaps exposed to something of his Eclectic thought but also that the Amherst Academy, perhaps under the influence of Coleman, cannot be considered a purely Scottish intellectual colony.[46]

The following is another (post-)Lockean poem about the mind and its "associations," but this time it pulls more eclectically in a Kantian direction:

> It is a lonesome Glee -
> Yet sanctifies the Mind -
> With fair association -
> Afar opon the Wind
>
> A Bird to overhear -
> Delight without a Cause -
> Arrestless as invisible -
> A Matter of the Skies.
>
> 4 Afar] remote - astray -
>
> (Fr873)

"Mind" and "association" are two terms that signal the place of this meditative poem in mixed philosophical conversation. They help generate a two-part, Lockean, associationist paradox: First, why is it that when we overhear a bird singing happily, we do not feel an unmixed ecstasy or beauty in our minds but rather a "lonesome Glee"? Next, how can that combined emotion of alienation and pleasure sanctify the mind with "fair association," that is, make it feel safe, certain, pure, and beautiful?[47]

As we have seen, analytical questions like this were especially attractive to Dickinson when they led beyond the explanatory power of their own terms. In this poem, true to the requirements of objective and inductive science, the song is "overheard" from a distance and the bird undisturbed by the presence of the investigator. But if the framework vocabulary for these questions put to nature is empirical and associationist, the reasons the speaker finds to explain the result of mental beauty are more speculative. Four things impress her about the encounter between mind and nature: the bird cannot be seen, it sings endlessly, it sings for no reason, and it sings alone (perhaps by opposition to the choral connotations of "glee").[48] Invisibility, arrestlessness, causelessness, and independence (or lonesomeness): if these features are intrinsic to nature, then natural philosophy—the empirical, inductive method—will not capture them or return an answer. Could it be that there is no finality or teleology woven into the fabric of nature? Could that non-finality be a source of both affect and song?

It is possible for readers to join their thought to these scientific and philosophical inquiries another way, especially if they are impressed by the parallel—established by the constant nineteenth-century equation of songbirds with female lyric poets—between a listener who overhears an overflowing, invisible bird singing inexplicably and a reader in the presence of poetry by an elusive author. In chapter 6 we will look more closely at poems that reflect Dickinson's transformative application of the Kantian-Romantic vocabulary of beauty and the sublime. Here it is enough to conclude that a Baconian mind fortified by Watts and Upham, thinking through difficult personal experience in the absence of a strong metaphysical discourse such as Christianity, and increasingly committed to the psychotherapeutic powers of lyric expression, would be well positioned to experiment with available philosophical vocabularies.

Dickinson comes closer than any of the Scots to the Transcendentalist view of the mind and spirit as active, speculative agents and to Kant's argument, expressed early in the *Critique of Judgement*, that "the supersensible" is an idea that "has certainly to be introduced as the basis of the possibility" of all objects of experience, even though "it cannot itself ever be elevated or extended into a cognition" (13). Indeed, she adheres to the strict limits on reason that Kant so painstakingly describes but his speculative followers so commonly ignore. The *Critique of Pure Reason* was a *critique* seeking to delimit the powers and applicability of reason. Kant makes this clear—"our entire cognitive faculty is presented with an unbounded but inaccessible cognitive field" (13)—and Dickinson, with her cognitive uses of "circumference," respects this inaccessibility or invisibility more faithfully than do Schiller, Fichte, Coleridge, or Emerson. We have seen that she was often only "able to testify" rather than explain or induce truths, and, like Kant, employed a wide variety of figures for mental failure, non-knowledge, and inexplicability. Philosophically, then, she stands out for her willingness to engage in neo-Kantian questions while resisting, at least in part because of her training in mental philosophy, the siren songs of Transcendentalism. Although her poems testify to the (for her very precious) inner experience of what Emerson in "The Oversoul" called a "Revelation" that is "always attended by the emotion of the sublime," she could never affirm with him that these "announcements of the soul are an influx of the divine mind into our mind" (392). In fact, as we have seen, if some secrets were irremediably a "Matter of the Skies," then this Kantian experience of reason's noumenal limitation could potentially become an explanans for a complex Lockean emotion like "lonesome Glee."

Dickinson's knowledgeable flexibility helps explain her appeal in a postmodern age awash in vocabularies from every discipline and cultural center. Too skeptical and analytical for the Transcendentalists, too speculative and exhilarated for the mental philosophers, too much a believer in lyrical language for either, she never stopped using their tools to scoop new turnpikes.

4

Amherst's Other Lexicographer

Maggie Tulliver . . . had so few books that she sometimes read the dictionary.

GEORGE ELIOT, *The Mill on the Floss* (1860)

People find difficulty with the aphoristic form: this arises from the fact that today this form is *not taken seriously enough*.

FRIEDRICH NIETZSCHE, *Genealogy of Morals* (1887)

A writer without either truth or genius, a mere uninspired, unfructifying logicker, is just the man to live in definitions.

HORACE BUSHNELL, *God in Christ* (1849)

Had we the first intimation of the Definition of Life, the calmest of us would be Lunatics!

EMILY DICKINSON to Elizabeth Holland (1877)

DICTIONARIES HAVE LONG BEEN America's most prestigious linguistic authorities. Valued for their erudition and utility, they are ubiquitous, trusted, and marketed in all sizes, shapes, languages, and media. But familiarity has bred indifference. The art/science of lexicography now produces such expected cultural furniture that it provokes nothing like the impassioned public debate and partisanship it did 150 years ago, when Noah Webster, Joseph Worcester, and their publishers waged an intense "War of the Dictionaries."[1] At that point the nation was itself in an acute and violent phase of self-definition, and arguments large and small coalesced around such topics as spelling, word meanings, linguistic and literary authority, nationalism, and the creation of a national culture. Far from being the sleepy, steady, but peripheral discourse we know, lexicography was then a volatile field on which questions of divine, human, and textual authority were played out publicly.

In a nineteenth century that Cynthia Wolff describes as a time of fading transcendence, lexicography can be seen as an acute and readily visible example of larger metaphysical, cultural, and political destabilizations. The dictionary wars brought the art/science of words into the national consciousness and joined it to a number of amorphously interrelated trends, both as an example and as an active agent: the literary problem of establishing an American culture, an American language, and an American sociopolitical identity; the language problems related to the ideology of the melting pot; the relationship to previous textual authorities such as the Bible, canonical literature, Johnson's dictionary, and scientific texts. For those who seek to join their thought to Dickinson's, the issue of word definitions represents a key mediation between her private poetic concerns and the larger, volatile cultural climate of metaphysical instability that included but far transcended the making of dictionaries.

Scholars have recognized for some time that Webster's 1844 dictionary is an important resource for reading Emily Dickinson's life and work. Like the King James Bible, it represents a vast semantic reservoir into which the poet liked to plunge, and both books help us understand how nineteenth-century New England interrogated, interpreted, and organized the known and unknown. Yet while critics and biographers have explored Dickinson's oppositional and dialectical attitudes toward the Bible in depth, they have not paid the same attention to her poetic definitions of things. The so-called definition poems deserve a close look, however, for not only do they represent an important part—at least a fifth—of all of her poetry, but also they contain some of her most topical and pragmatic lyrics.[2] The way they pursue discrete truths reveals her Aristotelian and Baconian sides—her epistemological desire to know, delimit, and express important areas of experience—while the lyrical strategies they employ reveal her creative, Kantian, Romantic sides. In previous chapters we have seen Dickinson use lyrics to weaken strong religious and philosophical discourses; here we will see her mix ordered thinking with a variety of poetic techniques to weaken one of the most powerful examples of strong metaphysics available in nineteenth-century America: Noah Webster's lexicography.

While Dickinson's lyrical definitions have not been ignored, they are, for several reasons, out of favor now, and little specific attention has ever been given to the relationships that exist between them and the form and content of Webster's dictionary entries.[3] As Margaret Dickie has noted, the first two feminist waves produced different Dickinsons, and neither the first wave's "revolutionary . . . enraged" poet nor the second wave's "complex and sophisticated" writer negotiating with "strategies of reticence and limitation" particularly resembles the kind of impersonal scientific observer or abstract definer that one might associate with lexicography (323). In fact, the various feminist Dickinsons mostly substantiate the opinion articulated by James McIntosh that Dickinson felt and expressed intense emotions but did not really think analytically about them.[4] "In her world," McIntosh writes, "spiritual and emotional states such as love, despair, and imaginative enthrallment can be felt and represented poetically but not pinned down, analyzed, or known" (2).

Recent emphasis on manuscript studies has also slighted the definitions, perhaps because they seem to offer themselves as preeminently "finished" right at a time when new appreciation is growing for writing as process and for poems as temporal objects. Yet as Jerome McGann's reading of "Experience is the Angled Road" suggests, a genetic awareness of textual variants and of the visual layout of Dickinson's manuscripts tends to reinforce the idea that the definitions are dynamic, process-oriented texts; they may ultimately become some of the manuscriptologists' favorite children (28).

Those who have studied the definitions have tended to misconstrue and oversimplify them, often by uncritically relying on Webster or other dictionaries to provide the standards for good definition.[5] Failing to meet expectations for a finished thought or a clear meaning, the poems have fared poorly among critics. Claiming, for example, that Dickinson knew "how to start" but proceeded "without a goal in view" (*Idiom* 94), David Porter suggests that her readers often "have a language experience without a completed conceptual experience" (93). He cites Millicent Bingham's comment from her introduction to the 1945 *Bolts of Melody* that "some poems trail off into a vague limbo" and concludes disapprovingly that Dickinson often drifted "toward an absolutely private lexicon" and wrote definitions that were not about reality but merely "about language itself" (105, 56, 121).[6] Sharon Cameron cites R. P. Blackmur's didactic and dismissive 1956 New Critical remarks to similar effect: "The first thing to notice—a thing characteristic of exercises—is that the order or plot of the elements of the poem is not that of a complete poem; the movement of the parts is downwards and towards a disintegration of the effect wanted. A good poem so constitutes its parts as at once to contain them and to deliver or release by the psychological force of their sequence the full effect only when the poem is done" (32). Building on these assumptions about how good poems are supposed to work, Cameron demonstrates that Dickinson's definitions are failures because they do not generate a "single effect." Repeatedly using the word "gratuitous" (34, 35, 38), she denounces them for being redundant and incoherent: they have "disengaged themselves from their contexts or have never sufficiently discovered them" (44). Resorting to a vocabulary of mental illness ("contiguity disorder"), she decides that they often "falsify the experiences they represent" (50). Even Jane Eberwein, much more sensitive and sympathetic to Dickinson's habits of mind and expression, especially in the definition poetry, speaks of "energy untamed," of "strong beginnings that occasionally seemed to go nowhere," and of "explicit organizational designs that sometimes broke down" (*Strategies* 128). Her more general comments eloquently typify the admiration, puzzlement, and frustration that, in varying measures, the definition poems have tended to produce:

> Dickinson's definition poems and her general concern with naming as an index of power also demonstrate her attentiveness to language and her concern that its force be respected. Yet diction often failed to encompass the inexpressible, as she signaled in an early definition poem, "'Hope' is the thing with feathers," that deliberately violates the lexicographer's cardinal rule about precision. What kind of "thing"? A birdlike thing as the feathers and song suggest: but the tenor overwhelms the vehicle, and the analogy breaks down in the puzzling conclusion with its absurd assumption that hope might ever go begging for help. Maybe hope is another kind of thing as well, infinitely suggestible, but never defined. (151)

From the perspective of beautiful and informative dictionary definitions, an "infinitely suggestible" quality would appear to be unwelcome.

Another view of Dickinson's definitional poetics does exist, however, and has been developed by Roland Hagenbüchle and Suzanne Juhasz, both of whom stress Dickinson's preference for process over and against the clarity, order, and stasis of dictionaries. In their readings Dickinson's sensitivity to the temporal dimension of thought and command of figural language work for rather than against the project of definition, and where others have been disappointed by conceptual imprecision or incompleteness, they tend, as I do, to see both a rich phenomenological attentiveness to the movements of consciousness during times of intense thought or feeling and an honesty about the elusive or indeterminate nature of the subjects defined.[7] They also stress Dickinson's technical control over tropes and her willingness to use abstruse verbal forms and thoughts to define perplexing topics.

As with the philosophical poems, the definitions best reveal their hermeneutic origins and contemporary value when they are understood as imbricated in larger discursive formations. Because the discourse of dictionaries was largely defined by Amherst's more famous lexicographer, Noah Webster, I start with him.

In 1828, after more than twenty years of labor, seventy-year-old Webster published his landmark *American Dictionary of the English Language*. Just two years later Joseph E. Worcester, the man who helped Webster abridge his vast work for a shorter edition, published a dictionary of his own. On November 26, 1834, an anonymous article in *The Palladium* accused Worcester of plagiarism; he responded; and their dispute unfolded in public newspapers. At first it was limited to the lexicographers themselves and their supporters and detractors, but over the years it widened until it earned the title "War of the Dictionaries" and became a public controversy: "College students in their rooms at night debated the merits of Webster and Worcester as hotly as their descendants now argue the relative puissance of regional football teams. The conductor of a local passenger train running into Worcester, from which city branch lines ran out to various towns including Webster, Mass., was in the jocund habit of shouting as the train slowed down, 'Worcester, Worcester! All change for Webster'" (Leavitt 53–54).

The war was fueled by both intellectual and economic factors. Not only did the two lexicographers have different ideas about how to produce a good dictionary—Webster's volumes emphasized nationalism, Calvinism, spelling reform, and prescriptivism, while Worcester's were more Anglophilic, international, and descriptivist—but also, commercially, dictionaries were increasingly important in a country that was rapidly absorbing immigrants and expanding its education system. The publishers of both dictionaries advertised aggressively and enlisted famous authors and statesmen for their cause. Worcester partisans included Longfellow, Hawthorne, Carlyle, and Horace Mann, while Webster's included Whittier, Ulysses S. Grant, Millard Fillmore, and Daniel Webster (Green 334, Leavitt 66). Historian David Micklethwait notes that in the 1850s, after Webster had died and George and Charles

Merriam had acquired the publishing rights to his dictionary, "a barrage of pamphlets" appeared—some forty-eight pages long—fired back and forth by the Merriams' and Worcester's publishers "with poor old Worcester as pig-in-the-middle" (282). During 1853–54, says Micklethwait, "the pamphlets whizzed to and fro, mostly missing the point, if there was one" (282). He sympathizes with Worcester, who could not avoid the "unpleasantness," but not with the publishers, whose pamphlets were "tedious, repetitive, humorless and unattractive" (283). They were ugly because they were "increasingly burdened with advertisements and testimonials for their respective dictionaries. The testimonials are from presidents of colleges, statesmen, distinguished scholars and writers, and are either commendatory circulars that such people have been persuaded to sign, or excerpts from letters written in response to being sent a free dictionary" (283). A later, humorous example from Ralph Waldo Emerson in 1878 typifies this situation. Upon receiving an unsolicited free dictionary from the Merriams, he gave them exactly the kind of quotation they were fishing for:

> Gentlemen,
>
> On my return home from the seashore a few days ago, I found the stately gift you had sent me to my great delight. In my youth my father gave me Johnson's dictionary: long after in Cambridge I became acquainted with Mr Worcester, and bought his book. Meantime, I have learned from good judges the superiority of Webster's Dictionary, and am very greatful to you for the gift.
>
> R. Waldo Emerson
> Mssrs. G. and C. Merriam. (August 21, 1878, *Letters* 6:313–14)

Bonanza! It was nothing less than an idealized conversion narrative. Emerson had progressed from Samuel Johnson (foolish youth) to Worcester (*politesse oblige*) to Webster (the best). His spelling of the word "grateful" suggests that he was in some need of this "stately gift."

By the mid-1850s the commercial machines were well in place, and dictionaries began carrying more and more pages of testimonials, sales figures, and cries of superiority. In my copy of the 1856 Webster's, the unnumbered pages of front matter include reproductions of the signatures of Millard Fillmore, Zachary Taylor, and James K. Polk, Daniel Webster and many other U.S. senators, and college presidents, newspaper editors, state governors, clergymen, authors, and other authorities. "It is with pleasure," they testify, "that we greet this new and valuable contribution to American literature. We recommend it to all who desire to possess THE MOST COMPLETE, AC-CURATE, AND RELIABLE DICTIONARY OF THE LANGUAGE." There is even a sycophantic letter written by the Merriams to Queen Victoria on the momentous occasion of their presenting her with a Webster's dictionary on behalf of the United States, "the republic which is proud to call England her mother country," followed by an affable reply from Prince Albert's secretary at Buckingham Palace attesting that the queen had placed the dictionary "amongst the few selected volumes which compose her own private library." Naturally, all of this took place when Webster—the arch-patriot who had insisted on writing an *American* dictionary—was scarce adjusted in the tomb.

When new editions (with pictures for the first time) of both men's dictionaries were published in 1859 and 1860, hundreds of luminaries and literati again weighed in. Oliver Wendell Holmes and Charles Dickens added their names to Worcester's side, though in general he remained the underdog, and the dispute over who had the biggest and best lexicon again flared up in newspapers, journals, and publishers' broadsides. The matter was basically resolved, at least commercially, in 1864, when the Merriams published an edition of Webster that would all but reign supreme in America for the next twenty-five years.

Such public disputes over who was the real linguistic authority and why generated a variety of responses. Comparative reviews of dictionaries proliferated, with journals and papers committing to one man's spellings and meanings as they might to a political candidate. (The twist, of course, was that the depth of these commitments could always be evaluated in the papers themselves.) And there were more lighthearted cultural echoes, such as the comic "definitions" that were a regular feature of *Harper's Weekly* in the 1850s: "*NEW DEFINITION.* A Lady: a sensitive plant, that thrives only in the centre of a large crinoline fence. Rarely seen, excepting by the most practiced eye" (July 25, 1857). Historians of lexicography have understandably treated the whole affair as a clash of American personalities and lexicographical styles as well as an amusing episode in Darwinistico-intellectual capitalism—a kind of orthographic-philological Coke versus Pepsi, or, given the ascendancy of Webster, Microsoft versus Apple. There is something undeniably humorous about the way, as early as the mid-1840s, as Joseph Friend has shown, the two men's dictionaries were able to symbolize "not only linguistic conservatives and moderates vs. radicals and liberals, but, with some inevitable extremist distortion and oversimplification, Anglophiles vs.

Americanizers, Boston-Cambridge-Harvard vs. New Haven–Yale, upperclass elegance vs. underbred Yankee uncouthness" (85).

Given the philosophical climate described in chapter 3, it is not surprising that the Yale-educated Yankee Webster, a founding father of Amherst College and the first president of its board of trustees, pledged absolute fealty to the strong metaphysical coalition between Common Sense philosophy, Lockean materialism, and evangelical Christianity. He traced the origin of different languages to Babel, used Locke's vocabulary of "simple" and "complex" ideas to describe how the mind processes dictionary definitions, and sowed Christian messages throughout the definitions.[8] (So thoroughly do his dictionaries reflect his faith that today the Christian Technologies company supports a searchable on-line edition of the 1828 *American Dictionary of the English Language*.) Jane Eberwein notes that Webster's dictionary probably reached Dickinson "with its painstaking elaborations on words with theological import" and makes the larger point that all of his books—spellers, grammars, dictionaries, atlases, behavior books, and many others—assumed or proclaimed ecclesiastical messages (*Local* 33).

As has been suggested, however, from the 1840s to the 1860s the business side of lexicography was propelling its science and art to the point of shaking its metaphysics: each new volume or edition of a dictionary had the potential to be received as both a repository of objective information, truth, and civilization and a partisan competitor seeking to distinguish itself in a brutal marketplace. With cultural authorities all but exhausted and with no higher linguistic authority to which to appeal, the lexicographers and their publishers resorted to fisticuffs. It was as serious and as funny as could be, as a March 10, 1860, illustration from *Vanity Fair* suggests (figure 3). Although this period has been cited as a time when competition forced lexicography to improve itself quickly, evolutionary accounts do little justice to the destabilizing effects of the long war. The many "testimonials," when they were not obviously mechanical, protested too much and contributed to a chaotic and shrill atmosphere that testified to a crisis in authority itself. Each famous name ran a constant risk of becoming a pedestrian signifier; when the most authoritative of authorities from all backgrounds and professions authorized themselves to evaluate, give political support for, or bless a dictionary—and when those authorities lined up so conflictingly—they nihilistically set the epistemological prestige of lexicography at odds with itself and made it, more and more obviously, a proxy for cultural battles of other kinds.

The very presence of competing lexicographies was another symptom of secularization and nihilism, of the highest values devaluing themselves. If lexicography before Webster and Worcester had always been an unstable mixture of philological science, authorial prestige, plagiarism, and creative art, then the heightened attention brought by the dictionary wars helped throw these loose categories into further doubt. Webster's attempts at spelling reform and idiosyncratic etymologies drew special criticism, and even the definitions themselves, those bastions of stability, reflected an ongoing crisis: Were they really the most secure uses of language, the final products of a deductive science and a strong metaphysics?

In the frontispiece, Webster promised "ACCURATE AND DISCRIMINATING DEFINITIONS, ILLUSTRATED, WHEN DOUBTFUL OR OBSCURE, BY EXAMPLES OF THEIR USE, SELECTED FROM RESPECTABLE AUTHORS, OR BY FAMILIAR PHRASES OF UNDISPUTED AUTHORITY." In practice, his citation strategy

3. *"Sporting Intelligences: The Battle of the Dictionaries." Cartoon in* Vanity Fair, *March 10, 1860. From Leavitt,* Noah's Ark *(1947).*

weakened this strong hermeneutic guarantee. Webster took many of his definitions from Johnson's dictionary but excised many of the illustrative quotations, and where he did so, Micklethwait explains,

> he nevertheless often kept in the names of Johnson's authorities, as well as furnishing authorities of his own. In Webster, therefore, a definition with no quotation is often followed by a name (sometimes by more than one), which may indicate any one of four different things. Many of them are easily identified, but there is nothing in the location to indicate whether such a name indicates (a) a reference book that provided Johnson's definition; (b) the source of Webster's definition; (c) the author of a quotation in Johnson, which Webster had taken out; or (d) the author of a passage that Webster knew, but did not put in. (178)

An example in Dickinson's family dictionary is the entry for "Circumference" (figure 4). We read, next to the first meaning, "Newton. Milton," and next to the second, "Milton. Dryden." Throughout the dictionary, readers are told only *that* such authors used words, not shown where or how, so the authoritative names are really just self-referential signifiers indicating fame and linguistico-cultural authority per se. To what extent could this don't-blink VIP status authorize and uphold the truths in a lexicographical system based on authority and precedent? Webster, who tried so hard to preside authoritatively over all these authorities and control the play of meanings in discrete lexicographical works, ultimately produced a series of proto-postmodern texts with the feel of dislocated reference, floating signifiers, and pastiche. As noted earlier, his volumes differed from Worcester's, but with the rapid advances in philology and the multiplication of lexicography's targeted demographics, they also differed profoundly from themselves: word lists, etymologies, and illustrations change a great deal in the major editions of 1828, 1841, and 1864. The very existence of a stream of new and improved lexicographical products disputed the claim to "undisputed authority."

Some of Dickinson's contemporaries were prepared to draw radically anti-foundationalist conclusions about the language game of lexicography. "No man is more certain to run himself into mischievous error," argued Horace Bushnell in 1849, "than he who places implicit confidence in definitions.

> CIR-CUM'FER-ENCE, *n.* [L. *circumferentia*, from *circum*, round, and *fero*, to carry.]
> 1. The line that bounds a circle ; the exterior line of a circular body ; the whole exterior surface of a round body ; a periphery. *Newton. Milton.*
> 2. The space included in a circle. *Milton. Dryden.*
> 3. An orb ; a circle ; any thing circular or orbicular ; as in Milton, speaking of a shield,
>
> > The broad *circumference*
> > Hung on his shoulders like the moon.

4. *"Circumference" in Webster's* American Dictionary of the English Language *(1844).*

After all, definitions will be words, and science will be words, and words, place them in whatever shapes we may, will be only shadows of truth" (73). For Bushnell, the post-metaphysical point to remember is that "language as an instrument" is "wholly inadequate to the exact representation of thought" (94).[9] And his pro-lyric, anti-lexicographical conclusion provides a timely rhetorical context for Dickinson's definition poetry: "Poets, then, are the true metaphysicians" because they understand the complexities of language better than lexicographers, and "if there be any complete science of man to come," the poets must be the ones to bring it (74).

Like much of literate America, Dickinson was exposed to the battles prevalent over words and meanings. The last explosive phase of the Webster-Worcester lexicographical furor coincided both with the Civil War and with the most creative period in Dickinson's life. Unlike Walt Whitman, however, who enjoyed reading different editions of dictionaries, considered writing one himself, wrote prose pieces describing the philosophical value of lexicography and linking it to geology, looked for his own coinages in new editions, and drew up long lists of words, Dickinson, despite close family ties to the Webster family,[10] did not get swept up in the politics of lexicography.[11]

Thus it is important to note that Dickinson's lyrical lexicography has origins much deeper than and different from simply perusing her dictionary: like the Bible, the dictionary was the object of critical interpretation, not naïve mimesis. In fact, Dickinson was much more likely to use her family's two-volume 1844 Webster's to press flowers than to check spelling or meanings.

She did not annotate it—aside from her father's signature, there are no pencil or ink marks in either volume—and seldom if ever riffed on the illustrative snatches of poetry or verse it provided.[12] Her niece Martha Dickinson Bianchi once claimed that Dickinson's dictionary "was no mere reference book to her," that "she read it as a priest his breviary—over and over, page by page, with utter absorption" (80), but beneath the façade of passive absorption was the lively, skeptical, conversational, experimental intellect we have seen in earlier chapters.

There is no written record of Dickinson's using the word "dictionary" at all. The term "Lexicon" appears in three poems, and taken together they form a clear and significant pattern: dictionaries are not sources of wisdom or inspirations for creativity; they are disappointingly limited tools that can answer only easy questions. One speaker reminisces about schoolchildren thinking of "Eternity": "Let Us play Yesterday - / I - the Girl at School - / You - and Eternity - the untold Tale - // Easing my famine / At my Lexicon - / Logarithm - had I - for Drink - / 'Twas a dry Wine -" (Fr754). This retrospective poem returns to the moment when a starving and thirsty child was first disappointed by horizontal solutions to vertical questions: the "Lexicon" and "Logarithm" provide temporary relief, not real sustenance. Similarly, the closing lines of "Forever at His side to walk -" sarcastically use the metaphor of the lexicon to indicate what humans most want but most lack: a reference book for the mysteries of life, death, and heaven: "And bye and bye - a Change - / Called Heaven - / Rapt neighborhoods of men - / Just finding out - what puzzled us - / Without the lexicon!" (Fr264). Finally, philology and the lexicon are useless against the trauma of grief:

> "Was Not" was all the statement.
> The Unpretension stuns -
> Perhaps - the Comprehension -
> They wore no Lexicons -
>
> But lest our Speculation
> In inanition die
> Because "God took him" mention -
> That was Philology -
>
> *(Fr1277B)*

"Was Not" is so unpretentious a phrase for death that it stuns human comprehension. Unlike the speaker, who relies heavily on complex, four-syllable Latin and Greek terms—"Unpretension," "Comprehension," "Speculation," "inanition" "Philology"—this poem's message bearers did not soften veracity through circumlocution; they "wore no Lexicons." And to the next, most painful question—Why did the person die?—Philology's terse answer only nourished further speculation.[13] All three of these poems recall "Shall I take thee, the Poet said," in which the speaker-poet tries but fails to find in "philology" the word most needed.

Along similar lines, Dickinson told Thomas Wentworth Higginson in 1862 that her "Lexicon" had for "several years" been her "only companion": "I went to school – but in your manner of the phrase – had no education. When a little Girl, I had a friend, who taught me Immortality – but venturing too near, himself – he never returned – Soon after, my Tutor, died – and for several years, my Lexicon – was my only companion – then I found one more – but he was not contented I be his scholar – so he left the Land" (L261). This letter has been taken to mean that Dickinson dearly loved her dictionary, but since her rhetorical goal is to highlight the straitened nature of her intellectual circumstances, it is clear that she is once more using "Lexicon" as a synecdoche for lifeless, limited knowledge. When no real tutor is available, it helps a little, but as Jane Eyre remarks to herself, "It's tough work pegging away at a language with no master but a lexicon" (Brontë 426). Higginson must have thought about the psychological effects of the two failed attempts at human tutorial and wondered as well why the second unidentified "he" was "not contented" that she be his scholar: Could her poor behavior really have caused him to leave "the Land"? Amazingly, Dickinson says just that, even as she asks a famous man she has never met to be her third tutor. Is the request audacious, hopeless, contrived?

Most of all it is inscribed in the tradition, both real and fictional, of tough-minded girls going it alone with textbooks and looking for a better way. As we will see in chapter 5, such a vision of learning, which lurks behind "Let Us play Yesterday," despite the presence of a schoolmate, was familiar to Dickinson from the novelists she loved and emblematized in scenes like that of young Maggie Tulliver studying a Latin grammar "much prettier than the Dictionary" by herself while her brother receives the instruction of the patriarchal pedagogue Mr. Stelling (Eliot, *Mill* 124). Most of the early letters to Higginson try to realize Maggie's dream that "she would go to some great man—Walter Scott, perhaps—and tell him how wretched and how clever she was, and he would surely do something for her," and this particular note is at least as calculating as it is self-deprecating (235). She may be a lonely girl with a "Lexicon," eclectically educated and temporarily untutored, but she may also be an American Elizabeth Barrett Browning.

Or even a Noah Webster, for unlike Whitman, Dickinson *did* produce a lexicon of her own—albeit a Borgesian one that defies classification. In fact, one can say that in writing substitute, experimental definitions for the nutritionless Webster, she took a step unlike any taken by (female) contemporary authors of fiction and poetry in redefining her cultural givens. To begin a list of Dickinson's *Bildungsroman* models for autodidacticism that will be continued in the next chapter, I cite here *Vanity Fair*'s Becky Sharp, a girl who hurls her graduation copy of Johnson's dictionary out of the stagecoach as she departs from Miss Pinkerton's school, "an establishment which has been honoured," Thackeray repeatedly tells us with great sarcasm, "by the presence of *The Great Lexicographer*" (3). Having symbolically and comically rejected her Victorian education and its monolithic language, Becky reflects, "So much for the Dixonary, and thank God I'm out of Chiswick" (8) (figure 5).

Dickinson, just as critical and still in Amherst, responds by writing a lyrical lexicon of some 250 poems. Most of it fits the old "hard words only" tradition of lexicography, since her definitional impulse was especially activated by aesthetic ideas and undefinable concepts and experiences: seasons, moods, extreme experiences, existential conditions, and abstract and metaphysical ideas.[14] As she put it in the poem "How Human Nature dotes / On what it cant detect -" (Fr1440), the "subjects that resist" are the most intriguing, and that fact is often made visible in striking opening lines: "Renunciation - is a piercing Virtue -" (Fr782);[15] "Remorse - is Memory - awake -" (Fr781); "Shame is the shawl of Pink" (Fr1437); "Fame is the tint that Scholars leave" (Fr968); "Death is the supple Suitor" (Fr1470); "Hope is a subtle Glutton -" (Fr1493); "*Speech* - is a prank of *Parliament* -" (Fr193); "'Hope' is the thing with feathers -" (Fr314); "'Faith' is a fine invention" (Fr202); "Faith - is the Pierless Bridge" (Fr978); "Prayer is the little implement" (Fr623); "Ideals are the Fairy Oil" (Fr1016B); "Dreams are the subtle Dower" (Fr1401); "Risk is the Hair that holds the Tun" (Fr1253).

But wait: Are not poets, by definition, terrible lexicographers? Are not the accents they place on suggestiveness, figurality, rhythm, symbolism, sound patterns, and all the other affective powers of language antithetical to the objective, informative, prosaic requirements of lexicography? Yes, but the

5. *Becky Sharp hurling her Johnson's Dictionary onto the stones. From Thackeray,* Vanity Fair *(1847).*

moment we lose our faith in grammar, as Nietzsche says, or take the linguistic turn, as Rorty says, a new, more postmodern kind of lexicography becomes possible in which semantically complexifying powers of poetic language become resources rather than obstacles. When definitions are no longer supposed to be products independent of language users, corresponding to unchanging, external reality, and guaranteed by a chain of authorities reaching heavenward to an ultimate Guarantor, they become weakened, co-created events involving language, lexicographers, and readers. It was Dickinson's "self-imposed labor," as Cynthia Wolff once put it, to "question God's authority and to free language from the tyranny of His definitions; thus the diction of her poetry is in the process of revising transcendent implication and pulling away from it even as the speaker addresses herself to God" (429). Responding to her epoch's impulses toward weakening and Baconian mental experimentation, Dickinson's definitions often repeat the initial gestures of metaphysically stable lexicography—headword, copula, explanation, and illustration—but ultimately take place less as exercises in linguistic correspondence than as post-metaphysical inquiries.

One might agree with all this and still wonder whether poems of the type "*X* is (figural elucidation and illustration)" should really be studied as a group or considered particularly "lexicographical." Literary history, after all, is littered with conflicted meditations on sunrises, and poets are always questioning God's motives and flirting with deconstructive paradoxes. Indeed the point is not that Dickinson's definition poems are essentially or programmatically lexicographical but that they engage strong metaphysical discourse by experimenting with lexicographical shapes. They are not primarily formal exercises directed at her dictionary but weakening responses to the kind of widespread, systematic assumptions about language and thought of which lexicography presents itself as a pure form: language as semantically stable, referential, sanctioned by God, absolutely transparent, and user-independent.

I have suggested that the contentious state of lexicography during Dickinson's formative years encouraged both awareness of and skepticism about its status as the highest science of words and meanings. But dictionaries are only the most salient manifestations of much broader cultural impulses toward definition: just as Dickinson lived in a time obsessed with mental process and responded to much more than the philosophy of her textbooks, so too was she surrounded by a wealth of quasi-lexicographical impulses and forms. Nineteenth-century America was saturated with verbal formulae sharing with dictionary definitions the mission of delimiting an essential truth or message: aphorisms, truisms, proverbs, platitudes, mottoes, axioms, maxims, epigrams, adages, sayings, apothegms, commonplaces, *sententiae*, moralities. The meditations in Martin Tupper's *Proverbial Philosophy* all have headword titles: Of Immortality," "Of Ideas," "Of Fame," "Of Society," "Of Solitude" are a few topics that Dickinson also treated. Many anthologies of flower sentiment attempted to define emotions like "Rage," "Sorrow," "Religious Fervor," "Misanthropy," or "Bashful Shame," [16] and Dickinson also knew many "single-topic" lyrics devoted to seasons (Longfellow's "Autumn" or "Spring," Blake's "Spring") or moods and emotions (Elizabeth Barrett Browning's "Grief," "Discontent," or "Exaggeration"; Emily Brontë's "Hope" or "Remembrance"). There were proverbs in the family's copy of Benjamin Franklin's *Poor Richard's Almanac* ("For age and want, save while you may; No morning sun lasts a whole day"), in Richard Chenevix Trench's *Proverbs*, and in the King James Bible, which also means everyday language: "Stolen waters are sweet, and bread eaten in secret is pleasant" (Proverbs 9:17).

Among the important literary sources for Dickinson's definitional art were the aphoristic and analytical lines strewn throughout realist fiction. Dickinson's grand, essentializing, existential throws of "There are" and "There is," which begin no fewer than twenty-five poems, are visible in her copy of *The Wit and Wisdom of George Eliot*, a collection of aphoristic snippets beginning with Dickinsonian lines such as "There is no despair so absolute. . . ." (49). There are, too, many typically Dickinsonian metaphorical equations: "Deep, unspeakable suffering may well be called a baptism" (44).[17] Examples of different kinds of definition were available in the many specialized lexicons of the day, including her family's 1855 *Dictionary of Congregational Usages* by Preston Cummings and the 1859 *Dictionary of the United States Congress* by Charles Lanman, and in the uniquely comparative style of Crabb's *Dictionary of Synonymes* (of which the family had an 1819 copy). They were also ubiquitous in the burgeoning textbook industry, including Dickinson's editions of Euclid's *Geometry*, Silliman's *Chemistry*, Day's and Greenleaf's math books, Upham's *Mental Philosophy*, Hitchcock's *Geology*, Paley's *Botany*, and others. Many of these books argued directly for the value of dictionaries[18] and stressed the idea that definitions were the bedrock of science and knowledge.[19]

With such a variety of sources it is not surprising that no clear definition of the definition poems has been reached. The problem is not so much that they have never been systematically identified, studied, and classified—although they have not—but that like other Dickinsonian mini-genres they cover a large spectrum that admits many valid classifications.[20] Because Dickinson's experiments with and on strong metaphysical discourses took so many forms, it is useful to provide here a taxonomy according to strategy and poetic technique. The following lexicographical zoology is neither exhaustive nor hierarchized—it could be expanded to include the "riddle" poems, for example—but the number of species does testify to the importance for Dickinson of many different definitional gestures:

1. *Essentials.* Some poems try to seize and present the fundamental essence or component parts of an experience or concept, for example, "The Truth - is stirless -" (Fr882). As the reading of "Prayer is the little implement" in the introduction shows, these poems can simultaneously pursue and challenge the project.

2. *Dialecticals.* In these poems, two opposing terms are introduced and defined by interdependent contrast and comparison. "Life is death we're

lengthy at, / Death the hinge to life." (Fr502); "Delight - becomes pictorial - / When viewed through Pain -" (Fr539).

3. *Differentials.* Sometimes Dickinson analyzes fine distinctions between neighboring concepts: "There is an arid Pleasure - / As different from Joy - / As Frost is different from Dew" (Fr885); "Suspense - is Hostiler than Death -" (Fr775). The following "differential" distinguishes between the related feelings/concepts of despair and fear and is typical of the technical compression of the definitions, their attention to the movements of consciousness, and their confident use of open-ended analogies:

> The difference between Despair
> And Fear - is like the One
> Between the instant of a Wreck
> And when the Wreck has been -
>
> The Mind is smooth - no Motion -
> Contented as the eye
> Opon the Forehead of a Bust -
> That knows - it cannot see -
> (Fr576A)[21]

This poem is philosophically associationist in the way it tries to distinguish between two emotional or mental states that rapidly succeed each other. The opening stanza installs a broad analogy: the difference between "Despair" and "Fear" is "like" the difference between the moment a wreck occurs and the moment afterward.[22] Whether the wreck is emotional, physical, private, or public, one experiences fear as it occurs and despair afterward.[23] Spare, the poem challenges us to supply our own detail, to imagine and align the two events of "Wreck" and "aftermath"; once we understand how we would feel during those two kinds of events, we will know the difference between fear and despair.

Differential poems like this clearly have a lot in common with the lyrics that experiment with mental philosophy. This one also makes sense as a response to Thomas Upham, who argues that sometimes, "especially when connected with permanent causes," fear

> gradually expands and strengthens itself, till it is changed into DESPAIR. The distinctive trait of Despair, in distinction from all other modifica-

tions of fear, is, that it excludes entirely the feeling of hope, which exists in connexion with fear in other cases. Despair may exist, therefore, in a greater or less degree, and with a greater or less amount of mental anguish, in accordance with the nature of the thing, whatever it is, which occasions it. When great present or future interests are at stake, and the mind, in relation to those interests, is in a state of despair, the wretchedness which is experienced is necessarily extreme. (473)

While for Upham the mind feels emotions directly, and the right combination—some fear, some anguish, no hope—is called "despair," Dickinson uses tropes to emphasize the process by which a despairing mind perceives. First, "The Mind is smooth" and has "no Motion" on its surface (underneath, perhaps, it teems with activity like the sea). The last three lines stretch out an analogy: the mind is like an eye "Opon the Forehead of a Bust -." In our mind's eye we see easily that a mind can be like an eye, but not so easily how it can be *contented* like an eye. Perhaps the despairing mind is peaceful because now, after the wreck, it has the leisure to gaze upon a fait accompli, no matter how catastrophic: the victim, which could be oneself, is irremediably a "Bust." So despair is distinguished from fear negatively: it involves no emotional haste or anxiety—possibly, with Upham, no hope—about what one must do.

Or is it, rather, that the despairing mind is to be identified with the eye sculpted on the bust itself? On second look, it is not easy to say where human consciousness is located or directed in this imagined scene. We are asked to create the subject-object pair of a mind looking at a bust, but we cannot know which pole, if either, to identify with. If the bust, then moving from fear to despair means realizing and accepting that one is permanently blind, that is, reaching the condition of contentedly knowing that one will never understand what has happened. Despair is then an epistemological condition, an accomplished nihilism. That readers will differ on whether or how to synthesize these interpretations reflects once more Dickinson's formal openness.

4. *Surprising Facts.* These poems announce and inform, asking and teaching us to see what we might have missed or redescribe what we thought we knew. Often they can be implicitly prefaced by a clause such as "Did you know that . . . ?" or "Would you believe that . . . ?" Did we fully realize, for example, that "God is a distant - stately Lover -" (Fr615), that "Pain - has an Element of Blank -" (Fr760), that "The Brain - is wider than the Sky -"

(Fr598), or that "There is a pain - so utter - / It swallows substance up -" (Fr515)?

5. *Self-corrections.* Many poems circle around a topic without ever reaching a conclusive statement. Often they repeat the definitional gesture by introducing a series of metaphors, nuancing the meaning and creating subtleties of mood without following any clear order or progression. "Grief" in one poem is a Mouse, a Thief, a Juggler, and finally a "Tongueless" witness who will not betray his secrets, even when burned in the public square (Fr753). In the famous "'Nature' is what We see -" (Fr721B) the poet corrects herself several times during the definition before concluding that "our Wisdom" is "impotent" to "Her Sincerity - ."

6. *Multiple Entries.* To certain important topics Dickinson devoted several different definition poems: death, consciousness, the self, grief, shame, loneliness, God, hope, fame, nature, beauty, ecstasy, awe, and exhilaration.

7. *Shades of Meaning.* These poems treat several forms of the same concept or feeling and demonstrate both Dickinson's dissatisfaction with received categories and meanings and her willingness to work with them rather than turn to neologisms. Training in the distinction-making techniques of analytical philosophy and science clearly influenced these poems, too, examples of which include "There is a solitude of space / A solitude of sea / A solitude of Death" (Fr1696), "There is another Loneliness" (Fr1138), and "Triumph - may be of several kinds -" (Fr680). Here are two more:

> There is a Shame of Nobleness -
> Confronting Sudden Pelf -
> A finer Shame of Extasy -
> Convicted of Itself -
>
> *(Fr668)*

> There's Grief of Want - and Grief of Cold -
> A sort they call "Despair" -
> There's Banishment from native Eyes -
> In sight of Native Air -
>
> *(Fr550)*

8. *Anti-definitions.* Dickinson sometimes defines ideas or experiences on the paradoxical grounds that they are, precisely, ineffable or undefinable. Such poems often treat aspects of sublime experience and articulate, through

a poetics of failure, some of life's most intense, complex, and inarticulable moments, emotions, and experiences: "'Heaven' - is what I cannot reach!" (Fr310); "To tell the Beauty would decrease" (Fr1689); "No Man can compass a Despair -" (Fr714).[24] Anti-definitions of ecstatic states reveal both a Burkean-Kantian desire to understand and express the sublime and a High Romantic high opinion of it as an extreme human possibility.

9. *Embedded Definitions.* Very often Dickinson includes short definitional thrusts in other poems. Sometimes these definitive moments support a tangential thought, clarify a term, or perform the role of a tested premise in a proof or chain of reasoning: "Power is only Pain - / Stranded - thro' Discipline, / Till Weights - will hang -" (Fr312). Sometimes they tumble very quickly upon each other: "Not so the infinite Relations - Below / Division is Adhesion's forfeit - On High / Affliction but a speculation - And Wo / A Fallacy, a Figment, We knew -" (Fr997).

To conclude this consideration of the scope and diversity of Dickinson's neo-lexicographical poems, it will help to examine closely one example of the way they articulate her postmodern, post-metaphysical philosophical stances. The 1865 "Aurora is the effort" can be considered an "essential" definition because it has something of the shape, confidence, and economy of a dictionary entry. Its mix of long words and brevity, however, also make it read like an ironic and cerebral aubade:

> Aurora is the effort
> Of the Celestial Face[25]
> Unconsciousness of Perfectness
> To simulate, to Us.
>
> *(Fr1002)*

This tiny lyric reproduces Kant's argument that the human mind has an "admiration of nature which in her beautiful products displays herself as art, not as mere matter of chance, but, as it were, designedly, according to a law-directed arrangement, and as finality apart from any end" (*Critique of Judgement* 160). Yet the poem questions that very last idea: How true is it that nature is beautiful, law-directed, and purposeful *apart from any ends*?

Put in prose, the quatrain says: at dawn (or perhaps during the Northern Lights, which "aurora" also meant) the celestial face—the skies, or nature, or God through nature—tries to show us a perfection that it is unaware of itself.

While the poem can be read as exuberant praise, for example, by gushing the third line, its difficult syntax and vocabulary seem to shade it over into a thoughtful, suspicious remark of the type: I wonder why so much effort went into making this beauty seem unstudied. It deviates only glancingly from Dickinson's habitual 8/6 iambics, but the missing beat at the end of the first line, in the place of an expected stressed syllable, can catch the mind; occurring as it does at the word "effort," the pause may draw attention to the forced quality of heavenly manipulation. The word "simulate" is also very strong and revives the nightmare of God as Cartesian Evil Deceiver, as Webster's definition makes clear: "The act of feigning to be that which is not; the assumption of a deceitful appearance or character. *Simulation* differs from *dissimulation*. The former denotes the assuming of a false character; the latter denotes the concealment of the true character. Both are comprehended in the word *hypocrisy*." [26] Aurora is beautiful but perfidious, and in the social universe that overlies the natural one in this poem, few things are more embarrassing than being caught assuming a false character.

"Aurora is the effort" thus features the kind of deconstructive paradox that both defines and destabilizes many of Dickinson's definition poems: the category of "the natural" transforms into the others that philosophers have always used to define it by opposition: the "social," "cultural," and "artificial." The specific terms the speaker uses to turn cosmology into cosmetics and make heaven's two-facedness the basis of a definition under erasure derive in part from the idea—circulating in Amherst thanks to Transcendentalism, Ruskin, Hitchcock, and the Hudson River school—that nature mirrors God's consciousness, that, as Barton Levi St. Armand puts it, "the sensuous veil of nature is but a protective covering over the naked creative spirit of the universe" (225). If nature is the medium through which we apprehend God, and atmosphere the agent of His consciousness, then landscapes and skyscapes seen at different times represent states of the divine mind. As Cynthia Griffin Wolff notes, Dickinson's religious tradition placed special meaning on "a small collection of natural events," especially dawn and dusk, both of which "were claimed as traditional symbols of the promised Resurrection: sunrise was the talisman of God's New Day, the rebirth into eternity; sunset was the sign of going home to the Father" (289).[27] Natural phenomena are at once unfolding texts we use to interpret God's attitudes and interactive conduits capable of reproducing those attitudes in our minds. Thus the test of many visual artists, especially luminists such as Thomas Cole, Jasper

Cropsey, or Frederic Church, is whether the canvas "expresses the 'effect' of a landscape, that quality of soul which animates, incarnates, and informs it" (St. Armand 226).

These aesthetic premises are quite in line with Dickinson's habit of trying to interpret nature's physiognomy, to discern "spiritual character from nature's physical features" (St. Armand 226). But the poem adds a neo-Kantian question about the morality of the process: What if natural beauty is not a faithful representation of divine mood and consciousness but an unethical simulacrum? Because the mind "cannot reflect on the beauty of *nature* without at the same time finding its interest engaged," argues Kant, and because one's interest is always necessarily moral, anyone who takes "an interest in the beautiful in nature can only do so in so far as he has previously set his interest deep in the foundations of the morally good" (*Critique of Judgement* 160). The poem's speaker takes an interest in the beautiful from precisely this perspective, wondering whether a stunning natural event represents an immoral attempt to seduce us: If aurora is presented "to" us rather than "for" us, does it not suggest that the contrived perfection is neither a "gift" nor a "needless show" but a dialectical move in an ongoing and perhaps eternal series of rhetorical performances? "Aurora," it turns out, needed redefinition because it represents that portion of the natural text that reveals rather than effaces questions about God's messages and motives.

In a lighthearted letter to her brother, Dickinson once wrote, "I have considerable work to arrange my emotions" (L167). Her many definition poems are further, and sterner, proof that she continued to work at it throughout her life.[28] In another early letter, well before her little force exploded into writing, Dickinson spoke openly and revealingly, again to her brother, about what she prized most in poetry: "I have read the poems, Austin, and am going to read them again, and will hand them to Susie – They please me very much, but I must read them again before I know just [what] I think of 'Alexander Smith' – They are not very coherent, but there's good deal of exquisite frensy, and some wonderful figures, as ever I met in my life – We will talk about it again –" (L128). "Coherence," "exquisite frensy," and "wonderful figures," that is, tropes: early on Dickinson recognized these as the qualities of good poetry (Smith was missing the first), and with hindsight we can see that they are visible par excellence in the definitions. Indeed the definitions are where Dickinson most explicitly tried to organize her explosion by imposing coherence on frenzy.[29] Like the "try-to-think" poems, the definitions are a place where the tension between imagination and reason, the defining tension of the Kantian sublime, is vigorously expressed.

Dictionary entries are not poems, and Noah Webster's lexicography overlaps with only some of the technical achievements, aesthetic logic, and sense-giving strata of Dickinson's. He aims for accuracy, not suggestiveness, seeks to eliminate rather than create doubt and obscurity, and many of his strong metaphysical techniques—such as relying on God, "respectability," linguistic transparency, stable meaning, and undisputed authority—are as different from Dickinson's as Jay from Bobolink. Thus, to get a full sense of the force of Dickinson's weakening innovations in lexicography, it helps to contrast her writing directly with his.

When America's foremost definer defines "define," he displays little of Dickinson's self-consciousness and irony; he makes no explicit reference to the activity of a dictionary, for example. He does, however, reveal the bases of his own poetics of lexicography and exhibit a good dose of his unique mixture of Calvinism and Enlightenment rationalism:

> DE-FINE', *v. t.* [L. *definio*; *de* and *finio*, to end, to limit, from *finis*, end; Fr. *definir*; Sp. *definir*; It. *definire*.]
> 1. To determine or describe the end or limit; as, to *define* the extent of a kingdom or country.
> 2. To determine with precision; to ascertain; as, to *define* the limits of a kingdom.
> 3. To mark the limit; to circumscribe; to bound.
> 4. To determine or ascertain the extent of the meaning of a word; to ascertain the signification of a term; to explain what a word is understood to express; as, to *define* the words *virtue, courage, belief,* or *charity*.
> 5. To describe; to ascertain or explain the distinctive properties or circumstances of a thing; as, to *define* a line or an angle.

After the etymology, Webster uses the first three meanings to express the notion of *fixing limits*, his examples stressing cartographical and political problems of determining land boundaries. Next he gives "define" the senses of determining, verifying, and explaining words. Yet despite the fact that the verb "ascertain" appears three times—and means, according to the author himself, to "make certain," "reduce to precision," or "establish with certainty"—Webster's delicate use of the passive voice in the fourth meaning registers his awareness that the lexicographer's job is not only to dictate the truth but to interpret how the general community assigns meanings to words. Explaining "what a word is understood to express" is a more community-based, historical, and hermeneutic challenge than merely explaining what a word expresses. Still, after reading all five meanings we are left with the strong impression that for Webster, such a vast project of explanation is eminently attainable in principle. His epistemological optimism, worthy of the Encyclopédistes, stems not only from his faith in God-backed word origins but also from his heavy reliance on written sources. He produced his dictionaries largely by collating authoritative texts, so the "community" he imagined, consulted, and interpreted, whose understandings of words he sought to express and whose pronunciations he long debated, was not primarily the increasingly diverse one of Anglophones. It was a huge collection of writings including American, French, and English dictionaries, books, and newspapers.

The complex fourth meaning also seems to be the most Dickinsonian, for it mentions the kinds of things Dickinson sometimes liked, in her own way, to define: emotions and character traits. And yet it goes out of its way to suggest four specifically *moral* words whose own "significations" one might "ascertain" by looking them up: "virtue," "courage," "belief," and "charity." The definitions for "virtue," "courage," and "charity" all cite scripture; the entry for "belief" does not quote the Bible directly but makes several references to the gospel and to "Christian belief."[30]

Taken as a whole, Webster's 1844 dictionary was and is for most readers beautiful in the commonplace eighteenth- and nineteenth-century senses of the term. It is well ordered, and its comprehensiveness and public authority project an air of certitude and control, altogether an attractive aura for which, as we have seen, there were good commercial reasons. Its definitions exhibit clarity, fullness, order, balance, completeness, and precision; they rarely challenge the senses, carry the mind to its breaking point, or incite passion. Moreover, although he respected, and even revered, the complexities and multivalences of words, Webster did not often wallow in paradox and would never have allowed himself to write, as did Dickinson, that the "Definition of Beauty is / That Definition is none -" (Fr797).[31] While they occasionally speak with great moral authority, his definitions more commonly ask to be processed and stored in the manner of a beautiful landscape painting, passively and pleasantly. Rather than aggravate or multiply our intellectual itches, the lists of meanings soothe us, inform us, and gently absorb our ignorance.[32]

By contrast, Dickinson's definitions reflect a poetics of the sublime, both in Burkean-Kantian senses and in the neo-Kantian senses extrapolated by such contemporary thinkers as Jean-Luc Nancy, Jean-François Lyotard, and Kirk Pillow. "I think there are reasons in nature why the obscure idea, when properly conveyed, should be more affecting than the clear," argued Edmund Burke in his 1757 *Philosophical Enquiry into the Origin of Our Ideas of the Sublime and Beautiful*, for it is "our ignorance of things that causes all our admiration, and chiefly excites our passions. Knowledge and acquaintance make the most striking causes affect but little" (57). The definition poetry often takes up obscure ideas and presents a determined consciousness coming to and galloping beyond its own limits, often through a process that challenges both author and reader. Webster's definitions aim to clarify one's relationship to external objects—kingdoms, countries, boundaries, words, geometrical entities—and his definitions derive methodically from a body of authoritative texts and personalities, including God. Dickinson's, despite their lapidary boldness and Websterphilic dedication to succinct and analytic language, are best understood not as parodic dictionary entries but as ironizing experiments on available vocabularies and as open-form, unauthorized meditations on Kantian aesthetic ideas.

The following poem immediately starts a conversation with ideas of ascertaining and delimiting, but then goes on to define the obscure idea of loneliness by the thought process one undergoes while experiencing the fear that one might become much lonelier still:

> The Loneliness One dare not sound -
> And would as soon surmise
> As in it's Grave go plumbing
> To ascertain the size -
>
> The Loneliness whose worst alarm
> Is lest itself should see -
> And perish from before itself
> For just a scrutiny -

The Horror not to be surveyed -
But skirted in the Dark -
With Consciousness suspended -
And Being under Lock -

I fear me this - is Loneliness -
The Maker of the soul
It's Caverns and it's Corridors
Illuminate - or seal -

3–4 plumbing / To ascertain] measuring / to register -   8 just a
scrutiny] simple scrutiny   9 Horror] chasm -   16 Illuminate -]
make populate - • [make] manifest

(Fr877)

Both a "surprising fact" and a "self-correction," this definition presents a well-polished thought in a single sentence with a long subject and a delayed main verb. This prose shape allows a series of hesitating statements to accumulate a combined force: "X, that is, Y, or, better yet, Z . . . *this* is what I fear."

This is loneliness, in an extreme form that is defined, like the one in "I tried to think a lonelier Thing," by implicit contrast to a more familiar, pedestrian kind. Each of the first three stanzas limns a situation in which one feels lonely and then senses or suspects that one's loneliness could become, or may actually already be, a much more terrifying and intolerable state that one "dare not sound." Those three stanzas compulsively revisit and rephrase the same instant of hesitation, when self-inspection threatens to reveal an unbearable fact or feeling of loneliness. As in other poems we have seen where the poet tries but fails to satisfy the demands of reason with imagery, the three circling stanzas show how frustrated and determined she is. The last stanza compromises with reason by getting more abstract: it draws back and presents a more engulfing fear, the fear that the earlier fear was well founded.

Thus the definition slowly circumscribes a liminal state in which one sees the long shadow of truly great loneliness on the lawn, when one naturally fears trying to "sound" it or, in analytico-Websterian language, "ascertain its size." With a loneliness as awful as this, would it be wiser not to know but to "surmise"? If the loneliness one knows, feels, and understands right now were to be compared with the loneliness that one *fears* one may *really* be feeling right now, then . . . the thought starts to produce an intolerable trauma from which all thought recoils. Is that unknown, adumbrated loneliness a permanent ontological estrangement, a grief, a nostalgia, an exclusion from one's most cherished earthly or heavenly community? The persona does not know and cannot or will not want to know. And that provides the experimental basis for the poem: How to define what it would be so much better not to know?

Even this brief paraphrase reveals that the poem does not share Webster's goal of removing doubt and obscurity. We sense, and perhaps fear, how impossible or naïve it would be to quote an "undisputed authority" on the subject, for what truly profound loneliness could really be communicated, shared, or universally imposed? By contrast, Webster seems jaded and genteel:

> LONE-LI-NESS, *n.* Solitude; retirement; seclusion from company. He
> was weary of the *loneliness* of his habitation.
> 2. Love of retirement; disposition to solitude.
> > I see
> > the mystery of your *loneliness.*   *Shak.*

Where Webster creates an aristocratic aura—a "love of retirement" from other people, a world-weary reclusiveness, and, for those who know their Shakespeare,[33] an appealing mystery—Dickinson fears that she might find unspeakable "Horror.'[34] Again, Webster's collectedness is beautiful, while the advancing, retreating, hesitating thought of the telescopic poem is more characteristic of the Kantian sublime: "The mind feels itself *set in motion* in the representation of the sublime in nature; whereas in the aesthetic judgement upon what is beautiful therein it is in *restful* contemplation" (*Critique of Judgement* 107). Nevertheless, besides the basic paradox of defining an emotion from within the experience of the emotion itself—during the fear of examining it further—there are other elements that make this poem a classic of sublime definition.

The defining consciousness constitutes its topic, loneliness, as a sublime object or an aesthetic idea. It is the kind of idea that, in Kant's critical philosophy, triggers a flood of associations, defies reason absolutely, and transcends the powers of language and imagination. In this poem the unimaginable, ungraspable, unexaminable, overwhelming loneliness triggers a strikingly gothic response. Afraid, seeking to express and perhaps thereby control her growing fear, the defining consciousness scrambles for familiar concepts and linguistic patterns to use prophylactically and avails herself of a series of gothic conventions: "Grave," "alarm," "perish," "Horror," "skirted in the Dark," "Consciousness suspended," "Being under Lock." The poem is gothic up to and including the final images of "illuminating" and "sealing" the "Caverns" and "Corridors."

To a point, then, one might wish to call this chilling lexicon "beautiful," since it emerges rather credibly in the night of thought, when the mystery of terrible loneliness is contemplated—just when, precisely (and this is rare in Dickinson), the speaker cannot seek consolatory recourse in language or images from the natural, social, or domestic worlds. There is a pleasing form-follows-function conceptual cleanliness in the way the speaker, threatened with an unspeakable loneliness, fails or refuses to draw upon quotidian figures, either to present or to encircle the fantastic power of the Bluebeard behind the locked doors of her consciousness.

Yet this orderly Hallowe'en beauty gives way to a meditative sublime when we realize how thought is failing to control the threat it is producing for itself. After two stanzas the definition seems to be at a standstill: it has tried twice to (anti-)define loneliness on the basis that it cannot be looked at or analyzed. Brita Lindberg-Seyersted once wrote that in "Emily Dickinson's poetic theory and practice there is not only reverence before the incomprehensible, but also an effort to view it as closely as possible and from as many angles as can be done" (104). Yet here the "incomprehensible" is terrifying enough to block the "effort to view it" entirely. The poem can proceed to become neither a public, authoritative, informative document à la Webster nor a self-clarifying act of philosophico-lyrical discovery.

What happens? Refusing to give up, the speaker *again* represents the logic of a blinding fear but now, in the third stanza, even more radically: the place occupied by the word "Loneliness" in the first two stanzas is now filled with "Horror," an immediate and intense term usually reserved for sudden, unbearable visual or emotional shock and not for gray, inscrutable loneliness.[35] "Skirted in the Dark" also implies more strongly than before that the horror *is* present and *is* close by, and the active verbs of the first two stanzas ("dare," "sound," "ascertain," etc.) are abruptly and completely replaced by disorienting, open-ended passive constructions without agents (e.g., "Consciousness suspended"—suspended by a person, loneliness, or God? Willingly or unwillingly?) And "not to be surveyed" is a particularly menacing phrase;

it means either that one *should not* survey the horror or that one *could not*, or both.

Although logically the first three stanzas are in paratactic apposition, and although they mirror each other structurally and say the same thing three times, their emotional echoes, like approaching footsteps, accumulate and sound louder and louder. The first stanza has a casual, colloquial feel: "would as soon," "go plumbing." The second is more threatening and strident, as the threat of death indicates, and the third is downright horrifying. In the last stanza, the lyric "I" finally appears for the first time, distraught, tentative, and confessional, and we realize that the fears expressed in the previous three stanzas are included in the larger, more intelligibly abstract fear that her earlier fear was correct, that *this* loneliness is indeed terrible, and that God has appointed it.

> I fear me this - is Loneliness -
> The Maker of the soul
> It's Caverns and it's Corridors
> Illuminate - or seal -

As is common in the definition poems, the final lines of the poem rely heavily on the reader, and the last stanza is a glittering gem in Dickinson's conversational, open poetics. Two particular difficulties stand out: the possible antecedents of "it's" (a frequent Dickinson spelling for "its")—one cannot be sure whether the "Caverns" and "Corridors" belong to the soul or to loneliness—and the physical, philosophical, and religious senses of "illuminate" and "seal." The possibilities deepen the mood of growing tension, uneasiness, and sense of failed progress brought about by the poem's obsessive repetition of style, meter, structure, and topic.

Like the emotional stakes, the interpretive stakes progressively heighten.[36] As in a film noir, the problems feel extremely important—What *is* this great, thought-defying loneliness?—but suspicions reign over truth. Dickinson prepares the moody semantic agony by using two lexicons with opposing connotations. One gothic strand, as we have seen, comprises mostly nouns, word-defenses thrown off by the speaker's unconscious. Each of these word-guards, however, is met in the poem by another term, usually a verb, from an equally well developed strand of scientific, analytic, definitive Websterian signifiers, summoned up and presented, this time, by the hyperconscious mind: "sound," "plumb," "ascertain the size," "see," "scrutiny," "survey." These words are the graphic traces of the lexicographer's or mental philosopher's attempt to find or impose coherence on and amid the frenzy of an inchoate emotion. Taken together, the gothic and Cartesian semantic chains define a bipolar atmosphere that is sublimely difficult to define.

The next poem also shows the tenacity of Dickinson's post-Websterian lyric speakers but relies more heavily on the implications of interlocking tropes. This time there are three tries at remorse; again, one try per stanza, and then, in the last couplet, a general statement:

> Remorse - is Memory - awake -
> Her Parties all astir -
> A Presence of Departed Acts -
> At window - and at Door -
>
> It's Past - set down before the Soul
> And lighted with a match -
> Perusal - to facilitate -
> And help Belief to stretch -
>
> Remorse is cureless - the Disease
> Not even God - can heal -
> For 'tis His institution - and
> The Adequate of Hell -
>
> 2 Parties all] Companies 8 stretch] *the* ch *over* <h>   8 stretch]
> reach   8 Of it's Condensed Despatch]   12 Adequate]
> Complement -
>
> *(Fr781)*

A commonsense understanding of remorse suggests that it, too, requires a divided self to be felt, for it is the emotional experience of remembering an earlier moment in which one did something embarrassing or wrong.[37] There is the older, remorseful self who regrets, condemns, and perhaps fears its former self, and that earlier one, lodged in the mind, who committed those "Departed Acts." The feeling of remorse accompanies the later self's attempt to confront or evade a previous self that, problematically, remains a remembered part of the remorseful one.

As was true for "The Loneliness One dare not sound -," in this poem a sudden equation in the first line emphasizes the mental rather than physiological components of the emotion and initiates a series of parallels and comparisons. Remorse, first, is an experience of memory "awake." The metaphor suggests alertness or attentiveness, but Dickinson insists that the rousing process is neither gentle nor private. Assigning memory the quality of a collective plurality, she imagines an army being blasted by reveille, its companies or "Parties" suddenly "all astir."

Next, consciousness becomes a house, with doors and windows, but the metaphors are carefully mixed: remorse is the sensation of the "Presence" of departed acts *to* the house of consciousness. The first stanza suggests that these personified "Acts" left the house and then turned around and came back to look in the windows and knock on the doors: they peer in, bang, and bother consciousness. To feel remorse is therefore to feel like a person trapped in a house under siege, with the added idea that the army at the door is composed of one's own paid mercenaries.

In the next stanza the past is placed before the soul and "lighted with a match," strongly suggesting that remorse sets one's memories aflame; yet in the next breath we learn that, "Perusal - to facilitate -," the mental match *illuminates* the memories. If both things happen—as they tend to when we imagine the scene—then Remorse's unique form of self-scrutiny is captured in the flickering logic of another vivid gothic scene: one's past is shrouded in eerie darkness; one peers nervously at it by the light of a match, seeking to dispel the mystery; and then suddenly it catches fire and incinerates one's whole being with guilt and pain.

Webster, for his part, eschews these cathartic metaphors of peering and searing and cautions us instead with an alliterative morality of crime and punishment:

> RE-MORSE, *n.* remors'. (L. *remorsus*, from *remordeo*.]
> 1. The keen pain or anguish excited by a sense of guilt; compunction of conscience for a crime committed.   *Clarendon.*
> 2. Sympathetic sorrow; pity; compassion.
>   Curse on th'unpardoning prince, whom tears can draw
>   To no *remorse.*   *Dryden.*
> [*This sense is nearly or quite obsolete.*]

That Dickinson's Remorse finally becomes a "cureless" disease suggests, contra Webster, that we passively endure it rather than initiate it; thus, the agent of the clause "lighted with a match" is not us but, as the last stanza suggests, a higher power. As she does in "The Loneliness One dare not sound -," Dickinson translates the intrasubjective experience of remorse to the ontological level, and remorse becomes an eternal, Kierkegaardian disease condition that God cannot heal: "'tis His institution - and / the Adequate of Hell -."

Our last example of Dickinson's sublime definition shows her using lyric effects such as alliteration and interlocking tropes to form a definition as thought experiment. Although it has received harsh criticism,[38] "Doom is the House without the Door -" is in fact a masterpiece of "essential" definition:

> Doom is the House without the Door -
> 'Tis entered from the Sun -
> And then the Ladder's thrown away,
> Because Escape - is done -
>
> 'Tis varied by the Dream
> Of what they do outside -
> Where Squirrels play - and Berries dye -
> And Hemlocks - bow - to God -
>
> *(Fr710)*

Perhaps, first of all, this poem belongs to the large group devoted to the theme of lingering "consciousness after death."[39] "Doom" is one of Dickinson's words for death, the doorless house suggests a grave, and the idea is present of a ladder being thrown away because death is final and one cannot climb back out. At the same time, the poem is a definition of a doom *emotion* and one of an equally large set of Prisoner of Chillon or Plato's Cave meditations that explore how human consciousness responds to various traumas and imprisonments. In this case the prison's walls are themselves ambiguous, and the poem relies for part of its effect on a typically Dickinsonian spatiotemporal sceneleseness. The radicality of the dislocatedness becomes evident if we ask a few basic questions: Where is the house without the door? Is it a dwelling in or on the ground, or a metaphor for a mental state? Is the ladder to climb up with, or down? We want to know such things, but we do not and seemingly cannot know, a situation shared by both author and reader in many definitions.

To get a richer sense of the countercultural form and content of this lyric, it again helps to compare with Webster:

DOOM, *n.* [Sax. *dom*; D. *doem*; Dan. and Sw. *dom.*]

1. Judgment; judicial sentence.
   To Satan, first in sin, his *doom* applied.   *Milton.*
   Hence, the *final doom* is the last judgment.
2. Condemnation; sentence; decree; determination affecting the fate
   or future state of another; usually a determination to inflict evil,
   sometimes otherwise.
   Revoke that *doom* of mercy.   *Shak.*
3. The state to which one is doomed or destined. To suffer misery
   is the *doom* of sinners. To toil for subsistence is the *doom* of
   most men.
4. Ruin; destruction.
   From the same foes, at last, both felt their *doom.*   *Pope.*
5. Discrimination. [*Not used.*]

This makes it clear that even before she began her definition, Dickinson framed the conversation by bracketing most of the meanings on Webster's (and her surrounding culture's) list. She meditates deeply on part of Webster's third meaning, "the state to which one is doomed or destined," and defines "doom" not as a discrete set of Websterian nominalizations—"Condemnation; sentence; decree"—but as a series of steps that form a template for a repeatable experience. If we accept the usual task of interpreting interconnected metaphors, we can reconstruct it. "Doom," that is, death or a mental state similar to despair or dread, is a *doorless* house; thus one neither knocks to inquire within nor walks in entirely by choice. We enter, then, or are ushered into doom "from the Sun," that is, from a psychic, emotional, or physical state of brightness and warmth, but we realize what has happened only later: we experience doom consciously only when it is too late to choose not to, when the ladder has been thrown away and escape made impossible. While at first it may seem to be the sun, or perhaps nature, that "puts us" into doom (rather than God, the final word of the poem), in fact the poem is deliberately obscure on the difficult question of causes: if anything, it suggests that we wander randomly into it. We just fall into doom-mood as we do into other emotional states whose beginnings and endings are unclear. But since "Doom" *is* a house, despite one's problematic entry, one (in some sense) lives in it, perhaps in figural contrast to a prison into which one is banished for a reason. Since we cannot get out, we take up residence and *think.*

Doom thereby becomes definable by a sequence of thoughts rather than a set of biological or physiological sensations. Structurally, a key moment of the doom experience occurs when we cease participating in the external world and our intense experiences of thought and emotion are activated. The phrase "varied by the Dream" is what shifts the poem inward and makes the objective or lexicographical perspective depend on that of the dead or despairing person. Once "in" doom, the speaker's consciousness fantasizes about "what they do outside." Distilled into that one cold Heideggerian pronoun "they," which he theorizes in *Being and Time* as *das Man*, the "they" who we all are before we reject our they-self, is a whole conspiracy theory of exclusion, accented in one way by the telling, tolling, monosyllabic étude in "d"—doom, door, done, dream, do, die, God—and in another by the many passive constructions which, as in the case of the loneliness and remorse definitions, strongly suggest a powerful agency without really explaining it: Who built this house? Who threw away the ladder? Why don't "they" outside let us out of our prison, or at least try? Why don't we contact *them*? The poem does not ask these questions directly but activates them by implication, an openist technique that both involves and disorients the reader.

Moreover, despite the way her thoughts are organized around the vast, indifferent "they," the speaker does not directly compare herself to other people. Left unfulfilled is the expectation created by the poem that the consciousness lingering in the house of doom will fasten on the joyous lives and activities of friends or family to define its own pain negatively. Instead, three carefully chosen, vivid, organic images are presented as occurring to the despairing consciousness trapped in the dark, doorless house/grave: squirrels, berries, and hemlocks. Each of these is simultaneously a concrete image and a figure for humanity in one of its fundamental phases or attitudes: squirrels *playing*,[40] berries *ripening*,[41] and hemlocks *bowing to God*. Symbolically, the activities of playing, dy(e)ing, and bowing to God also amount to a kind of summarizing digest, or total network, of life's activities, on the model of the school, the fields, and the setting sun in "Because I could not stop for Death -" (Fr479).

In the same way that the "meek members of the Resurrection" (Fr124B) in their "Alabaster Chambers" have, in some versions of the famous poem, a breeze laughing lightly above them, a bee babbling, and sweet birds piping in "ignorant cadence," these appealingly sensuous squirrels, berries, and hemlocks are sharply conceivable. Their beauty is mirrored by the singsong rhythm of the poem, a soft pattern that partially introduces the world's

physical pleasures into the despairing mind and incites a meditative yet ultimately lacerating experience of their absence.[42]

First, berries are dy(e)ing in either or both senses of the pun, and this
defines the thinking sensations that characterize doom in at least two ways:
when we are in a doom state we cannot pick, taste, or otherwise use the
bright, juicy berries before they die. Not only that, but their very bleeding/
dying is a figure for our own dying on the vine. And those happy squirrels,
we can just see them . . . they too could have been or could still be us, as they
play and eat berries and romp about on the hemlocks. And of course all too
well we know that we could have been more like those hemlocks, bowing
reverently before God, but we were not and are not. We are doomed.

Thus, all of this thinking, imagining, and mental composition not only
does not distract or give relief from doom but forms an integral part of it; the
fear that creative efforts would only intensify suffering haunts Dickinson's
therapeutic theory of poetic composition and prevents the definitions from
ever synthesizing into the Websterian beautiful. Here, in a gesture typical of
Dickinson, the doom dweller's absent pleasures and present sufferings are
both further intensified by the way the berries, squirrels, and trees *interact
with one another* to form a composite canvas of belonging, a communion in
the haze from which doom consciousness is, as it were, ultra-excluded.

As Elizabeth Perlmutter once noted in her short study of what she called
the "existential" poems—those that begin with clauses such as "there is"—
Dickinson tends not to recreate emotions or experiences directly but rather
to characterize them. There is "a sense of meditative experience," she concludes, "which has been rendered detached and abstract by prior assimila-
tion" (110). As is true of many of her definitions, Dickinson's "Doom is the
House" uses present indicatives rather than gerunds to identify the general
or universal properties of the experience, to produce an "objective" definition rather than a subjectivistic, lyricized opinion. Along with the opening
copula and the definite articles used throughout the poem, they represent
some of the metaphysically stabilizing features Dickinson retained from
wider lexicographical culture. Their consistent presence across the definitions confirms Dickinson's propositional, conversational seriousness, even as
she post-metaphysically makes them depend, along with the "detached and
abstract" experiences they define, on the ways individual readers repeat her
thought sequences and interpret her tropes.

"Doom is the House" begins by describing some of the lawlike features of
the experience of doom and then concretizes them by indicating the precise

images aroused in the "Dream." What would be hermeneutically unwarranted, if not unthinkable, for Webster is routine for Dickinson: to include in a definition poem both the universal, structural, and essential aspects of the emotion *and* a descriptive analysis of the workings of consciousness of the one involved in the experience, that is, the ongoing responses to the state being defined. No longer a passive consciousness ready to be impressed and educated, the participant-reader is brought—initially through identification with the lyric subject, then through an experimental rehearsal of the poems' figural logic—to ask questions well beyond the kind mentioned earlier. In the case of "Doom is the House," why does the doomed consciousness imagine *those* three specific things? If *I* were or am doomed, would I—shall I—imagine something else?

To take the poem as a self-experiment or self-test: How shall I interpret the final image of the hemlocks bowing to God? Do I think that hemlocks naturally look like that, and that the persona *qua* doom sufferer or the poet is innocently using a figure of speech? If so, then I can define doom primarily as a nostalgic reminiscence for nature's beauty. Or do I think instead that nature participates reverently in God's transcendence? If so, then I will (agenbite of inwit!) identify with a different kind of doom sufferer, one who regrets not bowing, who feels an infinite ontological exclusion. And if I see the hemlocks as figures for *people* who naturally bow to God—believers—then my doomed consciousness feels specifically distanced from the human community. Other interpretations are possible, but in all cases the open-endedness of this last figure is not so much an example of confused, vague, or gratuitous definition as one of a strong definition being weakened by the *Gedankenexperiment*-style guarantee that the reader will share in its event.

Because Dickinson's post-metaphysical lexicography works in many other ways than by opposition with Webster, it helps to compare her to other contemporaries. I choose the word/concept "experience" because it has so many definitions and connotations—Romantic, utilitarian, Lockean, evangelical, and Transcendentalist, among others—in Dickinson's surrounding culture. First, consider this classic from Benjamin Franklin's *Poor Richard's Almanac*: "'Experience keeps a dear school, but fools will learn in no other, and scarce in that;' for it is true, 'We may give advice, but we cannot give conduct,' as Poor Richard says" (31). This rather humorless conceit on the "costly school" of experience has the moralism and Enlightenment knowledge of unchanging human nature that typifies the *Almanac* as a whole. A slightly warmer version from the Donkey's Dictionary section of the 1858 *Harper's Weekly* reads: "Experience is a flannel waistcoat that we do not think of putting on until after we have caught cold" (January 2, 1858, 15a). It repeats Franklin's observation about experience teaching us badly and belatedly, but instead of stating a truth about other "fools," strains for a universal "we." The flannel coat appearing in the mind when one is freezing is the equivalent of Homer's "Doh!" on television's *The Simpsons*: Why am I so stupid that I never learn from experience?

In Webster's experience there is nothing funny. He emphasizes inductive reasoning, pragmatic wisdom, and morality: a person tries but fails to grow wheat in "clayey soil," and "experience proves" that it will not grow there; experience also teaches the "instability of human affairs" and "the value of integrity." His definition reveals a Lockean view of experience as a vast set of impressions that affect the mind and produce its "knowledge," and his un-Byronized definition reveals how little of "experience" he had absorbed from Kant or the Romantics. Emerson, by contrast, typically gives Idealist interpretations such as those in "The Transcendentalist" that stress the "imperative forms," "*Transcendental* forms," or "intuitions of the mind" through which human experience is necessarily acquired (198).[43] In "English Traits" he criticizes Englishmen for their relentless empiricism and argues (rather quantitatively) that "a good Englishman shuts himself out of three fourths of his mind and confines himself to one fourth. He has learning, good sense, power of labor, and logic" but unfortunately "repudiates" the idea that "experience must follow and not lead the laws of the mind" (*Essays* 903).

What about Dickinson? She too highlights the difficulty of learning something abstract or theoretical through experience and grapples with the Locke-Kant, materialist-idealist dispute:

> Experience is the Angled Road
> Preferred against the Mind
> By - Paradox - the Mind itself -
> Presuming it to lead
>
> Quite Opposite - How complicate
> The Discipline of Man -
> Compelling Him to choose Himself
> His Preappointed Pain -
> (Fr899)

The first stanza states a paradox as fact and challenges us to resolve or dispute it: the mind trusts lived experience more than it trusts itself. This is a paradox not merely because it is unclear why, given the option, one would prefer a road that is not straight, but because the mind cannot prefer something to itself without automatically preferring itself by exercising its power of preferring. The second stanza comments on that fact and can be read as either a Romantic affirmation or a teeth-gnashing condemnation of the way humanity has been abandoned to an inexplicable condition (cf. Fr581). Why are we "compelled" to choose the pain of experience when that choice is itself illusory? One thinks of the way Blake, in his influential *Songs of Innocence and Experience*, used "experience" as a general term for adult corruption and opposed it, as did Dickinson, to the "innocence" of children.

For a thoroughly exasperated Sharon Cameron, the "real problem" with this poem is that its focus shifts in the second stanza. There, she argues, "'The Discipline of Man,' an idiosyncratic but in no way interesting (because not made relevant) periphrasis for the mind, is called 'Complicate,' and this is then stated as the reason man chooses his 'Preappointed Pain,' itself an unexplained paradox" (43). I would point out, however, that in relevant contexts in Dickinson's poetry the word "discipline" means the unique and acute suffering of the human condition. (See: "I can wade Grief -" [Fr312], "I knew that I had gained" [Fr1033], and "The things we thought that we should do" [Fr1279].) The "Discipline of Man" is not a periphrasis for the mind alone; it is shorthand for the painful condition generated by the mind-experience predicament as a whole.

This crooked lyric both registers and protests the discipline of humanity. There is syntactic undecidability (how to parse "Quite Opposite"?), chicken-or-egg reasoning (the mind leads experience but chooses experience to lead it), and especially, at the end, a jarring false rhyme, both visual and aural, that clangs like a minor-chord *sforzando*: "pain" instead of the all-but-inevitable "plan." The sudden replacement (as we feel it) of "plan" by "pain" is both a miniature definitional performance of the whole poem and its knockout punch; it provides a disorienting instant when the smooth intellectual design is disrupted by an ugly shock, when *experience* overrides *mind*.

And yet—paradox—the mind seems to have planned the reader's experience very well: the words "Preappointed Pain" of the last line gather up and concentrate the many "p" sounds in the poem, at least one in every line, and release them against an unexpected sound—*ai*—introduced for the very first time in the just as unexpected last word of the poem: "Pain." The reader *understands* this disruptive, experiential pain—the loss or absence of the word "plan"—only by *feeling* it, but feels it only by understanding it, by planning and preparing for something else in the first place. For Emerson, "experience must follow" the mind, and for Franklin it should lead it. The knowledge they express is universal, so self-certain and reader-independent that it transcends human experience and strips it of its basic condition of non-knowledge. Dickinson resists these limited, binary options and restores the fullness, open-endedness, and uncertainty of human experience to the expression of it by creating for the reader a mental-experiential poem to perform.

"Dickinson chose to preserve the intensity of the performance at the cost of effortless intelligibility for her audience," writes David Porter, and that practice "can be seen as a radical mode of deconstruction" because it demonstrates "the enriching contest between figure and logic in the structure of language itself" ("Poems" 20–21). Indeed, Dickinson's performative, reader-oriented poems are so consistently pragmatic and experimental that she can also be credited with the general view that many ideas and experiences are better defined through performance and event than through analytic description. "Experience is the Angled Road" enacts an enriching contest between Locke and Kant—or more broadly life and thinking—by bringing thought to its limits and *then* using the lyrical properties of language to explore, enact, or experiment with what cannot be brought to univocal statement. Attributing to Dickinson Porter's insight about the costs of deconstructive performances to cognition, I look for it more generally in the warp and woof of the poems themselves and often find them valuably post-intelligible rather than gratuitously pre- or unintelligible.

Thus I insist on the post-metaphysical and deconstructive force of "Aurora is the effort," "Experience is the Angled Road," and myriad other definition poems because I think it is the best way to construct and understand the relationships between broader cultural contests (theological, philosophical, scientific, lexicographical, literary) and Dickinson's poems: her decentering approach to the dictionary and other defining authorities represents a rupture in the theocentric discursivity of her entire culture. Yet her viral suspiciousness rarely overthrows or directly opposes any specific doctrine or message, for it is not narrowly directed at Christian, Romantic, scientific, lexicographical, or any other single language or code. Defining on the slant, Dickinson reaches for deeply rooted semantic oppositions and deconstructs the movement in any language—God's, Upham's, Webster's—that propels thinking on the basis of absolutizing metaphysical distinctions. The dictionary was but one of many available, well-informed, authoritative but unimaginative interlocutors, and like the others, from priest to politician to father to literary critic to her own mind, it functioned most often as a necessary *foil*.

Let us now try one last time to imagine Emily Dickinson defining. Let her be concentrating intensely—we know how often she did this—and let her be thinking, sifting, and vividly imagining a specific topic, either a famously Dickinsonian one like death or awe or another subject such as loneliness or remorse. What really happens in an intensely thoughtful moment like this? The philosopher Jean-François Lyotard has posed a similar question and argued that, according to Kantian principles, any critical consciousness that is ready to pursue a "critique"—or in our thought experiment, a "definition"— has to be in a mood analogous to that of an observer before a painting. If the mind is not "lingering" before itself in a passive, reflective, unemotional state, then it runs the risk of empiricism, that is, of damaging and prejudging its investigations.

On the evidence of Dickinson's critical attentiveness to her own thought, so carefully described in such books as Stonum's *Dickinson Sublime* and Juhasz's *Undiscovered Continent*, one might be tempted to say that her mind "lingers before" and contemplates or scrutinizes itself like a painting whenever it seeks to define an emotion, idea, or experience.[44] This would help explain both the complicated imagery and the self-absorbing poetics that characterize the definitions. In the same way that Kant's *Analytic of the Beautiful* would be a propaedeutic to all critical thought, then, Dickinson's definitions would be an ideal entry into her poetics of frenzy, coherence, and wonderful figures. To a great extent, such a picture of the scene of Dickinson defining is both accurate and beautiful. In almost every case, however, we are also forced to try to think the way it includes the sublimely disruptive powers of frenzy and other emotions, states to which Dickinson was so very susceptible and for which she invented such a rich array of poetic techniques and definitional gestures.

5

Through the Dark Sod
Trying to Read with Emily Dickinson

> The final stage of the Pragmatist's Progress comes when one
> begins to see one's previous peripeties not as stages in the ascent
> toward Enlightenment, but simply as the contingent results
> of encounters with various books which happened to fall into
> one's hands.
>
> RICHARD RORTY, *Philosophy and Social Hope* (1992)

> Am I not a pedant for telling you what I have been reading?
>
> EMILY DICKINSON to Abiah Root (May 16, 1848)

> Through the Dark Sod - as Education -
> The Lily passes sure -
>
> EMILY DICKINSON (1863)

EARLY IN THIS BOOK we looked at how Emily Dickinson used the lyric form in ways that might help post-metaphysical thinkers recognize and redescribe their own contingency. We saw how she adopted a conversational hermeneutics and Eco-style open poetics that underpinned theoretical stances similar to Rorty's liberal ironist, Nietzsche's accomplished nihilist, and Vattimo's interpretive adapter and "weak" thinker. Her many poems on conversation showed an expansive awareness of how reading can shape the self, and her correspondence with T. W. Higginson revealed even more about the relationships she established between thinking and poetry. All this helped explain why, as we saw in chapter 2, she went so far as to develop the "try-to-think" subgenre to extend and experiment with thought itself. Chapters 3 and 4 then tracked a Dickinson weakening strong metaphysical discourses by acquiring and lyrically reshaping philosophical and lexicographical vocabularies and modes.

We have not yet asked, however, how Dickinson strategized *her* reading list. We have not seen her choose conversational companions or even endorse texts that might have directly inspired the kind of open, charitable, conversational hermeneutics she used to negotiate the denial of presence or "the weakened experience of truth." But if Emerson is right that some authors manage to say "that which lies close to our soul," then we might well ask: Who said the things that Dickinson herself was well-nigh thinking and saying? Who was she reading when she decided that reading could be camelizing or elasticizing, a life-preserving activity, a form of conditioning, a prophylactic?

Unlike Emerson, Thoreau, and Whitman, Dickinson did not keep a journal, so despite a century's worth of source studies we still know too little about the specific ways she read and responded to reading.[1] Given the interactive and reader-dependent qualities we have seen in her conversational hermeneutics, it is easy to suspect with Gary Lee Stonum that she wrote "reply" poems that are more directly allusive than has yet been shown ("Background" 53), and with her biographer Richard Sewall that she read "competitively," with her "whole being," as well as for companionship and inspiration (41, 43). Alfred Habegger, who has tried to set some of her fiction reading into the events of her life, lends support to my analysis in chapter 2 of the poet as a sometime Baconian experimentalist when he suggests that she used reading as a "kind of fieldwork, something experimental" (248). He argues that Dickinson stands out for the way she appears to have "defined herself partly through her books," and speculates that she improved her management of male tutors by studying the relationships between Jane and Rochester in *Jane Eyre* and the narrator and Paul Emanuel in *Villette* (227). Like the Victorian heroines, Habegger argues, she did not find "humble veneration" to be incompatible with "great strength," and even "exercised that strength as she read, seeking and extracting what she could make her own" (227).

All of this would help explain how the following 1863 poem analyzes and celebrates reading.[2] The first two stanzas locate the activity in the ongoing patterns of mental life, the third describes the emotional effects of reading on the self, and the fourth steps back to reflect on the value of books in our lives:

Unto my Books - so good to turn -
Far ends of tired Days -
It half endears the Abstinence -
And Pain - is missed - in Praise.

As Flavors - cheer Retarded Guests
With Banquettings to be -
So Spices - stimulate the time
Till my small Library -

It may be Wilderness - without -
Far feet of failing Men -
But Holiday - excludes the night -
And it is Bells - within -

I thank these Kinsmen of the Shelf -
Their Countenances Kid
Enamor - in Prospective -
And satisfy - obtained -

2 tired] Homely -   4 is missed - in] Forgets - for

(Fr512)

The first two stanzas show reading occupies us before, during, and after the books are opened and the mind engaged. Just as receiving praise makes this speaker think fondly of the pain that precedes it, the pleasure she enjoys when she reaches her "small Library" at the end of "tired" or (in the variant) "Homely" days makes her admire her own prior abstinence. As "Flavors" make delayed guests eager for the banquet they will soon attend, the distant aroma of good reading stimulates the time until she reaches the library. Then begins the "feast of reading" Dickinson described in an 1848 letter to Abiah Root, when the "Spices" join the food and expectation becomes event (L23).

The synopsized theory vividly presented in stanza three depends on an ambiguous guiding distinction between "without" and "within," one that evokes the interiors and exteriors of three different spaces all at once: the house, the speaker's room, and the speaker's consciousness. Each circumference reframes the activity and yields a different poem; taken together they confirm the presence of reading in, and its mobility across, the places and experiences of life. No matter how we construe the distinction, reading is affective and antisocial: inside the house, room, or mind, it produces such strong emotions and bright, noisy stimulation—"Bells - within"—that external events, natural or social, fade from consciousness. Who knows, it may be a "Wilderness" outside and people may be dying ("failing Men"), but reading grants us a "Holiday" from all that.

This euphoria may seem to paint reading as exhilarating rather than edifying, but the last stanza steps back from the internal pyrotechnics to remark on its value writ large. The speaker gives thanks to the "Countenances Kid"—leather faces, as in "kid leather"—and underscores the cordial, dependable relationship she has with books, the anthropomorphic language of "Countenances" and "Kinsmen" suggesting that they compare favorably to humans. In fact, unlike God, lovers, death, faith, and other "others" in the Dickinsonian world of object relations, books both announce and achieve high expectations: they "Enamor - in Prospective / And satisfy - obtained -." There "is no Frigate like a Book / To take us Lands away," she confirmed in another poem, for books are "the Chariot / That bears the Human Soul -" (Fr1286). It is no wonder, then, that she told Joseph Lyman that the "strongest friends" of her soul are "BOOKS" (*Lyman Letters* 76) or wrote poems like the following from 1882:

> He ate and drank the precious Words -
> His Spirit grew robust -
> He knew no more that he was poor,
> Nor that his frame was Dust -
> He danced along the dingy Days
> And this Bequest of Wings
> Was but a Book - What Liberty
> A loosened Spirit brings -
>
> *(Fr1593)*

But if reading is a holiday that loosens and liberates the spirit, satisfies, intoxicates, exhilarates, camelizes, elasticizes . . . then what do all these positive, affective responses imply about interpretive protocols? Do they translate to philosophical attitudes of weakening, interpretive application, openness, or hermeneutic conversationalism along the lines we have explored in earlier chapters of this book? To what extent did Dickinson learn her signature conversational and hermeneutic arts from reading?

It makes sense to read her favorite books. She never made a list, but three of them were novels: *The Mill on the Floss*, *Jane Eyre*, and *Aurora Leigh* (a novel in the form of an epic poem). Part of the flourishing nineteenth-century *Bildungsroman* tradition, they describe their protagonists' growth from childhood and analyze the interactions between female self and society, narrating the processes of what is now often called identity formation or self-fashioning: the self negotiates the expectations and constraints of marriage, education, work, class, family, service to society, religion, and other cultural standards. All three of the authors—as well as the fictional authors Jane and Aurora, who ostensibly write their own autobiographical *Künstlerromane*—represent important models of girls and women adjusting to the world through reading and writing.

And yet, might one not object that the genre of the *Bildungsroman* carries precisely the wrong ideology for postmoderns, that today's accomplishing nihilists have little to learn from its lengthy narratives of selves learning to conform or its paradigms of "formation" and adaptation to rigid constraints? Is it not counterintuitive to posit this Victorian prose genre as conversationally compelling for the paradoxes of post-Cartesian human agency "after the subject," in apocalyptic dialectics with the other? Surely the *Bildungsroman* cannot replace Dickinson's poetry in contemporary conversations about conversational hermeneutics, openness, vocabulary selection, anti-foundationalism, and post-metaphysical thought? No, not entirely. But although Dickinson's three favorite novels lack her lyrical array of voices, syntax, meter, vocabulary, and personae, and the unique uses to which she put them, they did—for reasons that are characteristic of the nineteenth-century female *Bildungsroman* as a whole—provide her with important models to incorporate into her reader's hermeneutics and writer's poetics. We can learn from thinking about how she might have done so.

Maggie versus Mr. Riley and Mr. Stelling; Jane versus Mr. Brocklehurst and John Reed; Aurora versus her aunt and cousin Romney: all three girls are subjected to uncharitable reading tests and admonitory patronizing by adult, usually male, authority figures. Beyond inviting readers to reconsider the fairness of the distribution of social and intellectual power—the girls acquit themselves well but get little for it—these scenes offer glimpses of the birth pangs of Rortian ironist consciousness. In reading, they acquire judgment, self-reliance, breadth, and alternatives to the master narratives in which they are raised. And as they defend and explain their reading, they turn their social weakness into philosophical strength: they learn to see many sides of questions and problems, use sincere and ironic language, and develop a keen understanding of the limits of the vocabularies in which they are described. In a manner especially legible to smart, iconoclastic female readers, Dickinson's triumvirate of companion thinkers spelled out possibilities for "weak" or "low" voices and generated the kind of proto-postmodern stances she would ultimately translate and extend in her lyrics, such as incredulity toward metanarratives, anti-foundationalism, and aggressive redefinition of cultural orthodoxies.

Most of all, these books' scenes of young girls reading show how the hermeneutic encounter with strong cultural discourses can sometimes be a dangerous, even fatal activity for the skeptical feminine self, but can also be the site where a rebellious heroine can develop the kind of ironic consciousness necessary to survive. In what follows I suggest that to the extent that her iconoclasm was compatible with one, Dickinson's interpretive community included fictional characters, and that she identified and experimented not only with their lives as such but also with the way they read and linked reading to life.[3]

Nineteenth-century fiction contains many scenes of boys and girls reading books and acquiring useful and useless knowledge. In *The Way of the World: The Bildungsroman in European Culture*, Franco Moretti notes that the English version of the genre generally took childhood much more seriously than the Continental. For him this is no accident: the more a given society "is and perceives itself as a system still unstable and precariously legitimized, the fuller and stronger the image of youth" (185). The category of "youth" in fiction therefore functions as something like a "*symbolic concentrate* of the uncertainties and tensions of an entire cultural system" and the arc of the youthful hero as the convention best allowing authors to explore the competitions and conflicts in social systems (185).

Moretti recalls *David Copperfield*'s total commitment to the "truth of childlike clairvoyance," apparent in the way young David becomes the "ethical-cognitive compass" and "ethical-hermeneutic foundation" of the entire novel (183). Whenever David meets a new character, the way he responds makes it obvious that the "'experience' of the adult reader proves to be absolutely superfluous," for it is always defeated by the superiority of the child's naïveté (183). Luckily, says Moretti, George Eliot came along to transform the entire landscape of the English novel by dismissing this simplistic and binaristic "judicial-fairy-tale model" in which everything was black or white and the child's intuitions unfailing. Her novels profoundly changed the "intellectual physiognomy" of protagonists because, as Moretti bluntly puts it, "now, thank God, they have one" (214). Released from binaristic strictures, the British fictional protagonist could become, much more interestingly and complicatedly, an adolescent struggling against society and advocating deviant and unacceptable expectations.

If, contra Moretti, we include Charlotte Brontë and Elizabeth Barrett Browning as part of the transformation, rather than just the backdrop against which Eliot revolutionized, then we do more justice to all three and make better sense of the strength and coherence of the message about the power and danger of reading available to readers like Dickinson.[4] In all three books, scenes of children reading in straitened circumstances are radical experiments in the making of human subjectivity, moments of heightened sensitivity to the conflict between cultural expectations and real possibilities. They are "radical" experiments because, in each case, the theoretical problem is even more primordial than the one Moretti identifies. Before these children can exemplify *Bildung*, become ethico-moral compasses, or be socialized into public manners and institutions, they must first be *humanized* into language and life itself. Maggie Tulliver, "gone nine, and tall of her age," begins *The Mill on the Floss* as an alien life form, and despite some creative attempts on the part of the narrator, she cannot be made to fit categories of either nature or culture (12). In the space of two pages, she is "half an idiot," "like a Bedlam creatur'," a "mistake of nature," and "a small Shetland pony." In one of the earliest of the book's million indications of her problematically un-fair skin, hair, and temperament, she is also said to have "a brown skin as makes her look like a mulatter" (12–13). Similarly, nine-year-old Jane Eyre is a "rat," a "mad cat," a "discord," a "rebel slave," and a "heterogeneous" and "noxious thing" (9–13). At thirteen, Aurora Leigh is a "wild bird scarcely fledged," brought to her aunt's "cage" (1.310).[5] These are not so much "children" as protoplasmic curiosities, the most unstable, precarious, and paradigmatically youthful kind of "youth" in the symbolic senses of Moretti. Accordingly, the scenes of these protagonists reading are hermeneutically rich points where their minds are shown projecting forward and identifying with new images, plots, and characters. The potent mixture of their eclectic reading, social pressures, and rigorous mental testing nourishes proto-weak, post-metaphysical philosophical stances in the child heroines.

Moretti's theory makes little of gender differences, but they heavily condition the scenes of reading in Dickinson's favorite novels. To see why, it is enough to glance at the way the young protagonist reads in Dickens's *David Copperfield*. As is true for Maggie, Jane, and Aurora, the adults around David make him uncomfortable, and he often escapes into the more hospitable warmth of reading: "I resolved to keep myself as much out of their way as I could; and many a wintry hour did I hear the church-clock strike, when I was sitting in my cheerless bedroom, wrapped in my little great-coat, poring over a book" (118). Just like Aurora, he receives a library from his father, a

> small collection of books which nobody else in our house ever troubled. From that blessed little room, Roderick Random, Peregrine Pickle, Humphrey Clinker, Tom Jones, the Vicar of Wakefield, Don Quixote, Gil Blas, and Robinson Crusoe, came out, a glorious host, to keep me company. They kept alive my fancy, and my hope of something beyond that place and time,—they, and the Arabian Nights, and the Tales of the Genii,—and did me no harm; for whatever harm was in some of them was not there for me; *I* knew nothing of it. (59–60)

Although these favorite titles obviously encourage a romantic view of life that competes with the realism of *David Copperfield* and Dickens generally, they help set David on his way to becoming a successful writer. Yet despite the latent Romantic-realist tension and the fact that storytelling could not be more central to the novel, Dickens does not draw actual scenes of reading with anything like the richness of the Brontës, Browning, or Eliot.[6]

The main reason is that in their *Bildungsromane*, the plots all but require the act of reading to become a site of full-blown hermeneutical analysis: girls turn to books with such hope and desperation[7] that without an explanation of it, their characters would be virtually incoherent.[8] The force with which reading catalyzes the self-interpretations and self-presentations of all three is visible in everything from Jane's enthusing over a book of British birds to Aurora furnishing an annotated childhood syllabus and anxiously insisting that "the world of books is the world" (1.748). It is as if everything surrounding the act of reading were potentially central to the girls' development. David frequently recalls his reading of the "Crocodile Book" but in a mode of comedy and nostalgia utterly unlike, as we will see, the girls' haunting textual encounters, and that is the point: he *can* emphasize the harmlessness of his library. He does not need the text, for he will have the world.[9] This is one reason why Dickens, an author Dickinson always liked, never captured her imagination with much more than his caricatures, turns of phrase, and humorous events and settings.

Jane, Aurora, and Maggie are more extreme examples than David of the "starving and thirsty" condition identified by Vivian Pollak as a "central tension" of Emily Dickinson's own life experience. Reading and education are the (sometimes unsatisfying) wines drunk by starving selves who, as Pollak describes it, suffer from an existential anorexia that is not so much a familial or psychological trait as a cultural condition shared by many nineteenth-century girls and women. It occurs in Dickinson's poems, she argues, because of the "parsimony of a stingy god; the inaccessibility of nature; and the failure of human love" ("Thirst" 63). The hunger imagery expressed in so many Dickinson poems about deprivation and compensatory hermeneutic nourishment—familiar to us already from our reading of "Strong Draughts of Their Refreshing Minds"—may owe something to the descriptions of her favorite child protagonists. Young Jane Eyre, after her mêlée with John Reed, begins "conceiving of starving [her]self to death" (13) and later, "brought low" to an isolated, penniless state, wanders "about like a lost and starving dog" (279). Browning's Aurora is, at the age of three, "A-hungering outward from the barren earth / For something like a joy" (3.889–90). And Eliot describes her young Maggie Tulliver as "thirsty for all knowledge" and affection, noting later that her "highly-strung, hungry nature" has "just come away from a third-rate schoolroom" (205, 311).[10] Whether or not these characters and descriptions directly inspired Dickinson's starving and thirsty personae, they suggest that her poems were not only self-interpretations but also contributions to wider cultural conversations.

Young, intelligent, hungry, spirited souls expanding their minds and confronting social constraints: this is the stuff of both cliché and compelling drama. Their feasts of reading are especially legible events in which religious, political, ethical, philosophical, and other codes battle for supremacy over girls' minds and souls. Recurring scenes include quasi-catechistical interrogations by authorities, usually older males, with young girl readers having their books slammed shut, thrown at them, or simply taken away. Such confrontational staging represented a theoretical counterweight to the dominant culture of literary reviews and mainstream fiction. Unlike sentimental antebellum American novels such as Susan Warner's 1850 *The Wide, Wide, World* or Maria Cummins's 1854 *The Lamplighter*, works in which, as Lisa Spiro points out, "the family comes together around the act of reading, enjoying productive leisure, intimacy, and comfort," Dickinson's favorite books displayed reading as contested and antisocial (57). This is one key to understanding why they *were* her favorite books.

In *Jane Eyre* the narrator obsessively charts her own early relationships with books, inviting readers to look over her shoulder and read along. She even provides exact quotations, proving that her childhood books are still with her many years later, and everything happens as if she cannot proceed with her fictional autobiography until she has communicated the way her habits of interpretation evolved through her childhood. *Aurora Leigh*, another fictional autobiography by another well-read orphan, similarly cannot get off the ground without lengthy analyses of books and learning, and while the first chapters of *The Mill on the Floss* ostensibly portray the Tulliver family deciding "how to find the right sort o' school to send Tom to," his clever sister Maggie is obviously the real problem: "'She understands what one's talking about so as never was. And you should hear her read—straight off, as if she knowed it all beforehand. And allays at her book! But it's bad—it's bad,' Mr Tulliver added, sadly, checking this blamable exultation; a woman's no business wi' being so clever" (16). It is the problem that Dickinson shares with the three young heroines: allays at their books, they have "no business" being themselves.

What is their business? This is a terrible question for all of them. To Higginson, Dickinson gave the famous, enigmatic answer of "circumference," by which she meant something like the interpretation and expression of the limits of thought and experience. Although critics will never be able to identify fully the origins of either her conversational hermeneutics or the unique poetics she adopted to pursue this business—anyway, such a strong metaphysical project works against her own philosophical preferences—a speculative analysis can nonetheless return results compelling enough to help us as we think and read. The complicated scenes of reading in the nineteenth-century female *Bildungsroman* were, for the right reader, potential instigations to the kind of weak, post-metaphysical conversational stances we have seen in previous chapters. To understand this, however, we must enter deeply into the details of how reading was written into Dickinson's favorite books.

George Eliot (1819–1880) and *The Mill on the Floss* (1860)

> No one who knew Emily [Dickinson] in life could ever forget
> her tenderness for Maggie Tulliver, whose adoration for her
> only brother Tom paralleled the deep affection between Emily
> and her only brother Austin.
>
> MARTHA DICKINSON BIANCHI, *The Life and Letters of
> Emily Dickinson* (1924)

The period reviewers of *The Mill on the Floss* sound like Dickinson critics. When they talk about the protagonist, Maggie Tulliver, they stress her indomitable spirit, her craving for love, and her difficulties with duty and religion. As is true of reviewers of the other two books I discuss in this chapter, they underscore the girl's cleverness and sensitivity but draw little attention to her obsession with reading. Because the scenes of reading are too numerous to treat exhaustively, I examine two key moments in Maggie's development: her autodidactic reading as a child and her transformative encounter as a teenager with Thomas à Kempis's *Imitation of Christ*.

The novel opens with a series of contrasts between the nine-year-old wild sprite Maggie Tulliver and her plodding, practical brother Tom, who is "slow with his tongue" and "reads but poorly, and can't abide the books, and spells all wrong" (18). The fact that Maggie knows how to read "almost as well as the parson" impresses her father but not everyone else: what kind of nine-year-old demonstrates intimate knowledge of Daniel Defoe's *History of the Devil* (12)? Why does her *Pilgrim's Progress* (such a good, strong book) fall open to the picture of Satan (16–17)? Ten years later, during an intimate conversation between teenagers, Maggie's friend and confidante, the "gentle unobtrusive" and "tranquil-hearted" Lucy, will come right out and say: "You know Shakespeare and everything, and have learned so much since you left school; which always seemed to me witchcraft before—part of your general uncanniness" (326, 313).

But at nine, when Maggie interprets Defoe for the eminent Mr. Riley, she assumes that he will have "a respect for her now; it had been evident that he thought nothing of her before" (16). Mr. Riley is unforthcoming behind his "high-arched eyebrows," and instead tests her further:

> "Come, come and tell me something about this book; here are some
> pictures—I want to know what they mean."

Maggie with deepening colour went without hesitation to Mr Riley's elbow and looked over the book, eagerly seizing one corner, and tossing back her mane, while she said,

"O, I'll tell you what that means. It's a dreadful picture, isn't it? But I can't help looking at it. That old woman in the water's a witch—they've put her in to find out whether she's a witch or no, and if she swims she's a witch, and if she's drowned—and killed, you know—she's innocent, and not a witch, but only a poor silly old woman. But what good would it do her then, you know, when she was drowned?" (16)

Mr. Tulliver is stunned. Mr. Riley ignores Maggie's interpretation and wonders instead how such an ugly volume has come to be among the Tullivers' books:

"Well," said Mr Riley, in an admonitory patronizing tone, as he patted Maggie on the head, "I advise you to put by the 'History of the Devil,' and read some prettier book. Have you no prettier books?"

"O yes," said Maggie, reviving a little in the desire to vindicate the variety of her reading. "I know the reading in this book isn't pretty—but I like the pictures, and I make stories to the pictures out of my own head, you know. But I've got 'Aesop's Fables,' and a book about Kangaroos and things, and the 'Pilgrim's Progress.'" (16–17)

Mr. Riley again has nothing to say, and Maggie's "free remarks" now make Mr. Tulliver uncomfortable. He tells her to "shut up the book" and suggests that his "child 'ull learn more mischief nor good wi' the books" (17). In what feels like a metatextual wink from Eliot, Maggie's "I know the reading in this book isn't pretty" invites readers to compare Maggie's text with Eliot's.

And indeed, while Jane and Aurora ultimately use their knowledge and resourcefulness to compromise and weave their way back into the social fabric, to very similar marriages and happy endings, Eliot explores a much darker outcome. Book 4, the middle book of *The Mill on the Floss*, has the Bunyanesque title "The Valley of Humiliation." It treats a transformative period in Maggie's life and education and represents a significant analysis of the reading life of nineteenth-century women generally. Chapter 3 of book 4, titled "A Voice from the Past," makes the immense wager that Maggie's life can be entirely restructured by reading a single text: Thomas à Kempis's early-fifteenth-century *Imitation of Christ*. Dickinson had witnessed and heard of any number of religious conversions achieved through preaching and social pressure; here was a rich description of how the act of reading could permanently convert the mind and sanctify the soul.

Depressed by a reversal of fortune, the four members of the Tulliver family are enduring a social ostracism with no end in sight. Maggie is sitting outside with a "battered schoolbook of Tom's" on her knees, a dry wine that gives her "no fortitude" in such a despairing time (229). In what looks like a stroke of good luck, Tom's friend Bob arrives with a collection of books to give her, many with pictures—"a superannuated 'Keepsake' and six or seven numbers of a 'Portrait Gallery,' in royal octavo"—and many others "cram-full o' print" (230). Maggie gratefully receives these volumes and hopes that they will address the problems of her life. The classics have become "bran" to her, as "flavourless" as "dry questions on Christian Doctrine," and she is no longer dreaming of more fanciful authors like Scott and Byron (233). No, she wants books that explain this "hard, real life" and offer some "key that would enable her to understand, and, in understanding, endure, the heavy weight that had fallen on her young heart" (234).

She turns to Tom's schoolbooks, which are very similar to Emily Dickinson's: "the Latin Dictionary and Grammar, a Delectus, a torn Eutropius, the well-worn Virgil, Aldrich's Logic, and the exasperating Euclid" (234). Like an optimistic liberal ironist, she thinks that "Latin, Euclid, and Logic would surely be a considerable step in masculine wisdom—in that knowledge which made men contented, and even glad to live" (234). And so she fills her extra hours with "Latin, geometry, and the forms of the syllogism," feeling an occasional triumphant thrill at being able to understand these masculine subjects (234). But the difficulties of culturally unsupported autodidacticism soon set in: taking her Aldrich out into the fields, she looks from "her book towards the sky, where the lark was twinkling, or to the reeds and bushes by the river, from which the waterfowl rustled forth on its anxious, awkward flight," but is startled to find that even when she does understand the masculine logic of Aldrich, the relation between it and "this living world" is, for her, extremely tenuous (234).

The crisis arrives. Looking back on her education as a whole, she summarizes and rejects it in devastating terms. The total critique of intellectual heritage that led Nietzsche to a philosophy of accomplished nihilism and, as we will see, Aurora Leigh to a positive program and a career as an author, becomes for Maggie the irrevocable rationale for a sudden, conservative turn toward "submission and dependence":

Poor child! As she leaned her head against the window-frame, with her hands clasped tighter and tighter, and her foot beating the ground, she was as lonely in her trouble as if she had been the only girl in the civilised world of that day who had come out of her school-life with a soul untrained for inevitable struggles—with no other part of her inherited share in the hard-won treasures of thought, which generations of painful toil have laid up for the race of men, than shreds and patches of feeble literature and false history—with much futile information about Saxon and other kings of doubtful example—but unhappily quite without that knowledge of the irreversible laws within and without her, which, governing the habits, becomes morality, and, developing the feelings of submission and dependence, becomes religion. (235)

That Dickinson was well prepared to understand Maggie's trials is clear from the fact that when, in 1848, she reached exactly the same point, she too worried deeply about the link between her education and her soul. This also must be quoted at length:

Father has decided not to send me to Holyoke another year, so this is my *last term*. Can it be possible that I have been here almost a year? It startles me when I really think of the advantages I have had, and I fear I have not improved them as I ought. But many an hour has fled with its report to heaven, and what has been the tale of me? I tremble when I think how soon the weeks and days of this term will all have been spent, and my fate will be sealed, perhaps. I have neglected the *one thing needful* when all were obtaining it, and I may never, never again pass through such a season as was granted us last winter. Abiah, you may be surprised to hear me speak as I do, knowing that I express no interest in the all-important subject, but I am not happy, and I regret that last term, when that golden opportunity was mine, that I did not give up and become a Christian. (L23)

Maggie takes the golden opportunity and gives up, and Eliot sets out to do what Dickinson's poem "I think I was enchanted" said could not be done: define the mental conversion occasioned by a single act of self-transformative reading. Having dismissed her education as so much malnutrition, Maggie analyzes the books she has before her and begins to read:

At last Maggie's eyes glanced down on the books that lay on the window-shelf, and she half forsook her reverie to turn over listlessly the leaves of the "Portrait Gallery," but she soon pushed this aside to examine the little row of books tied together with string. "Beauties of the Spectator," "Rasselas," "Economy of Human Life," "Gregory's Letters"—she knew the sort of matter that was inside all these . . . but *Thomas à Kempis?*—the name had come across her in her reading, and she felt the satisfaction, which every one knows, of getting some ideas to attach to a name that strays solitary in the memory. She took up the little, old, clumsy book with some curiosity: it had the corners turned down in many places, and some hand, now for ever quiet, had made at certain passages strong pen-and-ink marks, long since browned by time. Maggie turned from leaf to leaf, and read where the quiet hand pointed. . . . "Know that the love of thyself doth hurt thee more than anything in the world. . . . If thou seekest this or that, and wouldst be here or there to enjoy thy own will and pleasure, thou shalt never be quiet nor free from care: for in everything somewhat will be wanting, and in every place there will be some that will cross thee." (235–36)

Here the reader-text dialectic departs from the earlier ones in *The Mill* where Maggie demonstrated her independence. Removing the conversational, hermeneutic power from Maggie's mind, Eliot suddenly introduces a third term: the brown hand, reminiscent of the "Vision" that, as we saw in chapter 2, miraculously but secularly appears to the "Poet" in Dickinson's "Shall I take thee." This time, however, the strong metaphysical hand enables Thomas à Kempis to come to Maggie as a preinterpreted cultural inheritance, a previous reader who represents an anonymous, authoritative Christian tradition, waiting for her in the margins of her book.

The disembodied spiritual guide takes control and quashes Maggie's play with inherited vocabularies. No longer a liberal ironist, she is "hardly conscious" that she is reading at all. Her piercing eyes glaze over as her mind opens itself to pleasurable quiescence: "Forsake thyself, resign thyself, and thou shalt enjoy much inward peace" (237). Some twenty more lines of Thomas à Kempis are quoted, all encouraging self-abnegation and the suspension of the will, with the effect that a

strange thrill of awe passed through Maggie while she read, as if she had been wakened in the night by a strain of solemn music, telling of beings whose souls had been astir while hers was in stupor. She went on from one brown mark to another, where the quiet hand seemed to point, hardly conscious that she was reading—seeming rather to listen while a low voice said—

"Why dost thou here gaze about, since this is not the place of thy rest? In heaven ought to be thy dwelling." (236–37)

Maggie's powers of critical reading and questioning had only just crested with her critical deconstruction of her entire education to date, but they are now converted into listening and accepting.[11] As the obscure, distant text and interpreter redescribe her life, they form a single live, speaking voice, a commanding and unmediated presence rather than a conflictual site of interpretation where presence is painfully denied. Here "was insight, and strength, and conquest, to be won by means entirely within her own soul, where a supreme Teacher was waiting to be heard" (237). In this version of Emersonian abstraction, reading does not help one think but tells one what and how to think. So long nauseated by aimless autodidacticism and left "without the aid of established authorities and appointed guides," Maggie finds in the anonymous but supreme reader a premodern solution to her postmodern hermeneutic crisis. It is a new final vocabulary, a key to all mythologies, "a secret of life that would enable her to renounce all other secrets" (239). And once the brown hand is internalized, reading is no longer a difficult mixture of attraction and alienation. It is superfluous, and Maggie renounces it entirely.

In the young Maggie Tulliver, Emily Dickinson met the questioning, philological, spirited sides of her self and culture, and in the converted one she found the accepting, Christian, self-renouncing sides. This *Mill* chapter is the term between, the test of how far she could or should join her thought to the patterning power of tradition. We know that Dickinson took this test because her own copy of *The Mill on the Floss* is marked (probably by her own hand) at precisely the passage in which Maggie describes reading in her anonymously marked copy of *The Imitation of Christ*. Dickinson also had a copy of Thomas à Kempis, presented to her by Susan Gilbert Dickinson.

In fact, right at the time she discovered *The Mill on the Floss*, Dickinson was being pressured by the same forces that brought Maggie to conversion. On April 4, 1860, she received from her father a book of sermons by Harvard Professor of Christian Morals Frederic D. Huntington: *Christian Believing and Living*. He too quotes Thomas à Kempis, "Si crucem libenter portes, te portabit" (If you carry the cross willingly, it will carry you"), and preaches the "docility of the soul" (344, 515). Ten days later, an issue of *Saturday Review* appeared containing an article describing the trials of Maggie's life, her attachments to imaginative literature and mystical religion, and finally her struggle with "the fierce moral conflicts awakened by a passion to which she thinks it wrong to yield." The whole book "is entirely in the vein of Charlotte Brontë," writes the reviewer:

> *Mill on the Floss* shows that George Eliot has thought as keenly and profoundly as the authoress of *Jane Eyre* on the peculiar difficulties and sorrows encountered by a girl of quick feeling and high aspirations under adverse outward circumstances. But the objection which we feel to difficult moral problems being handled in fiction is certainly not removed by the writings of either of these gifted women. What does it all come to except that human life is inexplicable, and that women who feel this find the feeling painful? It is true that a girl like the heroine of the *Mill on the Floss* is not an improbable character. (April 14, 1860, quoted in Eliot, *Mill* 446)

Life is tough but inexplicable, and fiction cannot handle difficult moral problems. Such platitudinous self-satisfaction may help explain why Dickinson's favorite books pay so much attention to the hermeneutics of reading and to the fraught conversations that "not improbable" girls have with their culture.

Ultimately, however, Maggie represents the kind of hermeneutic catastrophe that only proves how real the dangers of reading were for Victorian girls who were learning to try to think. Her sui generis hermeneutic powers cannot withstand the forces marshaled against her: Thomas à Kempis comes to her in adolescence, in a time of radical self-doubt, when her family has been isolated and she is nauseated by her entire intellectual upbringing. This is the moment when things could turn out differently and she might become an accomplished nihilist, a liberal ironist, or an Emily Dickinson. But instead of camelizing or elasticizing, she petrifies: in spite of her natural intelligence and love of books, she relinquishes reading, never becomes a writer, and in fact dies.

"All men say 'What' to me," said Dickinson to Higginson, and Maggie is undoubtedly one of her kindred spirits: a girl who spooked authorities with bold interpretations and inappropriate books like Defoe's *History of the Devil* (L271). Yet Dickinson responded very differently to the same forces that presented themselves to Maggie. By the time she read *The Mill on the Floss* she was over thirty years old, and soon, on April 15, 1862, she would send her first letter and group of poems to Higginson. And just as important as her maturity at the moment when she was tested by Maggie is the fact that she had already internalized two other female characters, Jane Eyre and Aurora Leigh. Both of these girls had undergone similar hermeneutic tests and had escaped to become not just readers and thinkers but writers as well.

Charlotte Brontë (1816–1855) and *Jane Eyre* (1847)

> Oh what an afternoon for Heaven,
> When "Bronte" entered there!
>
> EMILY DICKINSON (1860)

In what biographer Alfred Habegger describes as her first encounter with a "major woman's text," Emily Dickinson read, and loved, *Jane Eyre* by "Currer Bell" late in 1849, when she had just turned nineteen (226).[12] As a literary critic she said little, but a girl who could fully enjoy contemporary favorites such as Longfellow's 1849 *Kavanagh* or Ik Marvel's 1850 *Reveries of a Bachelor* could only have been delighted by some of Brontë's innovations, such as the use of a plain, unidealized female protagonist to carry the narrative, the emphasis on childhood experience as potentially decisive for adult life, and the metatextual use of scenes of reading.[13]

The book begins on an English day so cold and rainy that nobody can go outside. Matriarchal Mrs. Reed is sitting by the fire in Gateshead Hall surrounded by her "darlings," children Eliza, John, and Georgiana (5). Jane, the nine-year-old orphan also under her care, has been "dispensed from joining the group," a privilege accorded only to "contented, happy, little children" (5). When Jane meekly inquires what she has done to deserve her exclusion, Mrs. Reed's sharp answers drive her to seek refuge in reading:

> "Jane, I don't like cavillers or questioners: besides, there is something truly forbidding in a child taking up her elders in that manner. Be seated somewhere; and until you can speak pleasantly, remain silent."
>
> A small breakfast-room adjoined the drawing-room. I slipped in there. It contained a bookcase: I soon possessed myself of a volume,

taking care that it should be one stored with pictures. I mounted into the window-seat: gathering up my feet, I sat cross-legged like a Turk; and, having drawn the red moreen curtain nearly close, I was shrined in double retirement. (5)

Brontë, or the older narrating Jane, presents reading as a religious ceremony, a procedure for contacting a new world and finding meaning when one's own is devoid of it. It is an exotic ritual, a secularized prayer that Jane performs "cross-legged, like a Turk," "shrined" in her sacred space of "double retirement from the world." By obvious opposition to the oral, public, distressing familial space controlled by Mrs. Reed and her children, reading is quiet, secluded, solitary, and potentially restorative. The surroundings are so carefully drawn that they transcend their function as realistic literary decor: "Folds of scarlet drapery shut in my view to the right hand; to the left were the clear panes of glass, protecting, but not separating me from the drear November day. At intervals, while turning over the leaves of my book, I studied the aspect of that winter afternoon. Afar, it offered a pale blank of mist and cloud; near a scene of wet lawn and storm-beat shrub" (5–6). Enclosed on the window seat with theatrical red curtains behind her, Jane is clearly a spectacle and a specimen under glass: "Come see *The Reading Girl*!" the text nearly proclaims. This forces Brontë's readers to become both playgoers and naturalists, to watch themselves watch Jane read and contrast their situation with hers. Jane's place is the precariously liminal one between two equally cold, inhospitable zones: the cultural sphere of the home where she is an alien and a prisoner, and the natural, equally forbidding sphere of the cold outdoors. Squeezed out of both habitats, belonging nowhere, thrown on her own resources without weapons or protection against any of these threats, Jane reads. At first this seems to promise either emotional compensation for the loss of Eden or escapist enjoyment during forced exile, but soon it turns out to be a more self-interpretive and creative means of winning agency.

Jane may be flustered, but she slips easily into her ritual and construes everything—the world outside as well as her book—as readable. Rhythmically, "at intervals, while turning over the leaves," from book to outside, outside to book, Jane "studies the aspect" of the winter day. It may be unpleasant inside and outside, but in Kantian aesthetic terms nature is still beautiful, susceptible of human cognition, and potentially "final" with it. Physically but not hermeneutically separate from culture and nature, Jane starts to see herself as a bird: "I returned to my book—Bewick's *History of British Birds*: the letterpress thereof I cared little for, generally speaking; and yet there were certain introductory pages that, child as I was, I could not pass quite as a blank. They were those which treat of the haunts of sea-fowl; of 'the solitary rocks and promontories' by them only inhabited; of the coast of Norway, studded with isles from its southern extremity, the Lindeness, the Naze" (6). Young Jane must have been quite serious about this bird book, we think, and must also have a strong memory since she is recounting so precisely an episode of reading from many years earlier. Like young David Copperfield, who enjoyed the pictures in Peggoty's copy of *Fox's Book of Martyrs*, Jane has deliberately chosen a volume "stored with pictures." But while David remembers little more than enjoying the time he spent reading— "I do not recollect one word," he makes a point of noting (145–46)—Jane remembers both the images and the way her mind was drawn away from them into the writing, the "letterpress," almost against her will.

Scenes of Jane reading are, in the Dickinson lexicon, italicized moments when the imagination is active and consciousness is especially open both to passive processes like perception and revelation and active ones like self-projection and self-definition.[14] Brontë is careful to document the way Jane both struggles against and yields to the power of the writing, her absorptive mind making her dangerously free to experiment with new images and define herself in new terms. Here the Rortian ironist's process of experimenting with vocabularies takes on gothic and Romantic contours:

> Nor could I pass unnoticed the suggestion of the bleak shores of Lapland, Siberia, Spitzbergen, Nova Zembla, Iceland, Greenland, with "the vast sweep of the Arctic Zone, and those forlorn regions of dreary space,—that reservoir of frost and snow, where firm fields of ice, the accumulation of centuries of winters, glazed in Alpine heights above heights, surround the pole, and concentre the multiplied rigours of extreme cold." Of these death-white realms I formed an idea of my own: shadowy, like all the half-comprehended notions that float dim through children's brains, but strangely impressive. The words in these introductory pages connected themselves with the succeeding vignettes, and gave significance to the rock standing up alone in a sea of billow and spray; to the broken boat stranded on a desolate coast; to the cold and ghastly moon glancing through bars of cloud at a wreck just sinking. (6)

We accept quite readily that in an illustrated book of British birds, Jane finds new lexical and visual vocabularies to fit her life and project it forward. She is attracted by the "forlorn regions of dreary space" presumably because they offer a symbolic language for her dawning, (over)dramatic conception of her situation as lonely seafowl in a frozen haunt: if I am a lonely British bird like these, then perhaps these places are my true home. Like the many names of places in Dickinson's poetry, from Vesuvius to Chimborazo, *Bewick*'s exotic names are irresistible: Siberia, Spitzbergen, Nova Zembla! (Are Lapland, Iceland, and Greenland lands of laps, ice, and green?) We transition into Jane's internal world and watch as the desolate images that end the passage become part of the vocabulary for her emerging self-conception: "the rock standing up alone in a sea of billow and spray," "the broken boat stranded on a desolate coast," "the cold and ghastly moon glancing through bars of cloud at a wreck just sinking." Borrowing and using the terms she is borrowing and using, we wonder how she will deal with her loneliness and the universe's cold indifference. Will she be a "wreck just sinking" with a "cold and ghastly moon" gazing upon her? Or a "rock standing up alone"? Young Jane does not ask these self-thematizing questions, but her attempts to redescribe herself in melodramatic terms are unmistakable both to the older Jane and to readers of *Jane Eyre*.

Already the scene has become less an event in the external plot sequence than an exposition of young Jane's interpretation and self-projection. In fact Jane's mind becomes so central that we are forced to pay increasing attention to the distinction between the old/narrating and young/narrated versions of Jane.[15] There is an unresolved tension in the autobiographical narrator's voice between the pride she takes in the achievements of her young mind—"I formed an idea of my own," a "strangely impressive" one—and the concern she has to represent her earlier child-self with the (now socialized) humility and distance that become her adult self. "Half-comprehended," "shadowy," and (in what shortly follows) "dim," "mysterious," "undeveloped," "imperfect"; all of these words for error and uncertainty emphasize young Jane's limitations as an interpreter, but they also highlight her openness to redescriptive edification.

The narrator's balancing act between youthful, rebellious, creative reading and mature, conservative certitude reveals itself most strikingly in the way words are given independent agency in Jane's consciousness: "The words connected themselves with the succeeding vignettes, and gave significance." The verbs are strong and active—"connected," "gave significance"—but their subject is not any aspect of Jane (her will, mind, or imagination). We are asked, somewhat improbably, to believe that the "words" on the page, not unlike the brown hand that enters Maggie's consciousness, do all the work. Why, after painting Jane's studiousness and precociousness, does the narrator suddenly oversimplify the ongoing psycholinguistic description by representing her as a passive, Lockean site of nonvolitional combinations? Why can the narrator not describe Jane's hermeneutic encounter with *Bewick's* in the terms of textual openness that young Jane is threatening to experience, the kind that readers like Dickinson were capable of glimpsing?

Giving the words the upper hand in the act of reading reflects a tergiversation caused by Brontë's competing expectations for the scene, one symbolic of the larger social competitions suggested by Moretti's theory. The "Reading Girl" set piece functions both as an anthropological study of a cultural practice and an event in the ongoing narration whose transgressive implications are hard to control. If Jane were allowed to choose and commit freely to the *Bewick's* images, it would endow her with so much self-awareness, ethical investment, and motivation that it would compete with the narrative of her development—among other things, her antisocial bitterness might become a fixed trait—and this would reduce the play, essential to the plot, between the defined older and the undefined, self-projecting younger Jane. The grammar thus preserves the passivity and open nature of Jane's mind *and* maintains her innocence: the words work *their* will on her, she does not work hers on them. But this is ultimately a dangerous game: How can a girl enjoy experimenting with vocabularies and Watts-style mind expansion, turning self-discovery into self-creation, without relinquishing her status as a Rousseauian Sophie?[16] Brontë's main target is the assumed cognitive innocence of girls, not the ethical, but the two are hard to keep separate.

Aside from the defensive and apologetic criticism of her younger self, Jane the older has little to say about how she has integrated or transcended Jane the younger. It is a problem endemic to autobiographical fiction but acute here because readers are invited to imagine a series of framed reading scenes: young Jane reading *Bewick's*, older Jane reading and writing the way her younger remembered self once read *Bewick's*; Brontë reading and writing both; everybody reading *Bewick's* and quoting it so that we can read it too— not to mention us, keeping all of these scenes in mind while thinking of Dickinson reading them. It is difficult to identify causal connections among these *mise-en-abyme* spectacles of reading, and just as difficult to identify wholly with either Jane. Has the older one become too metaphysically secure to understand her younger, "weaker" self? Is this what forces her to resort to Brocklehurstian formulae like "undeveloped understanding and imperfect feelings"? To watch the younger one's mind interact with her book, begin to use its images and language to organize her own self-understanding—in such a way that it even defies her own older self—is to recognize a model for Dickinson's complex, postmodern appreciation for split subjectivities and all the modes of reading from camel to elastic.

After Jane has set the historical precedent of resisting her torturer Master John Reed for the first time, and after she has been locked in the Red Room and liberated again, nurse Bessie offers her a tart and asks her if she would like a book. The "word BOOK acted as a transient stimulus, and I begged her to fetch *Gulliver's Travels* from the library. This book I had again and again perused with delight" (17). Crucially, however, this time the magic is gone, for "when this cherished volume was now placed in my hand—when I turned over its leaves, and sought in its marvellous pictures the charm I had, till now, never failed to find—all was eerie and dreary; the giants were gaunt goblins, the pigmies malevolent and fearful imps, Gulliver a most desolate wanderer in most dread and dangerous regions. I closed the book, which I dared no longer peruse, and put it on the table, beside the untasted tart" (17). Few readers, not Dickinson, could miss the point that Jane's cultural rebellion coincides with drastically altered conditions of interpretation. At precisely the moment when she defies the patriarchal order, we watch her lose the ability to eat and read. As the nutritive and medicinal properties of the "BOOK" evaporate, along with the charm from the "marvellous pictures," a proto-camelizing self that was approaching self-sufficiency turns into a *non-*reading self stuck with *just* herself, a Rortian ironist with no good vocabulary, forced into anorexic self-denial and unable to redescribe her intolerable circumstances.

If, in the eyes of the Reed household, a once docile girl has been made strange by disobedience, then in the eyes of Jane the same thing has happened with her "cherished volume," *Gulliver's Travels*: it rejects *her*, and she can no longer suspend her disbelief and take it as a "narrative of facts" (17). It is therefore important that the text made strange is a familiar favorite; it makes this an *unheimlich* moment, a liberal ironist's self-alienating, anti-edifying, vocabularistic crisis in which the things one knows and trusts most become frightening and alien. Perverted, though not entirely gone, are the dialectic of identification and self-discovery from *Bewick's* and the ability to gain productive "significance" by linking words to images. The giants are now "goblins," the pygmies "malevolent imps," and even the thoughtful Gulliver "a most desolate wanderer in most dread and dangerous regions." The polarity shift occurs across the whole text at once: Gulliver becomes a dark version of Jane's self-description, and so she closes the book, afraid of it and herself.

Dramatizing the way different but coherent editions of *Gulliver's Travels* are created by Jane's moods, the episode introduces a radically subjectivist perspective on reading that went largely unrecognized by period critics. The credibility and value of criticism was seen then, as it largely is today, to depend on notions of stable, impartial texts and meanings. Yet for a reader like Dickinson, scenes such as these from *Jane Eyre* raise valuable questions about the "open" hermeneutic consequences of a volatilized reading subject. The gothic-Romantic atmosphere of this experience with *Gulliver* repeats the Red Room terror of alienation from the human community; the difference is that now the threat has moved into the internal space of reading, that is, into Jane's psychology, and she cannot turn to books to lose and find herself *safely* anymore: the budding liberal ironist is confronted with a plausible but dangerous vocabulary. Like Dickinson's Watts and Eberty volumes examined in chapter 2, Jane's *Bewick's* and *Gulliver's Travels* include a great deal of mind-expanding long-distance travel, but as Jane's domestic universe takes on the attributes of the indifferent, alien universe, the once enticing possibilities for redescription turn from liberating to self-annihilating.

But Brontë seems determined to show a broad range of hermeneutic encounters. In a manner that recalls both Maggie Tulliver and the Dickinson we looked at in chapter 2, Jane next reveals herself to be a careful, sympathetic, but also transgressive reader of the Bible. Mr. Brocklehurst conducts the interrogation:

> "Do you read your Bible?"
> "Sometimes."
> "With pleasure? Are you fond of it?"
> "I like Revelations, and the book of Daniel, and Genesis and Samuel, and a little bit of Exodus, and some parts of Kings and Chronicles, and Job and Jonah."
> "And the Psalms? I hope you like them?"
> "No, sir."
> "No? Oh, shocking!" (27)

This time Jane is deviant because she prefers the epic and miraculous stories to the moralizing and faith-affirming Psalms. The whole scene prepares her for Rochester's later withering interviews and takes place as a parody of the way literary reviewers and other Victorian cultural authorities addressed and infantilized women readers. The point comes home when Brocklehurst gives Jane a "Child's Guide" that includes "an account of the awfully sudden death of Martha G——, a naughty child" (29).

Unfazed, Jane continues her defiance and, after she wins a heated verbal battle with Mrs. Reed, sits down to read yet again. Troubled by her own rhetorical victory, she feels that she "would fain exercise some better faculty than that of fierce speaking; fain find nourishment for some less fiendish feeling than that of sombre indignation. I took a book—some Arabian tales; I sat down and endeavoured to read. I could make no sense of the subject; my own thoughts swam always between me and the page I had usually found fascinating" (31–32). Now Jane explicitly intends for her consolatory reading ritual to *change herself*: she seeks a book that will give her "nourishment" for a "less fiendish feeling." But it is a disaster: earlier, the charm had left *Gulliver's Travels* but she had at least remained in its power, terrified but challenged by the uncanny reversal of its visual and narrative vocabularies. Now a similar hermeneutic event is so radical that it gives way to senselessness. Reading stops. We may be tempted to mark it all up to Jane's feelings of self-disgust and guilt following the argument, but the passage emphasizes her thought over her emotion: when she says, "My own thoughts swam always between me and the page," one can plausibly hear "*my own* thoughts" (nobody else's) or "my own *thoughts*" (not my emotions). Either way, Jane's mind is unacceptable to her culture, her family, and herself; her thoughts are so real and so intolerable that they destroy her most trusted source of losing and finding herself: reading.

Critics never remark that *Jane Eyre* begins as if it were set in Borges's "Library of Babel," where the plot turns on exposing its own future narrator to multiple and contesting hermeneutic paradigms. From this perspective Brontë's novel can be read as a postmodern fable in which the heroine's success depends on her ability to negotiate, and later narrate, a battery of bewildering interpretive initiation rites. Each of the early episodes features a different mind-text encounter and represents an aspect or stage of Jane's resistance and response to being constructed by society: rejected by her community, she projects herself into the universe through bird imagery; defying the patriarchal order, she is estranged from a favorite and familiar book;

under pressure from an obnoxious authority, her defiant reading of the Bible holds firm; another confrontation explodes the act of reading.

A reader like Dickinson could not miss the way Jane's struggles with reading place an important part of her psychological individuation outside the novelistic logics of character models and social aspirations. To devote so much early character development to reading weakens, in particular, the dialectics of positive and negative role models: yes, the plain-looking orphan Jane is "not Helen Burns" and "not Georgiana and Eliza Reed," but these oppositions based on rank and privilege lose much of their textual oxygen to the intrasubjective hermeneutics of reading. At the moments of self-creative crisis, when Jane's thoughts and projects could still become anything and are about to become something, at those moments when she *really* acquires the fortitude and independence to attract and defy a Rochester bored by the world's Blanche Ingrams, she imagines, identifies, and creates herself not so much through the Reeds as through reading.

Elizabeth Barrett Browning (1806–62) and *Aurora Leigh* (1856)

> Let who says
> "The soul's a clean white paper," rather say
> A palimpsest, a prophet's holograph.
>
> *Aurora Leigh*

To all evidence, Elizabeth Barrett Browning ranked first in Dickinson's private canon of inspirational woman authors, and the long "novel-poem" *Aurora Leigh*—some two thousand lines longer than Milton's *Paradise Lost*—first among books. She read it in 1859, the same year she learned that the George Eliot who had written *Adam Bede* was actually Marian Evans of Coventry, England.[17] She marked it more heavily than her other books, memorized passages from it, and wrote tribute poems to its author. If the plot of *Jane Eyre* has broad parallels with Dickinson's love life and emotional and intellectual temperament, then *Aurora Leigh* maintains many of these and adds key ingredients from de Staël's *Corinne* to the mix: the story of a girl who chafes against her conservative education, adopts a nonconformist intellectual life, and ultimately becomes, against tremendous social and familial pressure, a writer. Kathleen Hickock describes Mrs. Browning as systematically exploring "virtually all the women's roles with which the public was familiar in mid-nineteenth-century England" and rejecting conventional wisdom "at virtually every point" (131–32). Cora Kaplan suggests that the most revolutionary of the story's transgressions is the way Aurora is depicted as an independent writer: instead of merely romanticizing the life of a solitary woman author, Browning paints it more radically as "possible, interesting, and productive" (101). In all these ways, it is right to see Aurora as a model for Dickinson.

And like *Jane Eyre*, *Aurora Leigh* was also important for its study of the power and possibilities of the reading mind, and for the manner in which reading is linked to the rest of the heroine's life. When Dickinson mentions the book in a letter, she does not refer to the great credo about art and poetry in book 5, nor to its echoes of the *Jane Eyre* love plot. She draws attention to the way Browning, like George Sand, transcended the trials of painful education: "That Mrs. Browning fainted, we need not read *Aurora Leigh* to know, when she lived with her English aunt, and George Sand 'must make no noise in her grandmother's bedroom.' Poor children! Women, now, queens, now"! (L234). In neither case did the stifling circumstances of childhood prevent later artistic fulfillment.

Aurora Leigh is born in Italy to a Florentine mother and an English father; her mother dies when she is four, her father when she is thirteen, and she is educated in England by her father's sister. As with *The Mill on the Floss* and *Jane Eyre*, the opening sections of the book include many scenes of reading and education, and they are just as central to the full narrative.[18] Whereas young Jane stands out, however, against unintellectual characters, Browning makes a key figure of Aurora's spinster pedagogue, the "English aunt," who, Dickinson notes, caused Aurora to faint. Having "lived / A cage-bird life" as opposed to the wild bird Aurora, the arch-Victorian Miss Leigh attends a "poor-club" to prove her humility and a "book-club" to protect her from dangerous questions (1.302–5). Most of the first book of *Aurora Leigh* is a sobering, sarcastic deconstruction of the values and modes of indoctrination she embodies, and the way Aurora learns to combat her Victorian program represents nothing less than a how-to guide and philosophical template for smart, iconoclastic girls like Dickinson. It is a model of how an embattled liberal intellectual can set about redescribing her entire culture.[19]

Trying to think with Emily Dickinson, we benefit from looking in detail at Aurora's strategy. Although "feebler souls" would have succumbed to Miss Leigh's depredations, Aurora endures because she develops a multifaceted resistance (1.470). First, she draws solace and strength from her memory of retrieveless "relations in the Unseen"—her dead mother and father—and from the "elemental nutriment and heat" in the natural world (1.473–75). These sources are a constant shield from the life "thrust on" her by her circumstances, and they allow her to keep her inner life separate, with "ample room / For heart and lungs, for will and intellect, / Inviolable by conventions" (1.477–80). As the older Aurora retrospectively tells it, once she was possessed of a free, columnar self, she was able to rethink her reading, and her ability to alter her relationship with books is ultimately what allowed her to escape spiritual, intellectual, and even physical death.

There were two decisive steps: she rejected the social improvement model of reading and widened the canon of acceptable texts. The transgressiveness, at the time, of the second of these projects explains her insistence on both quantity—"I read much" (1.710)—and eclecticism: she read "books bad and good—some bad and good / At once" (1.779–80), as well as "moral books," "genial books," "merry books," "melancholy books . . ." (1.785–89), all before the discovery of her father's secret literary hoard. And *how* did she read them? It turns out that Miss Leigh caught hold of Aurora too late, for the teenager had already learned key lessons of self-reliance and skepticism. Her father had taught her "out of books . . . all the ignorance of men, / And how God laughs in heaven when any man / Says 'Here I'm learned; this, I understand'" (1.189–92). He had armed her for life against the authoritative and the sure, the brown hands, the Brocklehursts, and this negative knowledge prepared the way to Aurora's more individualistic mode of reading.

To "get the right good from a book," asserts Aurora, we must leap into a self-risking, sublime mode of textual encounter and "gloriously forget ourselves." Just as she rebelliously says her prayers "without the vicar," then, she reads books without

> considering whether they were fit
> To do me good. Mark, there. We get no good
> By being ungenerous, even to a book,
> And calculating profits,—so much help
> By so much reading. It is rather when
> We gloriously forget ourselves, and plunge
> Soul-forward, headlong, into a book's profound,
> Impassioned for its beauty and salt of truth—
> 'Tis then we get the right good from a book.
>
> *(1.698–709)*

Repudiating the calculation of "profit" from books, this theory, like Dickinson's tintinnabulatory hermeneutic holidays, demands that readers neither measure nor moralize but plunge soul-forward into texts with insouciant generosity. The value of the mediating critic, diminished already by Aurora's anti-canonical eclecticism, all but evaporates since it no longer means anything to know which books have which amounts of "beauty and salt of truth" in them.

If the narrating Aurora/Browning seems to be opposing one absolute metaphysics with another, then the "weakening" difference—as with the Dickinsonian ideas of reading as pleasurable feast, conversion experience, or elasticization—is that skydiving readers are, like Rortian ironists, metaphysically insecure entities, readily de-camelizing and losing themselves in books. Opposed to official culture's "wrong" good of moral improvement and social hierarchy and stability, Aurora's "right good" is emotional, personal, and experiential. The stakes become clearer as Aurora joins her ideas about reading to a theory of the soul, a complex passage worth quoting at length:

> The cygnet finds the water, but the man
> Is born in ignorance of his element
> And feels out blind at first, disorganised
> By sin i' the blood,—his spirit-insight dulled
> And crossed by his sensations. Presently
> He feels it quicken in the dark sometimes
> When, mark, be reverent, be obedient,
> For such dumb motions of imperfect life
> Are oracles of vital Deity
> Attesting the Hereafter. Let who says
> "The soul's a clean white paper," rather say
> A palimpsest, a prophet's holograph
> Defiled, erased and covered by a monk's,—
> The apocalypse, by a Longus! poring on
> Which obscene text, we may discern perhaps
> Some fair, fine trace of what was written once,
> Some upstroke of an alpha and omega
> Expressing the old scripture.

(1.815–32)

Unlike swans, people are born in ignorance and sin, with their "spirit insight" blocked by "sensations." The movements of inner life nonetheless reveal the presence of divinity, for the unexpected, unanalyzable spiritual quickenings in the dark are oracles that testify, as they did for Wordsworth, to immortality. In a direct attack on Lockean empiricism, Aurora quotes and rejects the dictum from *An Essay Concerning Human Understanding* that the "soul's a clean white paper," but instead of correcting it with the "sublime axiom," transmitted from Leibniz to the rest of European and American culture by Madame de Staël's *On Germany*, that "nothing was in the intellect other than sense experience, *except the intellect itself*" (*De l'Allemagne* 418),[20] Aurora likens the soul to a textual construct, a "prophet's holograph."[21] This metaphor, as does Locke's of the blank sheet of paper, postulates that the soul has unity, structure, and conceptual coherence, but only as an unreachable ideal or dream of coinciding zero degrees of writing and selfhood. Not only is the soul not a blank page; it is not an interpretable "first draft" from which other drafts emerge, either.

The contrast between mechanistic and hermeneutic philosophies could not be stronger. While, as we have seen, Lockean materialism encourages empirical and associative analyses of mental sequences, Aurora's theory of the soul-text instead requires a complicated historical and cultural hermeneutics. The soul is *never* available to be fully read, translated, or understood, for it is like a first draft made unrecognizable and unrecoverable by later processes of writing, "defiled, erased and covered" like divine truths scribbled over by lowly monks or an "apocalypse" overwritten by the obscene tales of some romance-writing Longus. Poring over the soul, one might be able to discern some "fine fair trace" of the original Logos, the pure "old scripture," but never the whole text, part of which has been permanently erased. It is therefore not a matter of retreating to the origins and reading the original document; the soul-text as palimpsest is inevitably, conversationally co-constructed by writings and readings.

From this postmodern announcement that subjectivity is structured by endless rewriting, we pass to the discovery of a huge cache of ink, the texts that will help *write* Aurora even as they help her learn to write: "Books, books, books" (1.833)! Among these, the dramatic, long-delayed arrival of poetry to Aurora's consciousness puts the finishing touches on her account of the writings that made her what she is. Hidden under her pillow, a book beats "in the morning's dark, / An hour before the sun would let me read! /

My books (1.842–44)"! The effusiveness of these and many more rapturous lines about poets and poetry helps account for the tone of Dickinson's tribute poem to Barrett Browning:

I think I was enchanted
When first a sombre Girl -
I read that Foreign Lady -
The Dark - felt beautiful -

And whether it was noon at night -
Or only Heaven - at noon -
For very Lunacy of Light
I had not power to tell -

The Bees - became as Butterflies -
The Butterflies - as Swans -
Approached - and spurned the narrow Grass -
And just the meanest Tunes

That Nature murmured to herself
To keep herself in Cheer -
I took for Giants - practising
Titanic Opera -

The Days - to Mighty Metres stept -
The Homeliest - adorned
As if unto a Jubilee
'Twere suddenly confirmed -

I could not have defined the change -
Conversion of the Mind
Like Sanctifying in the Soul -
Is witnessed - not explained -

'Twas a Divine Insanity -
The Danger to be sane
Should I again experience -
'Tis Antidote to turn -

To Tomes of Solid Witchcraft -
Magicians be asleep -
But Magic - hath an element
Like Deity - to keep -

(Fr627)

That the poem's "Foreign Lady" is Elizabeth Barrett Browning we know because the rhetoric of "witchcraft" and poets as "witches" is borrowed from *Aurora Leigh*.[22] The opening "I think" is sometimes glossed as a tentative "I suspect," but it works even better as an "I believe," or "I reason," confidently introducing the poem's narrative arc from the beautiful to the sublime, from how reading produced an enchanting feeling that led to a "Divine Insanity."

The "Dark" connotes several things. It reaches back to the speaker's self-description as "sombre" in the second line: "I realized it felt beautiful to be me," it suggests, "for my own darkness—of mood, thought, appearance—felt more beautiful as I read." It also refers to the night that surrounds the reader as she reads, as well as the ignorance, or the unknown, into which the reading mind projects itself. Above all, reading made the dark *feel*: the speaker was enchanted rather than taught, converted rather than enlightened. Like the self-abandoning Aurora diving for the "right good," or the young Jane Eyre with *Gulliver's Travels*, Dickinson's reading speaker is buffeted about by exciting images and states: all is confusion and synesthesia, not message. In fact there are multiple disorientations: temporal (noon and night), cognitive (Lunacy), and sensorial (light): "And whether it was noon at night - / Or only Heaven - at noon - / For very Lunacy of Light / I had not power to tell -."

One reason we read Dickinson today is that despite the fact that she has "not power to tell" the self-italicizing experiences brought on by reading, she resourcefully finds figural language to describe and analyze their ineffability. A three-part progression (bees to butterflies to swans) traces the onset of a transformative process with no natural end, as reading transforms the small, routine, minor, and mean into the grand, special, major, and important: "The Bees - became as Butterflies - / The Butterflies - as Swans - / Approached - and spurned the narrow Grass - / And just the meanest Tunes // That Nature murmured to herself / To keep herself in Cheer - / I took for Giants - practising / Titanic Opera - // The Days - to Mighty Metres stept - / The Homeliest - adorned / As if unto a Jubilee / 'Twere suddenly confirmed -." Reading has made the speaker's relationship to Nature grow hallucinatory and intimate: the morphing bees/butterflies/swans "spurn the narrow grass" and approach *her* instead. Nothing less will do than the rhetoric of religious conversion: the "Homeliest" day "adorned" and "confirmed" unto a "Jubilee."

Yet vivid and connected as these images are, and despite that fact that the conversion is a matter of "the Mind" and not of Nature or Heaven, the speaker again says she cannot analyze the process: "I could not have defined the change - / Conversion of the Mind / Like Sanctifying in the Soul - / Is witnessed - not explained -." As in the Brontë passage discussed earlier, where the narrator suddenly attributes all the power to the words themselves, the question is when a reader's headlong plunging ends and her conscious awareness, interaction, and hermeneutic engagement begin. Crucially, the last two stanzas propose that we can compensate for the total loss of agency we experience during reading . . . by rereading: "'Twas a Divine Insanity - / The Danger to be sane / Should I again experience - / 'Tis Antidote to turn - // To Tomes of Solid Witchcraft - / Magicians be asleep - / But Magic - hath an element / Like Deity - to keep -." The divine insanity produced by reading is but a higher form of sanity, a perilous but revelatory experience. Author-Magicians may be dead, "asleep," but because the magic of their writing is always alive, waiting to be awakened by a contacting consciousness, they feed an endless dialectic of holidays and workdays, of self-destructive and constructive reading.

In both Brontë and Browning, Dickinson found models of antiestablishment, hermeneutically inflected perspectives on reading. *Jane Eyre* provided a typology of different textual encounters and their roles in (de)constructing subjectivity, and *Aurora Leigh* added metavocabularies: a top-down critical analysis of Victorian culture's ideologies of reading; a post-Lockean theory of mind and reading; a postmodern view of the self as endlessly rewritten text; a Romantic theory of how to enjoy and use books.

In all three of the novels we have looked at, the plot elements at the center of so much nineteenth-century fiction—self, love, money, family, society—are conditioned and complicated from the start by the interactions the protagonists have with their books. Their broad message is that although reading may be the royal road to intellectual and emotional self-sufficiency, it is an angled path littered with unexpected obstacles and unpredictable outcomes. At any moment a girl can be repulsed or inspired by her education, brainwashed or emboldened, liberated or converted. Well-loved books can suddenly be made strange and new meanings discovered in or projected onto texts. Carried into adulthood, a hard-won education in critical reading can produce anything from the successful camel Aurora Leigh to the grotesque apotheosis of a reading life embodied in Dorothea Brooke's disastrous marriage to Casaubon in Eliot's *Middlemarch*. Carried into Dickinson's life, this education nourished an open-form lyric with postmodern powers of conversation much different from those of the *Bildungsroman*.

According to Moretti, the *Bildungsroman* lives and dies with the social problems it was invented to address. If so, its generic strength helps explain the power of these novels to attract and inspire Dickinson, a poet of weak thought, for their very triumph signals that society's "truly central ideologies" are not

> intolerant, normative, monologic, to be wholly submitted to or rejected. Quite the opposite: they are pliant and precarious, "weak" and "impure." When we remember that the *Bildungsroman*—the symbolic form that more than any other has portrayed and promoted modern socialization—is also the *most contradictory* of modern symbolic forms, we realize that in our world, socialization itself consists first of all in the *interiorization of contradiction*. The next step being not to "solve" the contradiction but rather to learn to live with it, and even transform it into a tool for survival. (10)

The fact that Dickinson's favorite novels were *Bildungsromane*, authored by women and featuring female protagonists, suggests that they helped her identify the contradictory ideologies and discourses surrounding her, learn to live with them, and make them "tools for survival." The scenes of children reading occur early in the books and early in the protagonists' lives, long before the crushing mechanisms of plot and social constraints can resolve them into the static states of fixed opinion, marriage, or death. Representing some of the most concentrated theoretical centers and avant-garde edges in the genre as a whole, the activities of these child hermeneuts help create the proto-postmodern spaces that Eliot called "the triple world of Reality, Books, and Waking Dreams" (*Mill* 225). This is the world where readers like Dickinson could begin to interiorize contradictions and learn to think about reading, thinking, and trying to think.

6

With Bolder Playmates Straying
Dickinson Thinking of Death

Perhaps Death – gave me awe for friends – striking sharp and early, for I held them since – in a brittle love – of more alarm, than peace.

EMILY DICKINSON to T. W. Higginson (February 1863)

The "they" does not permit us the courage for anxiety in the face of death.

MARTIN HEIDEGGER, *Being and Time* (1927)

Are you certain there is another life? When overwhelmed to know, I fear that few are sure.

EMILY DICKINSON to Charles Clark (mid-June 1883)

IN THIS BOOK WE have seen Dickinson in many postmodern roles: an accomplished nihilist, a liberal ironist, a poet of weak thought, and more. We have seen some of the major discourses in and against which she developed an open, conversational hermeneutics, and looked at how she used lyric poetry experimentally and therapeutically to pursue difficult projects of thought. Can all of this now be more closely connected to her existential poetry, to her frequent tries at thinking the limits of being? Is it possible that her signature poetics and philosophical orientation, the products of lifelong hermeneutic encounters with her culture, can help edify post-metaphysical postmoderns in circumstances where redescriptions are especially unsatisfying: in thinking of death?

In this chapter we look at how Dickinson's poetics of death converses with both her intellectual inheritances and her postmodern inheritors. Close examination of a single, usually neglected death poem shows her reworking the Romantic vocabulary of the sublime emerging from Kant, Wordsworth, and others in ways that predict twentieth-century articulations by Jean-François Lyotard and Jean-Luc Nancy. We also see how she adapted ideas of childhood, play impulse, and "naïveté" from the German Idealism of Friedrich Schiller to produce a logic of sacrifice and sovereignty along the lines of Georges Bataille. Once again, close reading and historicized hermeneutics are required for us to uncover the pragmatic and therapeutic potential in Dickinson's backward- and forward-looking existential experiments.

The early 1880s were traumatic years for Dickinson. During this final period of her life (she died on May 15, 1886) she endured the deaths of many friends and family members, and her search for a way to think of death may help today's readers find words for what they are well-nigh thinking and saying. Transpiring in a post-metaphysical perspective is the deceptively simple reminiscence poem from 1882: "Of Death I try to think like this" (Fr1588). Its striking, straightforward opening line conversationally announces the "like this" of interpretation as its main subject and then both prepares and deprives us of an interpretation of death. The question of how a consciousness can "try" to control the way death appears to it ultimately finds a complex (non)answer not in Christian or other visions, and not in personification—these options are explored in many other poems—but in a complicated figural pattern with many transitions which ultimately results in interrupted transcendence "at the end." Of course any effort to rethink death threatens to veer into received wisdom and standard cultural definitions; but "Of Death" works against orthodoxies by drawing on private memories and linking tropes in ways that do not result in a fixed position. The narrator describes an eyewitness account, and, as happens in Burke's and Kant's theories of the sublime, her experience of dangerous events from a safe distance inspires a strong response. Like the lexicographical lyrics, the poem draws on a sublime poetics and mimes but weakens its own ostensible metaphysical purpose, and like the Baconian try-to-think poems, it invites us to initiate our own thought experiment and reenact the way death proposes itself to our thought.

A first look at the poem shows that when the speaker tries to think in this way, her thought falls into two major parts, first evolving through several figures and then seeming to stray—perhaps following a hidden logic—to a vivid memory of a childhood moment when she saw a playmate confront "Doom itself" by leaping over a brook for a flower:

Of Death I try to think like this,
The Well in which they lay us
Is but the Likeness of the Brook
That menaced not to slay us,
But to invite by that Dismay
Which is the Zest of sweetness
To the same Flower Hesperian,
Decoying but to greet us -

I do remember when a Child
With bolder Playmates straying
To where a Brook that seemed a Sea
Withheld us by it's roaring
From just a Purple Flower beyond
Until constrained to clutch it
If Doom itself were the result,
The boldest leaped, and clutched it -

7 Flower] *written* flower Flower   15] Were Doom itself the
penalty -   16 boldest] bravest

(Fr1588)

Of Death I try to think like this. The present tense is difficult because it
might indicate recurrence—"of death I always try to think like this, this is
my general approach to death, my most advanced and profound thinking
on the subject"—but could also suggest urgency and immediacy: "of death
I am trying very hard, even as I write, to think like this." Since the speaker
proceeds to elucidate her thought not with grand systems and polysyllabic
words but with a personal childhood memory, the first line may also be read
as a humble, self-effacing preface. We may hear the characteristically "weak"
voice identified by Habegger saying, "Well, for what it is worth, here is a try.
This might be a way of thinking about death." Desperate or meditative, exploratory or persuasive, no matter which voice we choose to hear, this poem
is another of Dickinson's lyrical efforts to think the limit of being. And unlike
many poems—"Because I could not stop for Death -" (Fr479); "I heard a Fly
buzz - when I died -" (Fr591); "I died for Beauty - but was scarce" (Fr448)—
this one tries to think of death without developing the perspectival fiction
of having experienced it. The try of both thought and poetry is ultimately
distilled into the figure of the flower-jumping child.

Dickinsonian conversationalism is built deeply into the poem. The first stanza's near-prose feel, elegiac frame, and vivid present-tense narration of its own progress—this is how I think and remember—all contribute to form a setting that may be anything from quietly meditative to intensely argumentative. It opens a conversation with the second stanza, which seems to announce itself, in just as many voices, as a parable or an illustration of the first. Most of the tropes, scenes, language, and visions of community in the first stanza are meticulously yet mysteriously metamorphosed, echoed, or elucidated in the second. The speaker begins her meditation in the first stanza with the universal scene of a funeral and a group of mourners: *The Well in which they lay us.* This is in the present tense, and the community in view is public, adult, formal, lawful, civilized, ceremonial, and traditional. By stark contrast the second stanza, narrated in the past tense, describes a time long ago and a tribe that is private, playful, youthful, informal, and unlawful. It represents life as youth but also life at an earlier historical moment (the heroic or aristocratic age). In some ways these children also recall the hermeneutically open-minded reading girls we examined in the last chapter.

Both stanzas play with the same structure: a personal statement by a lyric "I" in the opening line is followed by a more far-reaching elaboration using the pronouns "we" and "us." Each stanza also features a provocative but sustained inversion in the use of articles, one that "openly" renders fluid the distinction between the perspectives of speaker and reader. The first stanza uses definite articles—"the Well," "the Brook," "the same Flower"—for a description that, as the plurals "they lay us" suggest, remains so general that it seems that it *should* require indefinite ones. Instead of trying to reenvision our grave as a well, any well, we are asked to think of it specifically as "the Well." Since we assume that Dickinson is writing abstractly and symbolically of wells, brooks, and flowers, this air of confident precision brings the first stanza to the brink of nonsense: What "Brook" in our past, exactly, threatened not to "slay" but to "invite" us? Surely it is presumptuous to assume that we have all already met with this fearful yet attractive Brook? One gets the eerie sense that one's own past is being included in a universal analysis of death that has been motivated by someone else's memory. And vice versa: the second stanza uses *indefinite* articles for an extremely precise private memory: "a" Brook, "a" Sea, "a" Purple Flower. Although the speaker now brings to mind this specific scene, these images are cited algebraically to suggest that we must all have some such memory and that anyone can use the vocabulary of her own experience to arrange an attitude toward death.

The first stanza involves a progression of figures (the grave is like a well, the well like a brook), and the second, relating a particular memory, turns the now-literalized brook into a figure for the sea. The explanation for the sweet-and-sour appearance of the first brook appears to be connected to the second brook's "roaring" and to the boldest child's unexplained leap, but it is not clear exactly how; among other things, the child is "constrained" by an unnamed force. Nor are we sure whether the brook seemed impressively vast and loud to all the "bolder Playmates" or just to the more timid and metaphorically minded speaker. Finally, the mythologically weighted and strangely exact "same Flower Hesperian" of the first stanza seems to translate into the more indeterminate "just a Purple Flower" of the second.

Is it the point that the leaping child is a version of Hercules, who, in his eleventh labor for Eurystheus, reached for the golden apples in the forbidden garden of the Hesperides? On the one hand, the child's separation from the community of children and leap for a flower is not heroic from any of the usual mythic or dramatic perspectives, since he or she does not seek glory or sacrifice anything for the group—at least the speaker does not think so—but acts for more personal reasons. And the child's object is *just* a flower, which seemingly subtracts the mythical element. On the other hand, the whole scene has enormous power to inspire and test the adult speaker's readiness to leap into the unknown of death. Indeed we might see the speaker herself as the Herculean figure, since in many versions of the story Hercules succeeds in reaching the Hesperian fruit only indirectly: he often talks Atlas into "leaping" for the apples in his place. Dickinson's speaker likewise watches the "boldest" child engage in an unmediated act of self-risk, and capitalizes on this to create a poetic thinking of death.

The overall result is a characteristically open-form poem that places several demands on its readers. Already it is clear that trying to think with this speaker means, at a minimum, trying to decide where and how to place ourselves in the imagined communities of adults and children, and whether to accept or adapt the progression of tropes. As interpreters, we must also negotiate the strangely inconclusive ending in which the child leaps and we are left guessing and thinking about why we were not told what happened. As individual thinkers, we are generally asked to experiment with the taxing yet theoretically palliative hermeneutic situation of thinking about our own death while creatively reviewing our memories.

Readers will differ on how well the speaker ultimately manages to mitigate death anxiety. Given the characteristically post-metaphysical perspectives we have seen in Dickinson, it is not surprising that this speaker does not posit death as something to pin down, represent accurately, or otherwise conceptualize on the basis of metaphysical principles. She thinks of her death not as a truth, essence, or event to simulate but as an always-impending, never-present state to be apprehended through responsible, introspective, and imaginative thought. The poem represents neither the analytic process of eliminating illusory understandings of death nor the creative attempt to construct death's best or most beautiful figural elaboration. It is neither summary nor critique of what the speaker has learned of death, nor even a statement of what she knows or wants to know of death. It is pragmatic and post-metaphysical, a try for useful thought rather than a reach for apodictic truth, and it showcases thinking as a conversational, lyric activity.

As the speaker tries to think "like this" rather than "like that," she makes detailed and interacting analogies and borrows from her heritage. Thus it helps to contrast the poem's thinking both with Dickinson's Christian options—visions of the afterlife, reunion with God, resurrection, and so on—and with Socrates' famous rationalistic argument. The "state of death," he says, can be only one of two things: either "the dead man wholly ceases to be and loses all consciousness" or death is some kind of "change and a migration of the soul to another place" (Plato 47). Either way, Socrates' mind is satisfied and his argument untouched by anxiety. The speaker's method departs from these patterns in part by integrating uncertainty deeply into the process of thinking of death. As is true of traditional vocabularies of the sublime, she emphasizes not the ultimate success or failure of reasoning but the effort of thought, that is, the experience of the resistance produced, as we have seen in earlier chapters, by the Kantian contest between reason and imagination. The way this poem negotiates that resistance is also noticeably different from the epistolary account we looked at in chapter 2, when the teenaged Dickinson repeatedly tried and failed to "realize" her own death as a potential, actualizable event. There she provided static imagery and got repeatedly stuck on the failure to harmonize reason and imagination, but here, as we will see, the dynamic figures both enact death's process of non-presencing and help create a desirable attitude toward it. In short, the speaker no longer calls on tropes to express or visualize the scene of her death but rather to help her deal with the way it does *not* present itself.

The sequence of images provides some of the poem's therapeutic, post-metaphysical power: first there is a grave (a point in the earth), then the grave becomes a well (still water), and then the well becomes a brook (running water), and finally, after a leap of thought through time and memory, the brook leads to the sea and the image of a child leaping to clutch a flower. Trying to bring death forth and into thought in a tolerable, credible way produces the Odyssean navigational track of an explorer departing from civilization: from a fixed point on land, thought sets off and runs to the infinite sea.[1] As is typical of the tradition of the sublime, this presentation emphasizes the complex emotional appeal of a scene that is both threatening and alluring. Not only is the brook that seems like a roaring sea a sublime image of fear, awe, and attraction, but the forbidden "Flower Hesperian" also "decoys" to greet and "invites" by a "Dismay" which is the "Zest of sweetness." The speaker's thought, after a tropological transformation of the way death comes to presence, has produced a past tense and, in the process, discovered or created a death that, after all, "was" not menacing but complicatedly *inviting*.

Because this process of thinking of death can be understood as an instance of what Gary Lee Stonum has called the "Dickinson sublime," it is helpful to recall here some key features of his study. Stonum shows that Dickinson's poems generally respond well to the way sublime experience was generally structured during the Romantic period. As outlined in Thomas Weiskel's 1976 description of "the orthodox Romantic sublime," the basic model of most philosophical (e.g., Burke and Kant) and literary (e.g., Wordsworth and Byron) versions of Romantic sublime experience boiled down to three phases. The first stage is simple being-there: one is as one is, minding one's business, moving unproblematically through the ordinary routines of life. The second stage is traumatic: one is suddenly overwhelmed or uplifted by an exciting, ecstatic experience. Perhaps one loses the sense of self or feels as if the top of one's head has been taken off. The third stage is reactive: one gains or regains a new coherence, a clearer view, and a (re)affirmation of a sense of totality, individuality, order, and identity.

So many of Dickinson's poems respond to Weiskel's basic scheme that Stonum does not even need to mention some of the most obvious examples. One definition poem, for example, restates the theory itself:

> Exhilaration is the Breeze
> That lifts us from the Ground
> And leaves us in another place
> Whose statement is not found -

Returns us not, but after time
We soberly descend
A little newer for the term
Opon Enchanted Ground -

(Fr1157)

Every element in Weiskel's account is clearly visible in this poem: starting from the "Ground" state of everyday life, "Exhilaration" lifts us up and brings us to a second, ineffable state. The third stage is reactive: the ordinary ground is now "Enchanted," and a new coherence is gained: "We soberly descend / A little newer for the term."

As Stonum's careful reading of many other poems demonstrates, Dickinson's overwhelming tendency is to cherish the second phase without spelling out in much detail the way the third differs from the first. More precisely, he shows that her poems generally *hesitate* between phases two and three, refusing to relinquish ecstasy but refusing, too, to offer any explanatory control over it.[2] As a rule, nothing is retained from the experience of the second phase: its "statement is not found." According to Stonum, the ambiguous times and spaces of Dickinson's settings also materially reflect her preference for the liminal experiential zone between the trauma and the anticipated resolution. Temporally, he argues, Dickinson's poems tend to prolong this "otherwise vague interval," while spatially their "scenelessness exemplifies the indeterminate relation between those two moments" (*Sublime* 180). "Exhilaration is the Breeze" is therefore exemplary for the way it prizes ecstatic experience but does not provide it with spatiotemporal setting, causal explanation, or visionary detail.

In Weiskel's terminology, also adopted by Stonum, all of this makes Dickinson's poetry more Romantically "sublime" than "visionary." Weiskel explains that in the writings of both Kant and Wordworth, the sublime often brings us "to the frontier of the 'invisible world'" but then "leaves us as soon as that world is consciously represented or given any positive content" (43). Because, in the model shared by both writers, the sublime "remains negative, dialectical, a movement between two states, an indeterminate relation," whenever the invisible world is thrown into serious doubt the whole "possibility of a sublime moment evaporates" (43). We can glimpse Dickinson's fluctuating attraction to these options in the way she so often narrates moments that defy narration: the act of dying, the transition between life and death, and after death. "Of Death I try to think like this -" ends with a dynamic, liminal, amphibious, stop-motion image of a leaping child, a figure for the kind of sublime thought process that simultaneously respects the Kantian restriction of reason in the noumenal world and yet peers at it and tries to think about it.

"Of Death," however, also suggests that if Dickinson's poetry interpretively adapts her precursors' model of the sublime, then it also ultimately exceeds the descriptive power of the visionary-sublime vocabulary. Unlike much Romantic poetry of either kind, for example, which strives to arouse emotion or illustrate belief, Dickinson's short poems often pursue a rigorous questioning and closely study mental movement. Because her process assigns an important role to imagery, it will help to consider another late poem that sheds light on the way Dickinson used tropes to structure sublime inner experience. Set against "Of Death," the poem suggests that our inability to understand the steps leading to and from a sublime experience is cognate with our inability to understand death. The two situations both call for and deny great efforts of thought and "face to face" confrontations:

No man saw awe, nor to his house
Admitted he a man
Though by his awful residence
Has human nature been.

Not deeming of his dread abode
Till laboring to flee
A grasp on comprehension laid
Detained vitality.

Returning is a different route
The Spirit could not show
For breathing is the only work
To be enacted now.

"Am not consumed," old Moses wrote,
"Yet saw Him face to face" -
That very physiognomy
I am convinced was this

(Fr1342)

"Awe" finds here a stripped-down Ovidian figural analysis recalling the houses of Sleep, Envy, Rumor, and Hunger in the *Metamorphoses*. According to the finely worked logic of the poem, one can neither "see" awe nor be admitted "to his house," although one can and perhaps must go "by" or "feel" his "dread abode." The poem therefore emphasizes not an original try at thinking that gives way to exhaustion and a breakdown in mental faculties but the movement between phases two and three: as soon as the "grasp on comprehension" is "laid," one awakens, flees, and yet finds that "vitality" is "detained." There is an invisible tractor beam surrounding the house of awe, and we do not even "deem of" (dream of, take consciousness of, form an opinion of) his constraining presence until we are already "laboring" in its aftermath. The idea that "human nature" has no direct cognition of awe but that we conceptualize it ex post facto in mediated fashion recalls Kant's argument that the "*astonishment* amounting almost to terror, the awe and thrill of devout feeling, that takes hold of one when gazing upon the prospect of mountains ascending to heaven, deep ravines and torrents raging there, and the like" is not "actual fear" but is produced by our "attempt to gain access to it through imagination" (*Critique of Judgement* 120–21). As we have seen in earlier chapters, it is when thought fails to satisfy its own demands that the sublime can begin. In Kantian terms, the sublime is occasioned by "the objective inadequacy of the imagination in its greatest extension for meeting the demands of reason" (121).

In "No man saw awe" the Kantian effect of being rendered ecstatic by the failure of one's grasping comprehension has a liminal phase two/phase three temporal component that is registered geographically: "Returning is a different route." One can neither "leave" the state of awe the same way one enters nor mentally reconstruct the experience. In other poems one may sometimes be "a little newer for the term" after experiencing an exhilarating phase two, but in "No man saw awe" the descent is carried out by rhythms beyond seeing and conscious understanding. What is left is the mechanical *corpus*: "The Spirit could not show / For breathing is the only work / To be enacted now." The speaker cites the searing theophany of Moses not for anything positive or visionary but because his gasping monosyllables register bare survival.

Now we are ready to see how "Of Death I try to think like this" relies on an isotope of the figural logic for sublime non-presence developed in "No man saw awe" but includes an important twist. Instead of a wandering, unexpected encounter with a traumatic experience, analyzed from the perspective of having survived it, Dickinson narrates a proactive, teleological attempt at thinking. Yet this positive thought project relies heavily on the interruptive force of the last lines: readers are made uncomfortably aware that the speaker knows but has not told what happened to the child, that she has installed the possibility of a transcendent answer and then post-metaphysically withdrawn it. There is, of course, physical momentum in the final image, and the scene implies some sort of splash, crash, death, or safe landing: happily or unhappily, the "boldest leaped, and clutched it -." For the speaker, the drama unfolded and became a memory long ago, so to all appearances she is exercising a divine reticence and, as in "Prayer is the little implement," we are left again with "Presence denied," forced to go over the poem for clues.

The hand on the flower, the last dash, and the blank page disorientingly combine to create a syncope of thought itself. Reinforcing the excruciating narrative inconclusiveness, the near-repetition in the rhyme "clutch it" / "clutched it" repeats the effect from "Because I could not stop for Death -," in which the unexpected duplication of a crucial word balks the poem (there it was "Ground / Ground"), as well as the reader's sensibility, the dramatic development, and one can even say all the forward progress of the speaker's and reader's minds. The strongly emotional verb "clutch" is itself on the limit between brushing lightly and holding tightly; here it connotes both the unstable grasp of a hand in motion (I *clutch* at straws) and the attractively unmixed attachment of a child (who *clutches* a teddy bear).[3]

The poem's final lines make it even clearer that Dickinson's goal is not to think more objectively about death than others in her adult community but to align her thoughtfulness with the child's paradoxically "thoughtless" thoughts before leaping for the flower. At the same time, it is clear that we have not yet really understood why the jumping child is such a powerful image in the first place. To do that, it is necessary to reconstruct more carefully the speaker's reconstruction of the child's pre-logical "logic."

Trying to think, narrating her reconstructed memory, the speaker in "Of Death I try to think like this" improvises the idea of a *constraint*: the child sees the flower on the other side of the brook, and then "Until constrained to clutch it / If Doom itself were the result, / The boldest leaped, and clutched it -." I do not believe that this is just her melodramatic way of saying that all death is difficult, that people are prone to reckless impulses, or that the hubristic youth, like Icarus, did not realize the dangers involved in soaring over the water. There is noticeably no psychological premise or truism given: the child is absolutely but inexplicably "constrained" to transgress, to risk, to seize what "decoys" and offers itself as forbidden. Despite the presence of the playmates, no sentiment of communal will seems to exist, so peer pressure also fails to explain the necessity that the thinker/speaker retrospectively identifies in the leaping child's action. The child may be the "boldest" of the "bolder Playmates"—the children are not distinguishable by sex, age, or any characteristic but boldness—but having great courage does not explain why one should feel constrained to clutch a flower.

So why the leap? Why does the speaker reconstruct the attitude of the leaping child as a necessity rather than a choice, and why the flower as a sublime Hesperian offering?[4] The way she tells it, her bold playmate considers the brook that "withholds" all of the children "by its roaring" and then leaps. Although the length of time implied in "Until" is richly open to interpretation, there is little if any thinking here, for the child does not examine and calculate the situation in any way. The child does not choose a course of action or strategize a means of obtaining the flower, does not willingly risk something (injury, life) in order to obtain something else (the flower and what it represents) because it is "worth it," does not hope, dream, imagine, or do anything that might be considered calculative. As a group, the children build no machines to get to the flower, they use no sticks to reach it, they do not plan and execute any concerted or communal action, they do not work together to achieve a goal, and they do not manipulate their environment in any way. They do nothing thoughtful, teleological, or technological whatsoever, and none of these possibilities even presents itself as a way to liquidate the constraint the child feels. The implication is not that a rational or technological solution to the problem of how to get the flower is "too troublesome." The child never thinks that way. Thus the fact that it is a child and a community of children is not just relevant, it is crucial. The scene is primal, before and beyond both civilization and scientific, experimental thought.

Before looking for vocabularies to describe and explain this, it is worth looking briefly at a companion poem in which Dickinson canvasses figures for the way they articulate an expansive, experiential *now*:

> How much the present moment means
> To those who've nothing more -
> The Fop - the Carp - the Atheist -
> Stake an entire store
> Opon a moment's shallow Rim
> While their commuted Feet

The Torrents of Eternity
Do all but inundate -
3 Fop - the Carp -] Dog - the Tramp -   5 shallow] fickle
7 Torrents] waters   8 all but] almost
(Fr1420)

If we include the variants, we have Fop, Carp, Atheist, Dog, and Tramp. Like the flower-jumper and other Dickinson children, these five figures represent attitudes that radically, even absolutely, renounce teleology in favor of an expanded experiential "now." The two animals are important because they represent the extreme limit of living outside the existential constraints of time consciousness, of living "in order to" or being-toward anything. The variety in this list only begins to reflect the lifelong care Dickinson gave to the problem of the meaning of a-teleological life—visible in the many meditations on Eternity as endless, unchanging presence—and the poem's first line invites readers to try to shift perspective and understand what a full, italicized experience of the now would really mean.[5] The poem is almost always read as criticizing these a-teleological figures from the superior perspective of those who wisely meditate on their last ends, but the high status of their representative and champion, the "boldest child" in "Of Death I try to think," suggests that the poem may also be celebrating those who dare to explore the limits of how much the present moment can mean.

One important context for Dickinson's flower-jumpers and now-italicizers is the theory of children and of play impulses Friedrich Schiller put forth in such works as *Letters on the Aesthetic Education of Man* and *Upon Naïve and Sentimental Poetry*. Dickinson almost certainly read the latter in translation in Frederic Henry Hedge's 1848 *Prose Writers of Germany*, a volume owned by the Dickinson family.[6] Using the German Idealist distinction between Reason and Understanding noted in chapter 3, Schiller distinguishes between two attitudes toward children. Our lower, mundane, ordinary faculty of understanding sees in children "an idea of weakness," one that provokes laughter and makes us feel our "(*theoretic*) superiority" (Hedge 374). But our more spiritual, intuitive faculty of Reason helps us see that "childish simplicity" is not a form of "folly, or imbecility, but a loftier (*practical*) strength, a heart full of innocence and truth," and our jest passes into admiration (374). We come to "lament that we are not like" the child (374).

The reason adults can be impressed by children and "experience emotion" in their presence, argues Schiller, is not that their "appearance of helpless-ness" gives us a sense of superior strength. On the contrary: children are "humiliating rather than gratifying to self-love," inspiring not because we can look down upon them "from the height of our power and perfection" but because we look up at them "out of the limitation of our condition" (373). In particular, the limitation of adults derives from the static condition we have attained. Our "definite mode" and "fulfillment" contrast sharply with the child's "bias and determination" and "boundless determinableness" (373). Using the premise that adults are not primarily moved by what the understanding sometimes mistakenly perceives as the "neediness" or limita-tions of the child, but rather by what our Reason intuits as "the appearance of its free and pure power, it integrity, its infinity," Schiller reaches his Idealist conclusion that children represent a specific kind of "actualization of the ideal": not "one fulfilled" but "one proposed" (373).

As we saw in chapter 5, Dickinson was attracted to the free and pure power of children and the ideal they propose to adult thought. The "boldest" child in "Of Death" recalls the wild young Maggie Tulliver and registers the poem's strong Schillerian undercurrent.[7] And yet "Of Death" also stages a scene in which a child exhibits modes of pure thoughtlessness, constraint, and self-sacrifice that Schiller's theory of children's naïveté does not quite explain. Being ultimately concerned with larger, un-Dickinsonian issues of building national culture, Schiller also does not think of children hurling themselves into the void, and does not develop an existential perspective on the basis of his theory of play impulse. Nor does the Kantian philosophy on which Schiller draws fully explain Dickinson's boldest child. Although Kant's *Analytic of the Sublime* could propose a detailed explanation for the combination of dismay, sweetness, and zest that characterizes the way the flower presents itself to the child or death to the speaker, the sacrificial logic of the child's "constrained" leap would be for it completely mysterious or arbitrary.

The same is not true, however, for the more Nietzschean thought of Georges Bataille.[8] On the one hand, for Bataille, children are not capable of eroticism and are therefore not human in the fullest sense. On the other hand, certain "adults," such as Gilles de Rais, of whom Bataille writes, "I insist, he's a child," manifest a savage, archaic childishness. He uses this medieval figure to bring into view a unique "childishness to which adult possibilities belong" (*Procès* 36). Rather than being understood as simply "infantile," these possibilities should be seen as "archaic." To the extent that

"Gilles de Rais is a child, it is in the manner of savages. He is a child as is the cannibal, or more precisely, as is one of his Germanic ancestors who were not limited by civilized preferences" (36). For Bataille, archaic childishness is aristocratic, and the "very principle of nobility, that which it is in its essence, is the refusal to submit to the degradation, the decay, which would be the inevitable effect of work" (48). Being of no interest in itself, work is always subordinate, something future-oriented that can only serve something else. Bataille excises the servility of the Schillerian project of self-education and national culture, retains the Romantic exhilaration of the sovereign now, and concludes in absolute terms that anybody who "wishes to escape servile life cannot, in principle, work. He must play. He must amuse himself freely, as does the child: free from his duties, the child has fun" (48).

Children share with the privileged social class the distinction of existing outside, or alongside, the regime of work. Both the "Playmates straying" in Dickinson's poem and Bataille's duty-free nobles exist beyond service and subordinate activity of every kind.[9] As we have seen, the children in "Of Death I try to think" do not accumulate or calculate in any way: they are not there to "gather" either thoughts or flowers while they may. They are a non-working, nonconversational, unproductive community, living like individual grasshoppers without thought of their futures and never sacrificing their "now" to any idea or plan; the child's leap is not the product of formic subordination. And like Adonis' anemone, the flower across the brook stands for riches unearned, ephemeral beauty, and total expenditure. Since the child's "decision" to jump for it is represented not as a product of thought but as an instinct, its meaning can be identified as the radically self-annihilating meaning of sacrifice and waste defined by Bataille: the child sacrifices all future-oriented calculating thought—such as, most important, the try of thinking with which the poem itself begins—in a recklessly obliterative now.

We are at this point in an even better position to understand why the thinker persona of "Of Death I try to think like this" should reconstruct the reasoning of the leaping child as reactive obedience to a constraint in the now rather than proactive calculation of costs and benefits: it makes the leap a powerful image of aristocratic sovereignty. For the thinking narrator, the child's very lawlessness provides a glimpse of an escape from servile thinking and throws into doubt the very project of "thinking of death"—the question the poem raises at the outset and rephrases in its abrupt non-ending. From Bataille's premises we may draw the conclusion that any representation—

whether in thought or on the page, in prose or in poetry—of one's own death to oneself is human, servile, and therefore anguished. Sovereign beings like the leaping child never invent or encounter any representations of their own death:

> Insofar as we are subordinate beings . . . we die humanly. Since dying humanly, in anguish, is having a representation of death that is permissible only by the doubling of the self into a now and a future, to die humanly is to have of the future being, of the being who counts in our eyes, the senseless idea that he is not. If we live sovereignly, the representation of death is impossible, because the present is not submitted to the demands of the future. That is why, in a fundamental way, to live sovereignly is to escape, if not death, then the anguish of death at least. . . . From the point of view of the sovereign man, the faintheartedness and the fearful representation of death belong to the world of practical affairs, that is, to subordination. (*Oeuvres* 269–70)

Thus, although the child's unthinking leap is sacrificial, a leap into the destructive force of nature, it is not suicidal since it does not involve in any sense a representation or a "try" at "thinking of death" or at ending life. The child's leap has no other sense than the meaningless meaning of the waste itself, in the gloriously aristocratic and beautiful expenditure of the self and all its resources.

The activity of children is decisive in the adult speaker's thinking of death both because they are "naïve" in the sense Schiller's Reason (but not his understanding) identifies—they represent an impressively unformed, free, playful power—and because they are archaic and sovereign in Bataille's sense: "not limited by civilized preferences." On the one hand, they are naïve, artless, and still free of the cognitive burdens of the faculty of understanding, and on the other, they are not working or seeking but *playing* and *straying*. Dickinson's children unthinkingly find themselves at the limits of their experience and perhaps, symbolically, at the limits of human experience as such.

In direct and painful contrast to the willfully exploratory thinking of the adult narrator/speaker—whose whole poem is *working* to think of death— the children's movements are purposeless. These are not pioneers, philosophers, conquerors, or try-to-thinkers but fops, carps, tramps, dogs, and atheists, lawless errant knights thrown to the edge of their world. Whereas

Hercules had to search for the garden of the Hesperides, traveling through all of Arabia and Asia to reach the edge of the known world, Dickinson's children arrive at the furthest reaches of geography and civilization through play. As was true for technological thinking, law and civilization do not even intervene at a distance as forms for them to transgress, so their freedom from the fact and idea of prohibitive law makes them ideal images of Bataillean sovereignty.

Using children to present a try at thinking of Death is thus a way of avoiding or preempting the premises of philosophical or Christian vocabularies that saturated civilized nineteenth-century adult conversations about death. The children in the second stanza are a Schillerian-Bataillean means for Dickinson to reach an order of thought unknown to the adult community of the first stanza, and to achieve in images the radical freedom that all conscious thought potentially has before death. It is precisely this thoughtless expenditure of the child's own being that attracts the aging poet's advancing thought, since the very try at thinking of death—perhaps emblematic of many attempts—now turns out, colored by the perspective of sovereignty glimpsed and extracted from a childhood moment, to have been servile, future-oriented, subordinate, and condemned to anguish. The strategies that the speaker has used to produce a "thinking of death" turn out to be all too Socratic and metaphysical: they labor to capture essential boldnesses of spirit and deed and then reasonably translate or transfer them into a thinking of death. (The calculative phrase "If Doom itself were the result" is not so much a description of the leaping child's thinking as it is the admiring speaker's own evaluation of risk.) Thus the speaker ultimately runs up against this growing conclusion: discursive thinking of death destroys discursive thinking of death by producing, from servile methods and premises, an awareness of the sovereignty of death itself. "Of Death I try to think like this" ends abruptly, then, in part because the servility of the try at thinking of death (in tropological or other terms) has recoiled on its own servile project like the rhyme expressing it.

How did the speaker reach this terrible paradox of asking for pragmatic help in thinking of death from a wildly aristocratic, sovereign, nonpragmatic child? To understand this, and to recognize something of the poem's value for post-metaphysical postmoderns, it helps to clarify the distinction between "dying without anguish" in the Schillerian-Bataillean sense and "dying without anguish" in the Christian or Socratic sense. Let us look briefly at how one of Dickinson's lyric characters goes gentle into the night:

So proud she was to die
It made us all ashamed
That what we cherished, so unknown
To her desire seemed -
So satisfied to go
Where none of us should be
Immediately - that Anguish stooped
Almost to Jealousy -

(Fr1278)

Here, instead of admiring and trying to translate the death of the other into an intuition of the way death comes to presence for themselves, this speaker's community grows petty and servile. The complacency of this proud, contented woman originates in the strong metaphysics that guides Christian visions of the next world. Life in this world, "what we cherished" seems "unknown / To her desire," and because she has seemingly managed a peaceful death based on a desire or faith her friends cannot fully share, their anguish stoops "Almost to Jealousy." The death of this *moriens* is precisely the kind idealized in a regime of strong metaphysics, where faith and reason seamlessly co-create the possibility for acceptance of death. But as we have seen, Dickinson's flower-jumper is not free from anguish in the sense of having internalized a consolatory metaphysics; he or she is free in the Bataillean sense of being outside all civilized preferences, all vocabularies, values, faiths, and representations.

To continue thinking without the foundations of strong metaphysics, Dickinson, as we have seen throughout this book, lyricizes and interpretively adapts the tensions between reason and imagination that she inherited. To understand the contemporary philosophical value of her attempts, it helps to compare her poetic (non)presentation of death with contemporary neo-Kantian versions of the sublime. Jean-Luc Nancy's elucidation of Kant's *Third Critique* has systematic recourse to precisely the kinds of figures and structures—tension, élan (leap), and suspension—to which Dickinson's poem commits so thoroughly in its try at thinking death. Most important, his sublime always involves, in Nancy's recurring phrase, the activity of "presentation without anything presented." According to Nancy, the profound logic of Kant's texts on beauty and the sublime is not one of either direct or indirect presentation: Kant does not aim to accomplish an indirect presentation of unrepresentable things by use of analogies or symbols, to figure the unfigurable, or to find the best descriptive language to designate pure kinds of absence or lack (*Finite* 224). The logic of the Kantian sublime should therefore not be confused with a logic of fiction or desire; it is rather something that "happens *in* presentation itself and *through* it but which is not presentation" (225), something like "illimitation" or "dissipation" or "overgoing." Nancy names this kind of presentation without anything presented "the sublime offering" (*l'offrande sublime*).

To understand what takes place in this kind of "offering," one must renounce the usual sense of imaginative presentation as the mind presenting and producing images to and for itself. This is because, in sublime feeling, the imagination neither simply generates nor perceives an image; the sublime is a broken tension, a suspended leaping forth which comes from being stopped, from reaching a limit while trying to reach further, beyond that limit:

> If presentation is most of all that which takes place in perception—to present is to render perceptible—, the sublime imagination is always on the order of presentation insofar as it is perceptible. But this sensitivity is no longer that of the perception of a figure, it is that of touching a limit, and more precisely it is found in the very *sentiment* that the imagination feels in touching its limit. The imagination feels itself passing by the limit. It feels itself, and has the sentiment of the sublime in its *effort* (*Bestrebung*), in its leap, in its tension, which makes itself properly known at the moment when the limit is touched, in the suspense of the élan, in the broken tension, in the syncope. (233)

Thus, according to Nancy, in a sublime experience one has the sentiment of touching one's own imaginative limit, of the mind feeling the failure to reach the limit for which it gropes. This is the Kantian tension between reason and imagination again, but the emphasis is on the mental movements during the experience—on the presentation without anything presented—rather than on the images called for or generated. This is also the difference between the epistolary Dickinson of chapter 2 and the more lyrical, Nancian Dickinson of "Of Death." There she wrestled nostalgically with the unpresentable, but here she concedes right away the unrepresentability of the unrepresentable and includes it in the try of thought.

Nancy's basic procedure is to posit the conscious experience of "perceiving a figure" and then to describe in terms of the sublime the feeling that accompanies the failure to achieve this. The imagination tries to perceive an image fully, to bring it into the senses, and in its failure to do so it finds, and feels, a limit. By proposing a kind of pure or immediate perception, Nancy can then point to a sublime (non)presencing that is only the activity of presencing, and its sentiment, without any actual presented content, material, or image. There is a difficulty with this strategy, for as Dickinson's reader-oriented and try-to-think poems so often show, there is no mental tension, no élan "as such"—every élan is singular because of its mood and local circumstance, and some are the product of the anguished human constraint of being toward death. To seek a vocabulary for the limits of presentation as such ultimately requires awareness of this fact. But despite a certain number of markers, there is little in Nancy's analysis to think this; he generally turns away from mood and individual circumstances and toward cognition as a play of seeing and interrupted vision.

While the verbs and images of Nancy's language are often anthropomorphic—touching, feeling, leaping—he resists the analogizing tendency of his own language and never imposes a developed lyrical figure on his thought. Indeed, if one reads Nancy's writings on the sublime with Dickinson's poetry in mind, her narration and imagery tend to join and converse with his thought, inhabiting and extending his exposition. His analyses, like those of much of the philosophical tradition of the sublime, are often limited to an abstract narration and description of mental events. By contrast, Dickinson's lyrics materialize these descriptions, not, as we have seen, by giving them "visionary content" but by dramatizing and individualizing the effects of sublime non-presencing on the lyric "I." For postmoderns, what is perhaps still more impressive is the way she lyricizes sublime offerings for pragmatic reasons, to help her think difficult existential situations like thinking of death.

This may help us better understand both Dickinson's specific decision not to represent the ending of the flower-jumper narrative and her more general refusal to "complete" the three-part structure of the Romantic sublime. The results of earlier chapters in this book allow us to see these things as reflections of conversationalism and weakened metaphysics, but from a Nancian perspective we can also see how they result from Dickinson's keen attention to the play of presentation in sublime experience. Her "hesitation" does not derive from any arbitrary preference for indeterminacy or obstinate refusal to answer questions; it is a way for her to avoid making the ontological mistakes of strong metaphysics, for example, looking for accurate descriptions and "presence" in a structure of being that denies them. In the case of the being-toward-death presented by the flower-jumper, Dickinson's lyric avoids all essentializing questions about what death really is and instead conceives of death as a sublime offering, a presentation without anything presented, a thought that is always impending and proposing itself to thought.

"Of Death I try to think like this" is both an intensely private meditation, not intended for publication, and a general analysis of how any and all of us might choose to think. Pragmatically, it records a try at transforming the permanent impotence of thought before death into the outraged Kantian imagination before the terrifying excess of the sublime. If, in an experience of the sublime, the mind continues to feel itself despite its impotence, and gains from this feeling the courage to attempt a radical presentation, then perhaps being-toward-death can be thought in the same way. To find language for this attempt, Dickinson does not develop the available rationalist premises of discourses such as Common Sense, Christianity, Transcendentalism, and Platonism, but post-metaphysically lyricizes weak options from her tradition. Adapting and combining Schiller's philosophy of children and play with her own idiosyncratic version of the Romantic sublime, she transforms the Romantic strong hero into the champion of the weakened experience of truth. Abstracting Dickinson and trying to think with one of her last and best leaps into the thinking of death, perhaps we too can learn to eschew the faithful optimism, reasonable skepticism, and Romantic visions of Protestant adults and suspend ourselves more existentially and sublimely in an imagined community of secular, archetypal, and sovereign children.

Notes

Introduction

1. Since 1998 a three-volume variorum edition edited by Ralph Franklin has been available which represents Dickinson's writing with more accuracy and detail than ever before; today there are also guides, biographies, concordances, Web sites, and reference and critical books of all kinds. The past several decades have seen great productivity from a number of scholarly approaches: feminism has helped place Dickinson within the gender expectations and limitations of her time; cultural studies have examined sociohistorical contexts from politics and the Civil War to popular culture and social class; and studies of Dickinson's manuscripts have brought us ever closer to the scene of her writing. So much critical activity suggests both that Dickinson remains an enigma, for the portraits do not agree, and that academic study of this poet may be reaching a complexity that does her justice, in which no single approach can be said to ground or preempt the others.

2. Those who have drawn from poststructuralism include Stonum, Loeffelholz, Porter, Cameron, Homans, Ladin, Hagenbüchle, McGann, Juhasz, Crumbley, and Henneberg. Loeffelholz brings Lacan and feminism together. Weisbuch attributes a "deconstructionist" attitude to Dickinson and adds that her "scenelessness is not simply a poetic technique but something of a metaphysic" (205).

3. I am adding to a list begun by Perloff; see "Emily Dickinson and the Theory Canon."

4. For typical examples, see chapter 1 of De Man's *Allegories of Reading* and the essay "Criticism and Crisis" included in *Blindness and Insight*.

5. Perloff speculates that Celan, Beckett, and Mallarmé appealed to poststructuralism because they produced worlds "in which there are no longer any certitudes to 'unname.'" Where Dickinson shows a "deep-seated skepticism about the cosmic order," Celan, in his translations, "has what Wortman calls 'a language grid'" (Wortman 141).

6. With few exceptions (e.g., Kimpel, Morey) Dickinson critics have maintained

the sharp distinction between poetry and philosophy. Charles Anderson made much of Dickinson's mental acumen but categorically affirmed that it "would do violence to her distinction as a poet to claim for her the status of a great thinker" ("Stairway" 35).

7. Dickinson resembles Amalia from Kafka's novel *The Castle*, the young woman who, alone in the village, decides to stop listening to the authoritarian and patriarchal "Castle-speak." Amalia has the confidence and self-reliance necessary to defy the institutions into which she has been thrown, but she offers no arguments, saying nothing about the political powers, historical circumstances, and sexual predicament that define her life. While Dickinson maintained a similar "prose" silence on such topics, her willingness to respond in poetry to the existential conditions of her life makes her less hermeneutically intractable than Amalia.

8. "There's nothing particularly exciting about Dickinson's views on her society," comments Tim Morris in his review of the 2004 *Historical Guide to Emily Dickinson*, "at least compared to Henry David Thoreau, Frederick Douglass, Elizabeth Cady Stanton, or Abraham Lincoln.... [H]er ideas about death, eternity, and sex are comparatively much more compelling" (118).

9. Those who see postmodern society fragmenting into smaller and smaller groups speaking "private" languages and codes can accept with Jameson that the cultural force of parody must be weakening, for as a stylistic option it depends on a linguistic norm against which to play deviant, eccentric voices. On this view, pastiche flourishes in postmodernity because it wears previous stylistic masks neutrally, with little faith in norms.

10. In *Cosmopolis*, Stephen Toulmin speculates about the paths modernity might have explored if Montaigne had been its founding father rather than Descartes, and concludes that the contemporary world has finally made its way back: now we find ourselves where humanists such as Montaigne, Rabelais, Bacon, and Erasmus left us, with the pressing question of how to remake ourselves in the absence of "the rationalist Quest for Certainty" (44). Emerson's *Representative Men*, a book Dickinson recommended, presents Montaigne as the best example of "wise skepticism" for his mixture of flexibility, pragmatism, and self-reliance.

11. "No law can be sacred to me but that of my own nature," reads one of Emerson's formulations of the self-reliant credo he shared with Thoreau and others. In "The Transcendentalist" he makes this autonomous self depend specifically on a pure form of philosophical Idealism. While the materialist "insists on facts, on history, on the force of circumstances and the animal wants of man," the Idealist insists on "the power of Thought and of Will, on inspiration, on miracle, on individual culture" (*Essays* 193). From the "transfer of the world into the consciousness," the "beholding of all things in the mind," he adds, Transcendentalist ethics "follow easily": it is "simpler to be self-dependent. The height, the deity of man is to be self-sustained, to need no gift, no foreign force.... [L]et the soul be erect, and all things will go well" (195). Despite her many meditations on the power of thought to create "self," "soul," and "identity," Dickinson rarely approached these more optimistic and Idealist Emersonian strains. Recognizing and respecting Kantian limitations on the reach of reason more than Emerson did, she regularly remarked on the mental conflicts and foreign forces inside her "own nature."

Since ". . . Myself - assault Me - / How have I peace / Except by subjugating / Consciousness?" she often wondered (Fr709). As Mary Janice Rainwater and others have noted, Dickinson understood better than Emerson that expectations based on confident self-reliance can result in pain and disillusionment as well as growth (56).

12. This book is not intended as a contribution to the long tradition of using absolutist, yes-or-no questions to organize studies of Dickinson: Was she a Romantic, a modernist, a Christian, a good poet, a lesbian, a feminist, a Transcendentalist, a LANGUAGE poet, a Civil War poet? The latest in this series is Virginia Jackson's *Dickinson's Misery*, which asks: Was she a lyric poet? Returning constantly to this question, Jackson shows that Dickinson's writing outstrips many models of the lyric and concludes, as had many before her, that we should not think of "the lyric" as a single reified, ahistorical genre. From the perspective of post-metaphysical hermeneutics that I am adopting in this book, the binary form that dominates the starting questions and critical gestures in essentializing language games too often holds out the false hope of epistemological contextlessness. (To suggest that one can answer the question whether or not Dickinson's poetry has anything like an "essence" assumes that the reader should hope for, and the critic provide, an objective, God's-eye representation.) Like many critics who begin with a strong metaphysical binary, Jackson ultimately overcomes it, admitting at the last minute that she has led her readers "to expect in conclusion an answer to the question of what it was that Emily Dickinson wrote" (235). There is no straight answer to that, of course, but the result of withholding the point so long is that Jackson cannot parlay it into anything like the promised theory of "lyric reading." Hermeneutic critics, more impressed from the outset by the variety of texts and languages we use to approach, interpret, and describe other texts, try not to lead readers by metaphysical expectations in the first place.

13. Since the moment Plato threw the poets out of his republic, the parlous question of how to describe (and usually hierarchize) the relationship between philosophy and literature has produced an endless array of language games. In this book I have tried not to impose a grid on Dickinson, preferring to work inductively from the poems. In any case her training in philosophy, as we will see in chapter 3, makes her something of a special case.

14. Dickinson's ethnographer persona is unmistakable in her description of her family in the second letter she sent to T. W. Higginson: "They are religious – except me – and address an Eclipse, every morning – whom they call their 'Father'" (L261). In the spring of 1846 she wrote to Root that the "few short moments in which I loved my Saviour" were a time when it was the "greatest pleasure to commune alone with the great God & feel that he would listen to my prayers" (L11). She lost "interest in heavenly things" by degrees, however, and the "prayer in which I had taken such delight became a task & the small circle who met for prayer missed me from their number" (L11).

15. The poem as a whole is often read as a straightforward prose statement reflecting skepticism. Philip and Carol Zaleski see it as a reflection of Dickinson's "idiosyncratic" and "jaundiced" religious views, for which they partially blame Emerson (280). They offer their own more optimistic definition of prayer in italics: *"prayer*

is action that communicates between human and divine realms" (5). Jane Eberwein emphasizes Dickinson's recurring worry about the audience for prayer as well as poetry (*Strategies* 256).

16. De Man pursues many variations on the argument that "two entirely coherent but entirely incompatible readings can be made to hinge on one line, whose grammatical structure is devoid of ambiguity, but whose rhetorical mode turns the mood as well as the mode of the entire poem upside down" (*Allegories* 12).

17. Often disparagingly associated with Mother Goose, the *Gilligan's Island* theme, and "The Yellow Rose of Texas," Dickinson's preferred poetic shape is reputed to be incapable of complex thought. John Crowe Ransom warned that ballad stanza was "disadvantageous if it is used on the wrong poetic occasion or if it denies to the poet the use of English Pentameter when that would be more suitable" (94). Like many, he saw pentameter as "capable of containing and formalizing many kinds of substantive content which would be too complex for Folk Line" and complained that Dickinson appeared "never to have tried it" (94). In this book, however, I never interpret Dickinson's meter as pentameter's poor cousin. I see it rather as a comfortable and flexible medium that enabled Dickinson to pursue many kinds of thinking, including logic, analysis, meditation, reverie, riddle making, and paradox.

18. Many poems respond to presence denied: "Of course I prayed" is another that dramatizes the disappointment of failed prayer; "Renunciation - is a piercing Virtue -" charts the paradoxical logic of "The letting go / A Presence - for an Expectation - / Not now -" (Fr782); the last line of "We pray - to heaven - / We prate - of Heaven -" is a question that summarizes the condition: "Where - Omnipresence - fly?" (Fr476).

1. Dickinson and the Hermeneutics of Conversation

1. Seminal works of these authors include: for Rorty, *Philosophy and the Mirror of Nature* (1979); *Consequences of Pragmatism* (1982); *Contingency, Irony, and Solidarity* (1989); *Objectivism, Relativism, and Truth: Philosophical Papers I* (1991), *Essays on Heidegger and Others: Philosophical Papers II* (1991), *Truth and Progress: Philosophical Papers III* (1998); *Philosophy and Social Hope* (1999); and *Take Care of Freedom and the Truth Will Take Care of Itself* (2005). For Vattimo: *The End of Modernity* (1991), *The Adventure of Difference* (1993), *The Transparent Society* (1992), *Beyond Interpretation* (1997), and *After Christianity* (2002). In 2004 Rorty and Vattimo co-authored *The Future of Religion*. Both have also received extensive criticism and commentary. See especially Alan Malachowski, ed., *Reading Rorty: Critical Responses to The Mirror of Nature and Beyond* (1990), and Santiago Zabala, ed., *Weakening Philosophy: Essays in Honour of Gianni Vattimo* (2007).

2. Rorty derives his language of self-creation through language creation from Alexander Nehamas's depiction of Nietzsche in *Nietzsche: Life as Literature*.

3. Critics of Rorty and Vattimo tend to fall into a few basic categories. One large group attempts to show that despite the two philosophers' lengthy arguments to the contrary, they are really just "relativists." Others try to reassert the rational

basis of faith or reimpose traditional aspects of foundational thought, such as metaphysically strong notions of absolute truth, universal reason, transcendental ethical imperatives, or correspondence theories of truth.

4. Rorty argues that Habermas's theories of things like "ideal speech situations" and "communicative action" are unrealistically rationalistic. For a reply that stresses the exemplary value of reason and consistency in conversation, especially philosophical conversation, see Bernard Williams's "Auto-da-Fé: Consequences of Pragmatism."

5. For another recent defense and illustration of the contemporary value of lyric poetry, see Charles Altieri, "Taking Lyrics Literally."

6. Ultimately the distinction Dickie proposes between narrative and lyric is too strong. Dickinson wrote narrative poems of many kinds, including straightforward storytelling ("The Malay - took the Pearl -") and metacommentary on established (often biblical) stories. Some polished narrative poems, such as "Because I could not stop for Death," include conversational and self-corrective processes of writing, thinking, and storytelling: "We passed the Setting Sun - // Or rather - He passed Us -" (Fr479).

7. See Eco, *The Role of the Reader*; Barthes, "From Work to Text"; Blanchot, *The Infinite Conversation*; and Lacoue-Labarthe and Nancy, *The Literary Absolute*.

8. In "Emily Dickinson and the Reading Life," Willis Buckingham describes Dickinson coming of age at a time "of reaction against one-way models of literary participation that imagined readers as self-indulgent recipients of authorial invention and genius. American literary culture of the 1830's and 1840's guards against solipsism by demanding that poetry work both centripetally, as individual illumination, *and* centrifugally, as sympathetic connection with others" (234). "Antebellum reviewers," he points out, tend to "uphold the paradigm of the giving genius and the gratefully receiving reader while insisting on a new set of pro-community relations in which readers are given a presumption of fraternity with writers" (235).

9. Other critics who have explored aspects of Dickinson's reader-oriented poetics include Keller, Weisbuch, Martha Nell Smith, Cristanne Miller, and Hagenbüchle.

10. To the extent that Dickinson is a radically reader-oriented poet, does not the role of the critic evaporate? While critics are no longer needed to produce unimpeachable arguments or evaluations, they can responsibly facilitate conversations by discussing individual poems, asking new questions, modeling conversation, pointing to uses of ideas or language that might otherwise go unnoticed or unintegrated, and so on. With Dickinson, one can hope to improve one's own conversations by learning how and why she used lyric poetry to converse with her culture and herself.

11. Rorty's *Contingency, Irony, and Solidarity* has been criticized both for the "elitism" of its well-educated, vocabulary-sifting liberal ironist heroine and for the strong distinction it proposes between private and public life. "Irony seems inherently a private matter," Rorty argues, adding that as he sees it, "an ironist cannot get along without the contrast between the final vocabulary she inherited and the one she is trying to create for herself. Irony is, if not intrinsically resentful, at least reactive. Ironists have to have something to have doubts about,

something from which to be alienated" (*Contingency* 87–88). Arguing that this privatized ironism functions as an unwitting apology for an unacceptable political status quo, Allan Hutchinson criticizes Rorty for spending most of his time talking about individual choices and actions rather than the "structural arrangements" of society (564–66). "Discrimination," contends Hutchinson, "is as much about the general effects of social practices as the intentions of individual actors" (565). Seeing Rorty's defense of individual self-creation over social commitment and engagement as resting "on an overly aristocratic and privatized view of society and social change," he argues that we should not encourage "the 'gifted' to read more books" but instead "chide them into using their gifts in programs to reduce illiteracy and improve education" (568). Criticism like this is roughly as valid or invalid for Dickinson as it is for Rorty, for she shared his commitment to—and much of his vocabulary for—the private sphere of self-creation.

12. Philosophers have suggested that Rorty's use of the term "redescription" relies too heavily on the very correspondence theories of truth he has rejected. Why "redescribe" rather than "reorganize" or "reconnect," wonders John McCumber, who also notes that one of Rorty's expositions of metaphor—as more like a strange noise or facial gesture than a meaningful sentence—competes with the idea of language as "description." He finds yet another incompatibility in the way the "interactive context" seems to disappear from Rorty's accounts of redescription (8). How, he asks, can Rorty's metaphors be conversational but his redescriptions monological? Without the context of a conversation, "redescription becomes the activity of an isolated ego, one whose relation to her audience is . . . wholly contingent" (8). While many of Dickinson's poems echo McCumber's questions, there are also many times—as when she distinguishes herself from other readers of the Bible—when she sides more with Rorty in postulating valuable "conversational" contexts in which one speaks mainly with oneself.

13. "Elastic, Elastical: Springing back; having the power of returning to the form from which it is bent, extended, pressed, or distorted; having the inherent property of recovering its former figure, after any external pressure, which has altered that figure, is removed; rebounding; flying back. Thus, a bow is *elastic*, and when the force which bends it is removed, it instantly returns to its former shape. The air is *elastic*; vapors are elastic; and when the force compressing them is removed, they instantly expand or dilate, and recover their former state" (Webster, *Dictionary* [1844] 569).

14. For studies of Dickinson's relationship to her religious culture, see Wolff, McIntosh, Eberwein, Lundin, Brantley, and Doriani.

15. In Vattimo's version of the history of Western culture, Christianity ultimately helped overthrow the objectivistic metaphysics that for centuries was used to defend it: "Christianity is the condition that paved the way for the dissolution of metaphysics and for its replacement by gnoseology—in Dilthey's terms, by Kantianism. The principles that inspired Descartes and Kant—the emphasis on the subject, the foundation of knowledge on a self-certain interiority—are the same ones that hold sway in modern philosophy. The latter remained, for a long time, a kind of metaphysics dominated by an objectivistic vision of interiority

itself, because the new principle of subjectivity introduced by Christianity did not immediately succeed" (*After* 107).

2. Trying to Think with Emily Dickinson

1. Kant describes the task of poets as "interpreting to sense the rational ideas of invisible beings," and explains that they manage to "body forth" aesthetic ideas better than philosophers. Readers of Dickinson will recognize her in his description of the poet's task and list of aesthetic ideas: "The poet essays the task of interpreting to sense the rational ideas of invisible beings, the kingdom of the blessed, hell, eternity, creation, &c. Or, again as to things of which examples occur in experience, e.g., death, envy, and all vices, as also love, fame, and the like, transgressing the limits of experience he attempts with the aid of an imagination which emulates the display of reason in its attainment of a maximum, to body them forth to sense with a completeness of which nature affords no parallel; and it is in fact precisely in the poetic art that the faculty of aesthetic ideas can show itself to full advantage" (*Judgement* 176–77).

2. Because our ideas and perceptions "are so mixed, compounded, and decompounded, by habits, associations, and abstractions, that it is hard to know what they were originally," the actions of the mind from infancy are comparable to those of "an apothecary or a chemist" who also receives materials from nature (Reid 14). Like the chemist, the mind purposely "mixes, compounds, dissolves, evaporates, and sublimes" ideas until "they put on a quite different appearance" (14). If, as we grow from childhood, our brains act as *unskilled* chemists and work randomly "by means of instincts, habits, associations, and other principles" before becoming capable of "deliberate acts of mature reason," then it is the job of philosophers to act as *skilled* chemists and "trace back those operations" (14–15). All of this explains the recommended Common Sense doctrine that one must unravel the mind's "notions and opinions, till he finds out the simple and original principles of his constitution, of which no account can be given but the will of our Maker. This may be truly called an *analysis* of the human faculties" (15). As we will see in chapter 3, Dickinsonian unraveling has consequences more skeptical and post-metaphysical than the discovery of original Common Sense principles and the will of God.

3. See Miller, *Emily Dickinson: A Poet's Grammar*, and Crumbley, *Inflections of the Pen: Dash and Voice in Emily Dickinson*.

4. For a historical study of Bacon, science, and evangelical religion, see Bozeman, *Protestants in an Age of Science*.

5. Watts often uses parabolic illustrations. Here is a tale about why one should fear self-certainty: "Arithmo had been bred up to accounts all his life, and thought himself a complete master of numbers. But when he was pushed hard to give the square root of the number 2, he tried at it, and laboured long in millesimal fractions, till he confessed there was no end of the inquiry; and yet he learned so much modesty by this perplexing question, that he was afraid to say it was an impossible thing. It is some good degree of improvement, when we are afraid to be positive" (8–9).

6. When Dickinson turned to poetry as a mode of experimentation in mental philosophy, she became a lyrical interloper in a tradition dating to Hume, at least, whose famous 1740 *Treatise* carried an important subtitle: *A TREATISE OF Human Nature: BEING An ATTEMPT to Introduce the Experimental Method of Reasoning INTO MORAL SUBJECTS.*

7. From the very the first pages of the text, Watts argues vehemently against dogmatism. There are "at present many difficulties and darknesses hanging about certain truths of the Christian religion, and since several of these relate to important doctrines, such as the origin of sin, the fall of Adam, the person of Christ, the blessed Trinity, and decrees of God, &c. which do still embarrass the minds of honest and inquiring readers, and which make work for noisy controversy; it is certain there are several things in the Bible yet unknown, and not sufficiently explained" (12). In all areas of learning, it is essential for you to maintain "a constant watch at all times against a dogmatical spirit" and to withhold judgment until you have "some firm and unalterable ground for it, and till you have arrived at some clear and sure evidence; till you have turned the proposition on all sides, and searched the matter through and through, so that you cannot be mistaken. And even where you may think you have full grounds of assurance, be not too early, nor too frequent, in expressing this assurance in too peremptory and positive a manner" (14).

8. Watts and others insist that their textbooks are starting points for individual self-analysis. In fact when Thomas Upham attempts to "indicate some of the prominent sources for self-inquiry," he offers a rather Dickinsonian list of experiences and ideas that "originate in consciousness": pleasure, pain, hope, joy, faith (140).

9. Many theoretical approaches and vocabularies can be used to describe Dickinson's mental activity. In *The Undiscovered Continent*, Juhasz identifies "dimensional" and "conceptual" vocabularies, while Stonum and Hagenbüchle use more process-oriented approaches.

10. Dickinson's textbooks of mental philosophy agree that the mind cannot easily treat itself as an object of science. Dugald Stewart, in *Elements of the Philosophy of the Human Mind*, remarks that "Cicero, and after him Mr. Locke, in illustrating the difficulty of attending to the subjects of our consciousness, have compared the Mind to the Eye, which sees every object around it, but is invisible to itself" (156). The Thomas Brown volume in Dickinson's library argues that both mind and matter must be analyzed, but that the mind yields knowledge less easily: "Nor, when nature exhibits all her wonders to us, in one case, in objects that are separate from us, and foreign; and, in the other, in the intimate phenomena of our own consciousness, can we justly think, that it is of *ourselves* we know the most. On the contrary, strange as it may seem, it is of her *distant* operations, that our knowledge is least imperfect; and we have far less acquaintance with the sway which she exercises in our own mind, than with that by which she guides the course of the most remote planet, in spaces beyond us, which we rather *calculate* than *conceive*" (108). For Upham, the problem is that we cannot "see the mind, nor is it an object . . . of sense. Nor, on the other hand, is the notion of mind a direct object of the memory, or of reasoning, or of imagination" (125).

11. "Should you think it breathed" means, is my thought now living on its own, apart

from me? It is Dickinsonian shorthand for an idea expressed by Emerson in "The Poet" when he described a poem as "a thought so passionate and alive, that, like the spirit of a plant or an animal, it has an architecture of its own" (450). Dickinson's remark "If I make the mistake" means, Have I included or omitted sounds, words, rhymes, ideas, or something else that might keep my thought from living on its own and becoming fully intelligible? And the question "What is true?" asks for Higginson's unadorned opinion.

12. The phrase "*they* look alike and numb" reveals an unexpected switch from singular to plural form; Dickinson had originally said "while *my thought is* undressed, I can make the distinction, but when I put *them* in the Gown . . ." (emphasis added). Thought thus exhibits a kind of conversational cell division, moving from single (when abstract, unwritten, available only to the thinker) to plural (when materialized in writing and available for readers).

13. "Of the important American writers of the nineteenth century, she is quite easily the most ignorant," ignorantly proclaims R. D. Gooder (64–65). He adds for good measure that she "not only had no power of discursive thought but she scarcely anywhere mentions any philosopher or theologian. Moreover, she was not well read, and had little power of talking about what she *had* read" (81). Since Dickinson spent her life reading and thinking, Gooder's comment can only mean that she did not read and think the things he thinks she should have, and not in ways he could appreciate. He chides Shira Wolosky for ignoring (in *Voice of War*) Emily Dickinson "the poet" in favor of Dickinson "the thinker," arguing that this was "not a good idea" because "the one thing that Emily Dickinson was unable to do was to think" (80). She herself "admitted it," he argues, in the "letter to Higginson: . . . 'when I try to organize—my little Force explodes—and leaves me bare and charred'"(80). Noticing neither the performative nature of Dickinson's comment in the local context of the letter and accompanying poems nor the way in which thought is developed as a central theme in the correspondence, Gooder reveals his adherence to a tradition that distinguishes so sharply between philosophy and lyric poetry, analytical and creative thought, that it renders Dickinson's hybridism unintelligible.

14. With this letter she includes five poems, including two with the mind as primary theme: "The Heart is the Capital of the Mind" (Fr1381) and "The Mind lives on the Heart" (Fr1384).

15. Thomas H. Johnson, editor of *The Letters of Emily Dickinson*, explains that Dickinson correctly guessed that Higginson was the author of an unsigned review of Lowell's *Among My Books: Second Series* in the March 1876 *Scribner's Monthly*. A second unsigned *Scribner's* review, of Emerson's *Letters and Social Aims* in the April issue, has not been identified as Higginson's (see L457, note). The second review reads like Higginson to me.

16. Dickinson's family understood how much she valued thought. Lavinia surely expressed the general sentiment when she explained that her sister "was not withdrawn or exclusive really. She was always watching for the rewarding person to come but she was a very busy person herself. She had to think—she was the only one of us who had that to do. Father believed; and mother loved; and Austin had Amherst; and I had the family to keep track of" (Bingham 413–14).

17. Dickinson asked Higginson during his first visit, "Is it oblivion or absorption when things pass from our minds?" and then, in the next letter, asked him "to forgive me for all the ignorance I had" (L342b, L352).

18. In another poem, pure thought has the power to produce enriching loneliness: "There is another Loneliness / That many die without - / Not want of friend occasions it / Or circumstance of Lot // But nature, sometimes, sometimes thought / And whoso it befall / Is richer than could be revealed / By mortal numeral -" (Fr1138).

19. "I tried to think a lonelier Thing" (Fr570) appears in fascicle 25 between the poems "A precious - mouldering pleasure - 'tis -" (Fr569) and "Two Butterflies went out at Noon" (Fr571). These last two were first published in 1890 and 1891 respectively.

20. I prefer the second interpretation both because Dickinson describes her poems as pragmatic responses to sudden emotion and because so many poems and letters think through the aftermath of traumatic experiences such as grief and loneliness. In December 1854, long before developing her signature modes of lyric expression, she wrestled in a letter to Susan Gilbert Dickinson with the difficulty of expressing extreme loneliness in words. At that point she was ready to declare visual art the superior medium: "Susie – it is a little thing to say how lone it is – anyone can do it, but to wear the loneness next your heart for weeks, when you sleep, and when you wake, ever missing something, *this*, all cannot say, and it baffles me. I would paint a portrait which would bring the tears, had I canvass for it, and the scene should be – *solitude*, and the figures – solitude – and the lights and shades, each a solitude. I could fill a chamber with landscapes so lone, men should pause and weep there; then haste grateful home, for a loved one left" (L176).

21. "Expiation" is one of the loneliest words in Dickinson's lexicon. This poem has the only recorded use in any poem or letter.

22. I disagree with Paul Muldoon's argument that this poem involves a commentary on the Civil War, that there is "no doubt that a strand" of this poem "refers to that 'Horror' involving 'Polar' opposites, North and South, between whom there falls a 'Partition'" (24).

23. The series of expeditions to the Arctic funded by Lady Franklin in search of her husband, Sir John Franklin, were much in the news in the 1850s; Dickinson read an April 1851 *Harper's* article on the subject (see Muldoon 13–18). She never forgot these events; in an 1885 letter she joked to her nephew Ned: "How favorable that something is missing besides Sir John Franklin!" (L1000).

24. See also "If I'm lost - now -," which ends: "I'm banished - now - you know it - / How foreign that can be - / You'll know - Sir - when the Savior's face / Turns so - away from you -" (Fr316).

25. The letter refers to the death of Leonard Humphrey on November 13, 1850.

26. Goethe's Romantic Werther is often lonely but sometimes consolable by others: "Sometimes I say to myself: 'Your destiny is unique; call the others fortunate—no one has been so tormented as you.' Then I read an ancient poet, and it seems to me as though I look into my own heart. I have so much to endure! Oh, were there other men before me as miserable as I!" (119).

27. Dickinson uses the word "partition" twice in poems and never in letters. In both

cases it unambiguously means the barrier/bridge between the living and the dead. See "In falling Timbers buried -" (Fr447).

28. James Guthrie selects one plausible account from the options opened up by the speaker: the process of word choice "has evidently made the poet's mind elastic enough to comprehend" the new portion of her vision (121). Watts justifies the search through philology by arguing that whoever "writes well in verse will often find a necessity to send his thoughts in search through all the treasure of words that express any one idea in the same language, that so he may comport with the measures or the rhyme of the verse which he writes, or with his own most beautiful and vivid sentiments of the thing he describes. Now by much reading of this kind we shall insensibly acquire the habit and skill of diversifying our ideas in the most proper and beautiful language, whether we write or speak of the things of God or men" (217).

29. Crumbley argues that this poem's dashes, variants, and general heteroglossia move a reader's consciousness from linear or monologic interpretations to spatialized ones. To the riddle of how a vision can be "crucial to the creative experience of a poet" but "not involve words," he suggests the solution of punctuation, specifically dashes (*Inflections* 147–52). For Guthrie, the poem records how Dickinson's "effort to find the word to fit the thought" was wider and deeper than a simple search for *le mot juste*; rather, it was "a consideration of the multiple possibilities of relation set up by different associations of words, like tumblers in a combination lock" (122).

30. Because they are so self-reflective and include carefully chosen word alternatives, poems such as "Shall I take thee" work against the view that Dickinson wrote in a heated passion. In his 1930 *Emily Dickinson: Friend and Neighbor*, MacGregor Jenkins describes her as a poet who wanted to "get the thing said" while it is "hot" and to utter her words "as quickly as possible" (54–55). He sees Dickinson's paradoxical mixture of raw passion and careful word choice as instinctual: "Every scrap written by her that I have ever seen and handled betrays this same sense of haste to get the thing said while it was hot, to send the message before the fine edge of its significance should dull. There was no pose in this. It was the one and only possible answer to an imperious demand of her nature to express the thought that flashed, to utter the words that rose in her heart and trembled on her lips. To utter them just as quickly as possible and in the briefest imaginable form. This led to an extraordinary terseness and directness in her verse and letters, and necessitated a careful choice of words. This choice was dictated more by instinct than by study, though she loved words and played with them, not with the cold calculation of a stylist, but in a passionate desire to use the one word which would express the subtlest shade of color, sense and meaning, which would translate for others the delicate fabric of her thought and emotion" (54–55). In my view Jenkins's strong binary oppositions between hot/cold, instinct/study, haste/calculation, and so on misrepresent the poet's complex self-awareness, philological sifting, and conversational hermeneutics.

31. The definition of "propound" in Dickinson's 1844 Webster's dictionary provides the suggestive setting of a Congregational church: "In congregational churches, to propose or name as a candidate for admission to communion with a church.

Persons intending to make public profession of their faith, and thus unite with the church, are propounded before the church and congregation; that is, their intention is notified some days previous, for the purpose of giving opportunity to members of the church to object to their admission to such communion, if they see cause."

3. Dickinson and Philosophy

1. The book fictionalizes a scene explored in many Dickinson poems of a soul stuck in a narrow circumference with a "natural enemy": itself. "He was allowed no books, nor pens, nor paper; for such was the established discipline at Fenestrella. . . . [A] book would have afforded a friend to consult, or an adversary to be confuted! Deprived of every thing, sequestered from the world, Charney had nothing left for it, but to become reconciled to himself, and live in peace with that natural enemy, his soul" (Saintine 15).

2. A variety of studies have touched on Dickinson's relationship to individual philosophers and philosophical questions, but none have delved deeply into the textbooks that permeated her culture. See Hagenbüchle, Grabher, Keller, Kimpel, Morey, Diehl, Wolosky, Loeffelholz, and Morris.

3. Historians of religion have different perspectives from historians of philosophy, and an important body of literature exists—much of it applicable to Dickinson's situation—on the relationship between Scottish philosophy and evangelistic religion in the new republic. For one such perspective, see Noll, and for a sympathetic and detailed account of McCosh and Scottish philosophy, see Hoeveler.

4. Whicher himself was following the precedent of Allen Tate, who in 1932 spoke in absolute confidence of Dickinson's "ignorance" and "lack of formal training" (159–60). Bypassing Dickinson's lifelong efforts to use poetry to try to think, he concludes more than once in his essay that she "cannot reason at all" (160, 164). Readers may find her "obscure and difficult," but this is never due to her "intellectualism" (164). Benilde Montgomery stresses a different, more spiritual side of the multifaceted Upham's possible influence in *Emily Dickinson and the Meditative Tradition*.

5. See Schmidt, *The Old-Time College President*.

6. When Humphrey ceased "to instruct the Senior class in Intellectual and Moral Philosophy," writes Tyler, a professorship in the department was "instituted for the purpose of relieving the President from those excessive labors, which, together with the unavoidable responsibilities of his office, and the peculiar anxieties growing out of the pecuniary condition of the College, were manifestly undermining his health. The Professor entered on his duties during the absence of Dr. Humphrey in Europe. And since his inauguration, the Professorship of Intellectual and Moral Philosophy has ceased to be connected with the Presidency. It was an important, it may almost be called a radical change. So far as that most important department is concerned, it was undoubtedly an advance. Intellectual and Moral Philosophy, not less than Mathematics, or Physics, is quite enough to task the energies and occupy the time of any Professor. Perhaps the change was indispensable, being at once the unavoidable effect of the growth of the College, and the necessary condition of its continued progress. But it contained the seeds of a revolution quite

unforeseen by the actors in it. And like other revolutions, it involved incidental dangers, evils and sacrifices. The President, who would be all that Dr. Dwight was in Yale College, or all that Dr. Humphrey was in the first twelve years of his connection with Amherst College, must be the principal teacher of the Senior class. The President, who would command the highest veneration and affection of the students, must be more than a police officer, or administrator of the government and discipline of the College—he must be the acknowledged intellectual, moral and spiritual, as well as official head of the Institution" (186).

7. Box 2, folder 5. These unpublished notes are held in the Frost Library at Amherst College.

8. Schmidt points out that the two most conservative colleges, Princeton and Yale, supplied fifty-eight college presidents to the seventy-five colleges in operation before 1840. They all brought Scottish Common Sense philosophy with them (27).

9. "Imagination is not prominent in his writings," Humphrey notes delicately of Fiske (*Memoir* 72).

10. According to Tyler, Fiske's "chief literary labor for the public was his edition of Eschenburg's *Manual of Classical Literature*. This book was commenced in the fall of 1834, and first published in April, 1836, carefully revised and reprinted in a second and third edition, and in 1843 it was stereotyped with such revision and additions as to make it substantially a new book. . . . Few classical text-books in this country have been so generally adopted as this manual, or retained their place so long in the College curriculum" (307).

11. Statistics compiled from information in Hitchcock's *Reminiscences* (44). This book is also the source for the chart of senior year requirements (53).

12. A short list of graduates with ties to Emily Dickinson would include Elbridge Bowdoin (1840; practiced law with Edward Dickinson 1847–55; lent *Jane Eyre* to Emily 1849), William Howland (1846; studied in Edward Dickinson's law office), Leonard Humphrey (1846), Samuel Fiske (1848), James Kimball (1849), John Laurens Spencer (1848), William Gardiner Hammond (1849), Benjamin Newton (1849; "her gentle, yet grave Preceptor, teaching [her] what to read" [January 13, 1854, L153]); George Gould, Henry Emmons (1854; with whom Emily went riding often in the summer of 1853), and Mason and Nelson Green (1850, 1855). Emily's brother Austin was an Amherst graduate (1850), as were cousins William Cowper Dickinson (valedictorian 1848), John Graves (1855), and Perez Cowan (1866).

13. Phrases such as "mental and moral" occurred frequently in the print culture of the day, including in the title of Samuel Sidwell Randall and Henry Stephens Randall's 1844 *Mental and Moral Culture, and Popular Education*. In December 1852 Dickinson adopted it humorously to refer to herself as "a mental and moral being," and her father used it less sardonically on the floor of the House of Representatives in Washington, D.C., two years later (L97; Leyda 1:307). In a letter to Mrs. Holland, Emily refers to the homeliness of those who have not "mental beauty" (L321); another time she jestingly takes a letter from Austin away from her father, "fearing the consequences on a mind so formed as his" (L44).

14. "In *Aids to Reflection* Coleridge makes a strong distinction between what is spiritual and what is natural and in so doing eliminates the need to reduce the one to

the other. He argues that the faculties by which we perceive these different spheres of reality are as different as the spheres themselves, although these faculties somehow reside in a single human mind. The *Reason* is the supersensuous, intuitive power, at once the source of morality and of the highest kind of intellection; the *Understanding* is the humbler servant who works by combining and comparing ideas derived from sensation, who helps us reflect and generalize—the faculty Locke had mistaken for the whole of the mind, in other words" ("Assault" 354). It should be noted that this understanding of the distinction, while dominant among the Transcendentalists, represents Coleridge's distorted reading of Kant.

15. In like fashion Upham brings in Coleridge to refute his doctrine of the body at the Resurrection. Coleridge worries that since we are judged for deeds done with a live body and soul, when the body is dead and the deeds forgotten, we cannot understand the justice meted out; he proposes that we will be clothed with a "celestial" body instead of a terrestrial one, one that will restore the record of past experience. Upham responds: "The power of reminiscence slumbers, but does not die. At the Judgment-day, we are entirely at liberty to suppose, from what we know of the mind, that it will awake, that it will summon up thought and feeling from its hidden recesses, and will clearly present before us the perfect form and representation of the past" (190).

16. "Delight should be intermingled with labor, as far as possible, to allure us to bear the fatigue of dry studies the better. Poetry, practical mathematics, history &c. are generally esteemed entertaining studies, and may be happily used for this purpose" (Watts, 135).

17. Hedge cites Brown's *Lectures on the Philosophy of the Human Mind* as an excellent book "for persons who are forming the intellectual and moral habits" (quoted in Martin 16).

18. Dickinson's teacher of mental philosophy at the academy was Caroline Hunt, who also taught the class that was congratulated four years earlier in the anonymous letter in the *Courier*. "She was a *smart* old woman," Edward Hitchcock recalled in his *Reminiscences* (Leyda 1:73).

19. Upham explains right away on the opening page that while "our youth should be made acquainted with these principles, it is impossible that they should go through with all the complicated discussions," and concludes his preface by noting that the book is intended to assist "those youth who need some knowledge of Mental Philosophy, but are not in a situation to prosecute the subject to any great extent" (iii, iv). Watts invites girls to read his book: "Let it be observed also, that in our age, several of the ladies pursue science with success; and others of them are desirous of improving their reason even in the common affairs of life, as well as the men; yet the characters which are here drawn occasionally, are almost universally applied to one sex; but if any of the other shall find a character which suits them, they may, by a small change of the termination, apply and assume it to themselves, and accept the instruction, the admonition, or the applause which is designed in it" (xv).

20. Often an American third-party broker performed the abridgment. In the same way that Joseph Emerson, the pedagogue who so inspired and influenced Mary

Lyon, adapted Watts's *On the Improvement of the Mind* by adding a preface, rules for teachers, and running questions at the bottom of each page, Amherst College's Jacob Abbott adapted Abercrombie's books on intellectual and moral philosophy. In the preface to the abridged *Philosophy of the Moral Feelings*, Abbott explains that the "original treatise of the author is published entire, without alterations or omissions," and that his own introduction is "to be carefully studied by the pupil as the first lesson" (Abercrombie iii). "It is of great advantage to the powers of the mind," he says encouragingly "to be practised a little in early life, in thinking and reasoning on metaphysical subjects" (13). Like many of the books' authors, he explains "physical" as that which can be perceived by the senses and studied through corresponding physical sciences. "But there are certain other realities with which we are conversant, that lie beyond these, as it were, and are of a different nature altogether: —the powers and faculties of the mind, various moral truths, the principles of duty, and other similar topics. They are totally different in their very nature from the others. They can neither be seen nor heard nor handled. They are in no place, and have no relation to time. You cannot illustrate them by models or by diagrams. In fact the whole field in which they lie is entirely *beyond*, as it were, the material creation. Hence they are called meta-physical; the affix *meta* having the force of *beyond*" (14).

21. In his 1997 introduction to Reid's *Inquiry into the Human Mind on the Principles of Common Sense*, Derek Brookes describes basic elements of Scottish philosophy: for Reid the goal of thinking and reasoning was to produce true beliefs, the epistemological standards governing the sciences of both nature and the mind were provided by Isaac Newton, and the mind was structured by innate faculties—memory, imagination, consciousness, and others—each of which had its own mode of functioning in the economy of mental process.

22. The trying-to-think, ready-to-experiment Dickinson would have been especially prepared for others, for instance, Thomas Brown describing the anxieties of what she herself would later call "circumference." The fact that a human being "should be at once arrested by the narrow circle which nature has traced around him," he explains, "and yet constantly reminded, that, beyond these limits, there are objects which he is never to attain—that he should be able to reason, till he loses himself, on the existence and nature of these objects, though condemned to be eternally ignorant of them—that he should have too little sagacity to *resolve* an infinity of questions, which he has yet sagacity enough to *make*—that the principle within us, which thinks, should ask itself in vain, what it is which constitutes its thought, and that this thought, which sees so many things, so *distant*, should yet not be able to see itself, which is so *near, that self*, which it is notwithstanding always striving to see and to know—these are contradictions which, even in the very pride of our reasoning, cannot fail to surprise and confound us" (Brown 108–9). Elsewhere Brown discusses at length the situation of a mind closed off from all sensory input, a structure Dickinson adapted for her poems about isolated tomb-consciousness (413).

23. Hickock was perhaps the "most widely read early American textbook writer of the German idealist tradition," notes Rand Evans. He "was influential in the

shift of American academic thought toward German idealism as the century progressed" (47). See Hickock's *Rational Psychology* (1848) and *Empirical Psychology* (1854).

24. Along with the many associationist techniques and questions Dickinson discov-
ered in her philosophy textbooks, she also found analyses of almost every emo-
tion and mental faculty that she wrote about. Several poems feature memory:
"That sacred Closet when you sweep - / Entitled 'Memory' - / Select a reverential
Broom - / And do it silently - // 'Twill be a Labor of surprise - / Besides Identity
/ Of other Interlocutors / A probability - // August the Dust of that Domain - /
Unchallenged - let it lie - / You cannot supersede itself, / But it can silence you."
(Fr1385). Fiske's lecture notes distinguish carefully among remembrance, memory, and recollection: "Remembrance: The recognition of any former notion or
state of mind—or the having any state ever before had, together with the feeling
that it has been in the mind before. Two elements 1) conception or apprehension
{Simple suggestion} 2) notion of past time {Relative suggestion} To be distinguished from Memory only as the term Memory designates the Faculty, rather
than the act or state—from Recollection, as the latter is Remembrance that arises
under the existence of desire" (box 2, folder 4).

25. Dickinson had already been exposed to the controversy over Brown and his "he-
retical" attempt to move beyond Reid and Stewart. In chapter 17, "Of Improving
the Memory," in her edition of Watts's *Improvement*, the editor steps in with
the following note, in brackets in the text: "[*Brown's Suggestion.*—Dr. Thomas
Brown appears to have made an unhappy mistake in relation to this subject. He
would substitute the term *suggestion* for *association*. But these words, according
to established usage, signify very different things; as different, as any cause and
effect. *Association* seems most happily to express that uniting or union or con-
necting of ideas, in consequence of which, one will suggest the other, or recall it
to the view of the mind; or at least, tend to this effect. If the word *recollection* did
not happily express the thing intended, suggestion might be substituted for this
purpose. But with no shadow of propriety, can it be applied to that exercise, by
which ideas are received into the mind, by being united with others, or for that
union of ideas, which are said to be treasured up in the memory, in consequence
of which union, one idea will suggest another; or in other words, may be recalled,
or recollected, by means of its associate]" (Watts, *Improvement* 163–64).

26. Margaret Landes points out that Brown's rejection of a core doctrine of associationism—that "the units" dealt with are even 'ideas' at all, i.e., sensations and
transformed sensations"—made him a maverick in the philosophy of associationism (460). For a poet who trades heavily in mental experience, it is surprising
that Dickinson never speaks of the mind having, creating, generating, accepting,
arguing with, or otherwise manipulating "ideas." The Rosenbaum *Concordance*
lists only a single use of "idea" and no "ideas" in all of Dickinson's poetry. By
contrast, there are sixty-nine uses of "thought" (sometimes as a verb) and five
"thoughts." It is as if Dickinson deliberately avoided the word "idea," either
despite or because of the way it was commonly used in the Lockean tradition to
mean both concept and percept (or sensation). Along with her attraction to the

various processes of thought described in chapter 2, she may have thought that "thought" better reflected dependency on both mind and brain.

27. In the Dickinson copy of Thomas Brown's *Lectures on the Philosophy of the Human Mind* (1848), in the chapter on "Mental Identity," a handwritten note, perhaps by Austin, at the bottom reads: "for the lesson in remainder of this chap merely state the two objections used against mental identity" (122).

28. Textbooks point out that there is no notion of duration without the succession of thoughts in the mind. But such observations do not address Dickinsonian questions of how consciousness behaves during mysterious limit conditions of temporality, for example, the "time" spent in the grave waiting for the resurrection or the "time" of immortality. The temporalities explored in poems such as "Because I could not stop for Death" (in which centuries seem "shorter than the Day") are anticipated by textbook examples like Upham's of a person sleeping "with a perfect suspension of all his mental operations from this time until the resurrection. . . . Ten thousand years passed under such circumstances would be less than a few days, or even hours" (128).

29. Upham's description of associational disorders matches Higginson's account of his interview with Dickinson. Upham: "Their thoughts fly from one subject to another with great rapidity; and, consequently, one mark of this state of mind is great volubility of speech and almost constant motion of the body" (250). In the spirit of "Much Madness is divinest Sense -" (Fr620), in several 1850s letters Dickinson humorously problematizes her own "insanity" or "Femina Insania." "Insanity to the sane seems so unnecessary—but I am only one, and they are "four and forty" she says to Catherine Scott Turner (Anthon) in 1859 (L209). In an 1856 letter to Elizabeth Holland she spins a mechanistic fantasy of her body and mind going haywire: "Should my own machinery get slightly out of gear, *please*, kind ladies and gentlemen, some one stop the wheel. . . ." She signs the letter "Mad Emilie" (L182). See also L77, L107, L185.

30. Dickinson's many poems scrutinizing fame have precursors in Upham's analysis of the "disordered action of the desire of esteem" (459). Anybody who inordinately exercises this propensity, he argues, "tends to *disorganize* the mind" (460). "It is nearly impossible that the pillars of the mind should remain firm" in this case, and in fact when such people do not receive the applause they love, "they are apt to become melancholy, misanthropic, and unhappy in a very high degree" (460). See also Stonum's analysis of the paradox of claiming an "affective" poetics for a poet who did not publish or try to find readers (*Sublime* 102).

31. Helen Vendler has built a theory around the idea that Dickinson was a "chromatic" thinker.

32. Helen Hunt Jackson's "Thought" similarly emerges from pure philosophy. In his *Short Studies of American Authors*, Higginson recounts the story of Emerson and this poem: "When someone asked Emerson a few years since whether he did not think 'H. H.' the best woman-poet on this continent, he answered in his meditative way 'Perhaps we might as well omit the *woman*;' thus placing her, at least in that moment's impulse, at the head of all. He used to cut her poems from the newspapers as they appeared, to carry them about with him, and to read

them aloud. His especial favorites were the most condensed and the deepest, those having something of that kind of obscurity which Coleridge pronounced to be a compliment to the reader. His favorite among them all is or was the sonnet entitled

THOUGHT

O Messenger, art thou the king, or I?
Thou dalliest outside the palace-gate
Till on thine idle armor lie the late
And heavy dews: the morn's bright, scornful eye
Reminds thee; then, in subtle mockery,
Thou smilest at the window where I wait
Who bade thee ride for life. In empty state
My days go on, while false hours prophesy
Thy quick return; at last in sad despair
I cease to bid thee, leave thee free as air;
When lo! Thou stand'st before me glad and fleet,
And lay'st undreamed-of treasures at my feet.
Ah! Messenger, thy royal blood to buy,
I am too poor. Thou art the king, not I.

Emerson enthusiastically claims that the 'uncontrollableness' of thought by will has never been better expressed by words than in this sonnet; and there are others which utter emotion so profoundly, and yet with such artistic quiet, that each brief poem seems the summary of a life" (41–42). This allegorical poem recapitulates the logic of Dickinson's "Shall I take thee." Jackson's "Thought" is the messenger that the "I" tries unsuccessfully to control. Thought lies about, mocks me, and refuses to cooperate; then, when I give up trying to think, thought suddenly provides me with treasures. It turns out that "thought" is the king, not me.

33. Gall's famous series on phrenology was translated and published in six volumes in the "Phrenological Library" in Boston in 1835. The Quesnay selections were published in *Observations on Surgical Diseases of the Head and Neck: Selected from the Memoirs of the Royal Academy of Surgery of France*, ed. and trans. Drewry Ottley (London: The Sydenham Society, 1848), 57–58. Quesnay describes a case where surgeons find a "splinter in the substance of the brain" (56), and one in which a man "received a blow on the head, which drove a splinter into the brain about an inch deep; this wound almost immediately caused severe symptoms" (56). I do not know whether Dickinson saw these particular volumes but suspect that she had met with similar scientific discussions of splinters in the brain.

34. Gilbert and Gubar claim that this poem is "frank in its admission that madness is its true subject, and that psychic fragmentation—an inability to connect one self with another—is the cause of this madness" (628). Poems like this can also be interpreted as experiments designed to test the strength and applicability of theoretical premises circulating in mental philosophy and physiology. In the poems of mental experience different readers will hear different voices: autobiographical, scientific, meditative, rational, irrational, and so on.

35. Bergson writes: "What we really need to discover is how a choice is effected among an infinite number of recollections which all resemble in some way the present perception, and why only one of them—this rather than that—emerges into the light of consciousness. But this is just what associationism cannot tell us" (*Time* 164).

36. One poem restates a Kantian argument against the *Ding-an-sich*: "Perception of an Object costs / Precise the Object's loss - / Perception in itself a Gain / Replying to it's Price - // The Object absolute, is nought - / Perception sets it fair / And then upbraids a Perfectness / That situates so far -" (Fr1103B). Many others can be seen to reflect a Kantian Copernican turn, especially if it is construed as a moment of weakening, not as the "strong" search for foundations or a priori conditions but as an inquiry into the shaping, hermeneutic powers of the mind: "Heaven is so far of the Mind / That were the Mind dissolved - / The Site - of it - by Architect / Could not again be proved - // 'Tis Vast - as our Capacity - / As fair - as our idea - / To Him of adequate desire / No further 'tis, than Here -" (Fr413).

37. Tyler reports that at Amherst in 1824 optional instruction "is also offered in the Hebrew, French and German Languages, to such as wish it, for a reasonable compensation" (131). George Bancroft and Thomas Cogswell taught German in their school in Northampton beginning in the 1820s. "Why should a group of [Carlyle's] essays giving biographies and critical accounts of German authors become the rage of intellectual Boston? By 1833 the mania for all things German had become so strong that James Freeman Clarke was almost ashamed to confess to his friend Margaret Fuller that he did not enjoy Goethe's poetry" (*Cambridge History* 2:362–63).

38. Leyda reproduces some of Dickinson's German homework and notes that her father gave her a copy of *Ollendorff's New Method of Learning to Read, Write, and Speak the German Language* (1:98). "You will not I know care," Joseph Lyman writes to his fiancée Laura Baker, "if I continue to write to such friends as our sweet Mintie [Wharton] and to Emily Dickinson who used to read German plays with me and sat close beside me so as to look out words from the same Dictionary—10 years ago" (July 30 1856, *Lyman Letters* 58).

39. Coleman was the principal of Amherst Academy from 1844 to 1846, a position his assistant Jesse Andrews also held (Whicher 45). Emily and Lavinia were close friends with Coleman's daughter Eliza, whom they visited in Philadelphia in 1855. See Strickland, "Emily Dickinson's Philadelphia."

40. At first the noisy debate over Kant causes Carlyle's Schiller to examine his doctrines carefully. Then, under the influence of Reinhold, who saw Kant's system as both "more poetical" and "grander" than that of Leibniz, he becomes still further inspired (173). A system "which promised, even with a very little plausibility, to accomplish all that Kant asserted. . . . to explain the difference between Matter and Spirit, to unravel the perplexities of Necessity and Free-will; to show us the true grounds of our belief in God, and what hope nature gives us of the soul's immortality; and thus at length, after a thousand failures, to interpret the enigma of our being—hardly needed that additional inducement to make such a man as Schiller grasp at it with eager curiosity" (172–73).

41. In 1870 Samuel Bowles sent his two daughters to Berlin to study German. Ac-

companying them was Dickinson's good friend Maria Whitney, a professor of German at Smith College in Northampton; she too had trained in Germany.

42. New England's Germanophilia was connected to its mind mania. One important source of German thought was the *Encyclopaedia Americana*, edited by the German Francis Lieber, which began appearing in the late 1820s, and Hedge's enormous *Prose Writers of Germany*, with long chapters on Kant, Schiller, and many other thinkers, poets, and writers, appeared in 1847. In 1844 Orestes Brownson published a three-part critical analysis of Kant in *Brownson's Quarterly Review*, a journal of general interest; he provides a brief history of philosophy in which he shows that the rationalist Cartesian "I think" and the materialist Lockean "I feel" have both proved inadequate.

43. Arguing that it is crucial to place Dickinson in the context of the 1850s religious currents, Habegger says that "the single most important" of these was "the growing tendency within orthodoxy to question the primacy, even the necessity, of a rationally articulated faith. *Was* it so vital, after all, to have correct abstract doctrines? Wasn't there also a true religion of the heart that would do just as well, and which could be expressed 'aesthetically' rather than abstractly? Such questions, particularly as worked out by Horace Bushnell and Edwards A. Park, New England's boldest Protestant thinkers, helped make feasible Dickinson's work as poet" (310). The *Republican* likened Wadsworth to Bushnell on October 22, 1850, for his style of argumentation: "rapid, unique and original, often startling his audience, like Dr Bushnell, with a seeming paradox" (Leyda 1:181). In his eminently poststructuralist text *God in Christ*, Bushnell speaks fondly of a Goethe able to avoid the fate of becoming another "dull proser" or "male spinster of logic" by embracing contradictions and antagonisms (68).

44. Breazeale points out that this is exactly what happened to Amherst professor Julius Seelye's uncle Laurens Hickock in his *Rational Psychology*. He "rejected Kant's strictures on the limits of reason with respect to the noumenal realm and offered his own novel solution to the antinomies of pure reason, as well as a new path to knowledge of what lies beyond nature (which he called 'the Absolute'). With this new, more robust conception of 'reason,' Hickok believed that he could avoid the problems of skepticism and pantheism that seem to cling to Kant's own philosophy of religion" (230).

45. In 1831, for example, when his wife, Ellen, died, Emerson "distracted himself by reading new books—a lifelong pattern that explains why major intellectual expansions in his life so often followed personal losses. He began Victor Cousin's *Cours de l'histoire de la philosophie*, whose sympathetic treatment of Indian philosophy and religion gave him far better knowledge than he had acquired while doing hurried research for 'Indian Superstition'" (*Cambridge History* 2:92). For a recent account of Cousin's role in founding intellectual history, see Kelley, *The Descent of Ideas: The History of Intellectual History*.

46. Nor was Dickinson the only Amherst-born teenaged girl working on her German and mental philosophy. Helen Hunt Jackson described her life as a sixteen-year-old to Julius Palmer on March 8, 1850: "I acquired a tolerable good knowledge of German (and as I knew that he [her father, Nathan Welby Fiske] had often

occasion to refer to books in that language, I pleased myself with the idea that I might make my knowledge of it, useful to him). I read three new Latin authors. . . . I devoted a great deal of time to Intellectual Philosophy, which I knew to be one of his favorite studies" (quoted in Phillips, *Helen Hunt Jackson* 11).

47. Three poems help elucidate Dickinson's complex understanding of "sanctification." In "The Malay - took the Pearl -" the speaker is afraid that "the Sea" is "too much / Unsanctified - to touch -" (Fr451). In "I think I was enchanted," sanctification is sudden, inexplicable, permanent, beautiful, and total: "I could not have defined the change - / Conversion of the Mind / Like Sanctifying in the Soul - / Is witnessed - not explained -" (Fr627). In "The Robin is the One," "Sanctity" connotes peacefulness and, along with "Home" and "Certainty," counts as one of the "best" things: "The Robin is the One / That speechless from her Nest / Submit that Home - and Certainty / And Sanctity, are best" (Fr501C).

48. Webster's 1844 dictionary gives two definitions for glee: "Joy; merriment; mirth; gayety; particularly, the mirth enjoyed at a feast"; "A sort of catch or song sung in parts."

4. Amherst's Other Lexicographer

1. For accounts of nineteenth-century lexicography, see Micklethwait, Friend, and Green. Easily the best resource available on Webster and Dickinson as lexicographers is the Emily Dickinson Lexicon project overseen by Cynthia Hallen. See http://edl.byu.edu/.

2. Critics who have given sustained attention to the definition poems include James S. Leonard as well as Sharon Cameron, whose *Lyric Time* includes the chapter "Naming as History: Dickinson's Poems of Definition" (26–55). Much of Cristanne Miller's *Emily Dickinson: A Poet's Grammar* is relevant to a study of definition poems, and the book also includes a brief section titled "Noah Webster and Lexicography" (153–54). Harold Bloom's gushing chapter on Dickinson in *The Western Canon* celebrates her tremendous powers of cognition and describes her unique ability to "unname." Susan Howe's equally gushing *My Emily Dickinson* enthuses about Dickinson's transgression of traditional gender limitations and hints that Dickinson's redefinitions were part of a liberatory literary project: "For this northern will to become *I*—free to excavate and interrogate definition, the first labor called for was to sweep away the pernicious idea of poetry as embroidery for women" (17). Suzanne Juhasz, *The Undiscovered Continent: Emily Dickinson and the Space of the Mind*, contains some of the most nuanced thinking on the definition poems specifically, and the emphasis in her 2000 essay "The Irresistible Lure of Repetition and Dickinson's Poetics of Analogy" on the moving parts of definition parallels my own. She explains how in Dickinson's poetry "the analogical structure itself denies any literalness to the definition that has been advanced and ends, or does not end, really, by giving the reader the sense that definition is not conclusive but ongoing" (23–24). Critics who have written less systematically on the definitions include Porter, Perlmutter, Howe, Weisbuch, Crumbley, Benvenuto, Hallen, Blackmur, Doriani, Winters, and Hagenbüchle.

Of Dickinson's three best biographers (Sewall, Wolff, and Habegger), only Wolff discusses the definition poems at any length (476–81.) and makes more than passing reference to Webster (91–92).

3. There has been very little explicitly comparative work done on Webster and Dickinson. The question is still open whether, as Susan Howe and others have suggested, Dickinson's poetic mind worked creatively with the graphic and/or visual aspects of Webster's text.

4. As Eberwein's nuanced readings of the definition poems attest, the second wave came much closer to seeing the defining Dickinson. See *Strategies of Limitation*, 146–55.

5. In 1938 Yvor Winters objected to Dickinson on moral grounds. After accusing her of employing "the familiar device of using a major abstraction in a somewhat loose and indefinable manner," he went on to explain his own view of how one should treat the boundaries of human knowledge: "It is possible to solve any problem of insoluble experience by retreating a step and defining the boundary at which comprehension ceases, and by then making the necessary moral adjustments to that boundary" (32, 33).

6. Porter's quotation of Bingham is misleading. As the full context reveals, Bingham's comment applies to one poem only and is not intended to characterize Dickinson's poetics per se. Rather it is meant to show that Dickinson "sometimes used the same stanza in two different poems. 'When what they sung for is undone,' the second stanza of 'A pang is more conspicuous in spring,' is also the beginning of another poem which trails off into a vague limbo. Such overlapping provides plenty of pitfalls for an unwary editor" (x–xi). See Fr1545.

7. In contrast to Hagenbüchle and Juhasz, Porter writes that "her characteristic poem is repetitious, lacking in development, sometimes petering out in the closing stanzas, often incapable of endings, and riddled with the obscurities of private reference, syntactic ellipsis, and grammatical distortion" (*Idiom* 134).

8. Webster's description of definition relies heavily on the Lockean theory of simple ideas combining into complex ones: "*Definition* is such an expression of the several ideas involved in a word, as to communicate them to a person who does not understand the word; or the unfolding of some conception of the mind, answering to the word, or term which is the sign of that conception. Definitions, to be useful, must excite in the mind the precise ideas which common usage has annexed to the word. If they do not, they mislead the inquirer. In definition, then, the original ideas from which a complex idea is formed, must all be enumerated, and in the proper order. But although this precision is necessary to a perfect definition, yet in practice, definitions may often be shortened by the use of complex ideas, instead of the simple ideas which from them; as the complex ideas are well understood to contain simple ideas" (*Manual* 118).

9. Here is a fuller sample of Bushnell's anti-lexicographical vehemence: "No good writer, who is occupied in simply expressing truth, is ever afraid of inconsistencies or self-contradictions in his language. It is nothing to him that a quirk of logic can bring him into absurdity. If at any time he offers definitions, it is not to get a footing for the play of his logic, but it is simply as multiplying forms or figures of that which he seeks to communicate—just as one will take his friend to differ-

ent points of a landscape, and show him cross views, in order that he may get a perfect conception of the outline. Having nothing but words in which to give definitions, he understands the impossibility of definitions as determinate measures of thought, and gives them only as being *other forms* of the truth in question, by aid of which it may be more adequately conceived. On the other hand, a writer without either truth or genius, a mere uninspired, unfructifying logicker, is just the man to live in definitions. He has never a doubt of their possibility. He lays them down as absolute measures, then draws along his deductions, with cautious consistency, and works out, thus, what he considers to be the exact infallible truth. But his definitions will be found to hang, of necessity, on some word or symbol, that symbol to have drawn every thing to itself, or into its own form, and then, when his work is done, it will be both consistent and false—false because of its consistency" (57). *God in Christ* was much debated in the early 1850s; the Dickinson library contained two books by Bushnell.

10. Noah Webster was a close friend of Dickinson's grandfather, a co-founder of Amherst College, and the first president of its board of trustees. Emily was great friends for several years with Webster's granddaughter Emily Fowler, eventually Emily Fowler Ford. For over ten years Webster lived in Amherst, writing the bulk of the 1828 *American Dictionary of the English Language*. The Dickinson family owned a revised 1844 two-volume edition, a reprint of the 1841 edition published in Amherst by J. S. & C. Adams.

11. Whitman's lifelong interest in lexicography has received limited but excellent critical attention, none of which mentions Dickinson. Ed Folsom has shown how Whitman collected dictionaries and interpreted their lists of words as the repositories of his culture's most active elements. Inspired by his dictionaries (he owned many but was partial to Webster), Whitman linked etymology to recent trends in science: "The science of language has large and close analogies in geological science, with its ceaseless evolution, its fossils, and its numberless submerged layers and hidden strata, the infinite go-before of the present" (quoted in Folsom, 17). The ever-expanding and transforming nature of dictionaries also made them a perfect parallel for (and instance of) his increasingly inclusive vision for the growth of American democracy: individual words, like people, carried the historical roots of American culture while simultaneously representing contemporary demographic transformations and multiethnic realities. In short, dictionaries were, as Folsom writes, "the ultimate example of texts that demanded reader response, texts that furnished the hints for endless poems to come" (16).

12. Despite her reputation for difficulty, Dickinson did not deliberately lard poems with obscure or difficult words. Leafing through the 1844 dictionary, I am struck by how many a poet could have used if she were interested in displaying vocabularistic virtuosity: *margatiferous* (pearl-producing), *oscitant* (yawning), *philomath* (lover of learning), *sombrous* (gloomy), and thousands more. I suspect that Dickinson acquired most of her words through conversation and reading, occasionally using the dictionary and other sources to "search philology." There is little to suggest that she used lexicons as primary resources for either writing or thinking.

13. Franklin's note explains: "Too early to refer to her father's death on 16 June

1874, the poem may respond only to the biblical passage to which it refers, Genesis 5:24: 'And Enoch walked with God: and he *was* not; for God took him.'"

14. There is disagreement about how many definition poems there are and when they were written. For Wolff, "Emily Dickinson wrote a great many poems of definition, especially in the later years of her life" (352). But for Eberwein, "1863 brought a great rush of definition poems in an apparent attempt to impose order on experience and arrive at communicable generalizations" (*Strategies* 146). Both positions are defensible; they simply result from different criteria for definition.

15. James Leonard reads "Renunciation" precisely as if it were a full, finished statement: "This definition and redefinition has the effect of bringing the abstract term into focus, delimiting a boundary around the term within which it can be examined as finite, concrete, specific" (19). Camille Paglia characteristically emphasizes the image of violence, arguing that "Renunciation" "is piercing because it is a self-blinding, like Oedipus with the golden brooches" (632).

16. See Sarah Josepha Hale, ed., *Flora's Interpreter; or, The American Book of Flowers and Sentiments*, 7th ed. (1839) (Boston: Marsh, Capen & Lyon). Many such anthologies were published in the nineteenth century; for a partial list, see Richard Sewall, *The Life of Emily Dickinson*, 2:671.

17. George Eliot writes that in "our times of bitter suffering, there are almost always these pauses, when our consciousness is benumbed to everything but some trivial perception or sensation. It is as if semi-idiocy came to give us rest from the memory and the dread which refuse to leave us in our sleep" (50). Dickinson's analysis matches, but characteristically extends to a paradox on time perception: "Pain - has an Element of Blank - / It cannot recollect / When it begun - Or if there were / A time when it was not - // It has no Future - but itself - / It's Infinite contain / It's Past - enlightened to perceive / New Periods - Of Pain." (Fr760).

18. Jane Taylor's *Physiology*: "Every family and school should possess a Dictionary of the English Language, as a book of constant reference; for with an imperfect knowledge of the accurate meaning of words, it must follow that an imperfect understanding of facts is conveyed to the mind when reading upon any subject" (6).

19. In Dickinson's edition of Jeremiah Day's *Introduction to Algebra*, for example, we read: "The foundation of all mathematical knowledge must be laid in definitions. A *definition* is an explanation of what is meant, by any word or phrase. Thus, an equilateral triangle is defined, by saying, that it is a figure bounded by three equal sides. It is essential to a complete definition, that it perfectly distinguish the thing defined, from every thing else. On many subjects it is difficult to give such precision to language, that it shall convey, to every hearer or reader, exactly the same ideas. But, in the mathematics, the principal terms may be so defined, as not to leave room for the least difference of apprehension, respecting their meaning. All must be agreed, as to the nature of a circle, a square, and a triangle, when they have once learned the definitions of these figures" (2–3).

20. Although it is possible to classify the poems in many different ways, there are some natural divisions of theme and topic. In a class of emotions, for example, one might place poems on such topics as hope, remorse, anguish, and shame. Other classes could be invented for natural events such as sunsets and seasons,

or for metaphysical topics like death or God. One could also arrange the poems chronologically, or study their fascicle contexts; such methods might possibly highlight the various biographical, historical, social, and other contexts for the definitions. Still another approach would be to isolate the basic shapes or forms of definitions, of which Sharon Cameron has found two and James Leonard four. "The first group of statements," writes Cameron, "contains the copula as the main verb, and their linguistic structure is some variation of the nominative plus the verb 'to be' plus the rest of the predicate. The characteristics of the predicate are transferred to the nominative, and this transference becomes a fundamental aspect of the figurative language" (*Lyric* 29) Others "attempt to establish a single aspect or identic property of the thing being defined" or else "personify characteristic actions and attributes of the subject under consideration, distinguishing and so defining them" (30). Many, she suggests, are "frankly aphoristic" (30). Leonard limits the term "definition" to "those poems whose PRINCIPAL EFFECT is to convey the essential nature of an abstract idea or type of material object" (18) and enumerates as follows: "Direct definition," "definition through antithesis," "unlabeled definition," and "definition by dissection" (18). More generally, in his now classic essay "Sumptuous Destitution," Richard Wilbur suggested that Dickinson's lifelong creative appropriation of Calvinist terminology made "redefinition" a key aspect of all of her work. Since she "would not let that vocabulary write her poems for her . . . [the words were] taken personally, and therefore redefined" (53).

21. Franklin notes that a copy of this poem was sent to Susan Dickinson in about 1864. See Juhasz, *Undiscovered*, 36.

22. A similar poem defines the difference between "the form of Life" and "Life" by comparing "Liquor at the Lip" with "liquor in the Jug" (Fr1123).

23. The poem also supports the opposite hypothesis—perhaps one feels "despair" first and "fear" second—and thereby suggests that these terms, like magnets or human consciousness, have reversible polarity.

24. A long philosophical tradition, stretching from Plato and Aristotle through the scholastics, William James, Amélie Rorty, and today's virtue theorists, psychologists, and cognitive scientists, attests to the difficulty of defining human emotions. The edition of Upham's *Elements of Mental Philosophy* that Dickinson knew stressed the limitations of language and the primacy of consciousness: "We are dependent for a knowledge of the interior and essential nature of emotions, not upon verbal explanations and definitions, which are inadequate to the communication of such knowledge, but upon Consciousness. It is a species of knowledge which the soul reveals to itself by its own act, directly and immediately. While, therefore, we do not profess to define emotions, in any proper and legitimate sense of defining, we may commend them without impropriety to each one's internal examination" (269).

25. It is possible that Shakespeare's sonnet 33 provided Dickinson with the phrase "celestial face," as well the sun and sky as figural sites of personal disappointment:

> Full many a glorious morning have I seen
> Flatter the mountain tops with sovereign eye,

Kissing with golden face the meadows green,
Gilding pale streams with heavenly alchemy;
Anon permit the basest clouds to ride
With ugly rack on his celestial face,
And from the forlorn world his visage hide,
Stealing unseen to west with this disgrace:
Even so my sun one early morn did shine,
With all triumphant splendour on my brow;
But out, alack, he was but one hour mine,
The region cloud hath mask'd him from me now.
Yet him for this my love no whit disdaineth;
Suns of the world may stain when heaven's sun staineth.

26. Unless otherwise noted, all dictionary entries are taken from Dickinson's two-volume 1844 Webster's. Published in Amherst by J. S. & C. Adams, this is not a new edition but an exact reprint of the 1841 edition.

27. Dickinson was familiar with many poems about the morning. A long essay titled "Poetical Imagery: The Morning" was dedicated to the topic in an 1848 issue of *The Indicator* and mentioned examples from Chaucer, Dante, Milton, and many other poets. See *The Indicator* 1, no. 3 (August 1848): 65–69.

28. Dickinson was not alone, of course, in trying to analyze and order her emotions. There is a long history in the West, before and after Kant, of trying to define them by translating them into symbolic, technical, imaginative, and other creative or systematic languages. Dickinson has a place with the poets and thinkers who emphasize the feel of emotions as well as with behaviorists and philosophers who try to establish "causal chains" that lead to them. As a rule, Dickinson was much less interested in the circumstances that surround an emotion than in its associated changes in consciousness. "More often," Eberwein has said, "this poet omitted narrative detail entirely to leave the reader with the intense emotional and imagistic sensation of an event but without any situational context" (*Strategies* 139). Stonum concurs: "Again and again in her poems Dickinson represents the effects on a speaker's mind of objects, events, and persons whose identity the reader can often only guess at" (*Sublime* 89). Profoundly indifferent, too, to the Aristotelian question of the moral appropriateness of emotions, Dickinson's poems reject the long line of thought that treats them as basically noncognitive. While on the one hand she does describe and celebrate the madness that belongs to some of them, she also tends to agree with William James's position that they are a special kind of perception. Indeed much more than physiological details, she often uses the changes in perceptive and imaginative experience to give precision to her definitions of emotional states.

29. The situation of mental tension that Dickinson described to Higginson in her famous explanation of her writing process—"When I try to organize, my little force explodes"—was captured by Georges Bataille as a crisp, universal principle: "We achieve ecstasy through a contestation of knowledge" (*L'Expérience* 24).

30. Christian terms, italicized and summarily dropped into the definition of "define," were personally important to Webster: in 1808, two years after publishing

his smaller *Compendious Dictionary* and four years before moving to Amherst, he underwent a profound evangelical conversion. Aside from the term "belief," however, a word she scrutinized in many poems and letters, those four terms are remarkably rare in Dickinson's writings and never the explicit subjects of definition poems. For an account of Webster's tumultuous life during this time, see Harlow Unger, *Noah Webster: The Life and Times of an American Patriot* (265).

31. Webster's faith in ultimate reason becomes especially palpable in his definition of the word "paradox": "A tenet or proposition contrary to received opinion, or seemingly absurd, yet true in fact." For a discussion of Dickinson's use of paradox, see Brita Lindberg-Seyersted, *The Voice of the Poet*, 104.

32. According to Blackmur, reading Dickinson's poetry provokes a "multiplicity of irritation" (79).

33. Webster's quotation is from *All's Well That Ends Well* 1.3. (When the Countess discovers that Helena loves her son, she is able to diagnose Helena's mysterious "loneliness" as a case of unrequited love.) But as is often the case, Webster has borrowed and edited the entry from Johnson's 1755 dictionary, curtailing the illustrative quotations. Johnson's "loneliness" reads:

> Loneliness. n.s. [from lonely] Solitude; want of company; disposition to avoid company.
> The huge and sportful assembly grew to him a tedious loneliness,
> esteeming nobody found since Daiphantus was lost.   Sidney
>   I see
> The mystery of your loneliness, and find
> Your salt tears' head.   Shakespeare

34. Dickinson often experimented with the paradoxes of loneliness. "It might be lonelier / Without the Loneliness -" begins one 1863 poem (Fr535) in which the speaker fears that hope might "intrude upon" or even "blaspheme" the "sweet parade" of ordained suffering that defines acute loneliness. She opened an 1863 letter to the Norcross cousins with the striking comment, "Nothing has happened but loneliness, perhaps too daily to relate" (L285). Any who doubt that Dickinson felt deep, frightening loneliness might also consult Ellen Louise Hart and Martha Nell Smith, *Open Me Carefully*, 51ff.

35. Dickinson often treats emotions usually construed to be "violent" as, in fact, "calm" and vice versa. One traditional philosophical difference between the two is that the "violent" emotions have a physiological component, while "calm" ones like loneliness are predominantly mental or psychological.

36. One can see the speaker's compulsive repetition and rephrasing as a sustained attempt to "try to think" an aesthetic idea. Kirk Pillow describes what happens to the Kantian imagination when it tries but fails to control the many associations incited by such an attempt: The flood of allusion and implication set loose by the aesthetic idea provides imagination 'a multitude of kindred presentations' . . . that it apprehends as an expanding series. Imagination seeks to *comprehend* this multiplicity as a unified whole, but the boundless wealth of the aesthetic ideas soon overwhelms it" (86).

37. In *The Long Shadow*, Clark Griffith plausibly reconstructs the narrative of the

poem as follows: "Faced by the record of her own corruptions, Miss Dickinson's speaker begins by trying to stretch belief around the offenses—and, failing in that, ends by believing that she herself has been offended. She perceives the darkness within as radically alien to her own being, and as a cause not for shame really, but for unremitting wonder" (204). For Daneen Wardrop in *Dickinson's Gothic*, this poem exemplifies Freud's notion of recurrence and promises that "there is a way to escape consciousness" (164.).

38. Sharon Cameron finds that the second stanza does not clarify the first and argues that the reader simply cannot "see a coherent picture" (*Lyric* 37). The poem "leads the writer to interpretive despair, for there is no way to figure the confusion that ensues" (36). The poem receives a more persuasive and positive reading by Paul Crumbley in *Inflections of the Pen*. It also provides the central figure—a doorless house—for Maryanne Garbowsky's book-length analysis of Dickinson's "agoraphobic syndrome that left her in fear of the outside world" (22).

39. Other examples would include "I heard a Fly buzz - when I died -" (Fr591), "I died for Beauty - but was scarce" (Fr448), and "Safe in their Alabaster Chambers -" (Fr124).

40. Dickinson aligns herself with squirrels as figures of practicality in "Experiment to me": "But Meat within, is requisite / To Squirrels and to Me" (Fr1081). The squirrels in "What shall I do when the Summer troubles -" function similarly to those in "Doom is the House" in that they are figures of fun and self-fulfillment that the suffering consciousness must endure while she misses her lover: "Oh, when the Squirrel fills His Pockets / And the Berries stare / How can I bear their jocund Faces / Thou from Here, so far" (Fr915)?

41. Franklin corrects Johnson's "Berries die" to "Berries dye." Both terms are present in the pun, but Franklin's ripening (rather than moribund) berries reinforce the idea that the speaker's trapped consciousness imagines and dwells on beautiful things.

42. In his associational analysis of "contrast," Upham argues that when a person suffers greatly, his "extreme misery aggravates itself by suggesting scenes of ideal happiness, and his mind revels in a paradise of delights merely to give greater intensity his actual woes by contrasting them with imaginary bliss" (156).

43. In "The Transcendentalist" Emerson roots "experience" deeply in the Kant he had learned about through de Staël. "It is well known to most of my audience, that the Idealism of the present day acquired the name of Transcendental, from the use of that term by Immanuel Kant, of Konigsberg, who replied to the skeptical philosophy of Locke, which insisted that there was nothing in the intellect which was not previously in the experience of the senses, by showing that there was a very important class of ideas, or imperative forms, which did not come by experience, but through which experience was acquired; that these were intuitions of the mind itself; and he denominated them *Transcendental* forms" (*Essays* 198).

44. A great many poems begin in the present tense, in a state of hesitating yet heightened thought or emotion: "I do not care - why should I care / And yet I fear I'm caring" (Fr1534), "I am alive - I guess -" (Fr605), "We dream - it is good we are dreaming -" (Fr584), "I am ashamed - I hide -" (Fr705).

5. Through the Dark Sod

1. For studies of nineteenth-century reading habits in America, see Richard Brown, Machor (*Readers*), Baym, Tompkins, and Pawley. For studies of Dickinson's reading in particular, see Keller, Diehl, Kirkby, Rainwater, Pollak ("Allusions"), Capps, Sewall, Loeffelholz (*Frame*), Wolff, Buckingham ("Reading"), and Stonum ("Background"). There is also a wealth of feminist literature on Dickinson, much of it devoted to her relationship to other women writers. For Dickinson and Charlotte Brontë in particular, see Habegger, Farr, and Homans; for Dickinson and Browning, see Bogus, Moers, Rainwater, Walsh, Gilbert and Gubar, Pollak, Cristanne Miller, and Loeffelholz (*Frame*); for Dickinson and George Eliot, see Homans and Cary.

2. It might seem possible to study Dickinson's reading habits by looking at wider patterns among her peers. Christine Pawley argues that "by conceiving of readers as members of a particular kind of reading community, historians can find a way not only to link those apparently disparate elements—reader and text—but also to elaborate on who readers were, and thus to shed light on how these specific readers read" (144). Richard Brown's *Knowledge Is Power: The Diffusion of Information in Early America* analyzes three specific female readers and the way they absorbed "affective information" through literary and other texts. In practice, however, it proves difficult to construe Dickinson as a representative of specific social groups, so even the best descriptions of shared reading practices, such as those of Machor and Buckingham, remain suggestive.

3. The methods of historicists like James Machor, who has identified thorough-going antifeminist bias in nineteenth-century review culture, sometimes leave too little room for the countercultural readers that their theories, taken sociologically, almost predict: faced with clear and deep-rooted hypocrisies, some people during this age of burgeoning individualism surely ignored or distrusted the culture of literary reviews. In Dickinson's case, skeptical poison was poured into the porches of her ears by Amherst students, the sarcastic Samuel Bowles, and many others who fueled her tolerant attitude, confident iconoclasm, and wit. In an 1850 letter to Abiah Root, she mocked review-style moralizing discourse systematically: "Now my dear friend, let me tell you that these last thoughts are fictions – vain imaginations to lead astray foolish young women. They are flowers of speech, they both *make*, and *tell* deliberate falsehoods, avoid them as the snake, and turn aside as from the *Bottle* snake, and I dont *think* you will be harmed" (January 29, 1850, L88). The pithy *vita* she sent in her second letter to Higginson shows that she received at home the kinds of "contradictory scripts" Machor identifies in the periodicals: a stream of instructions that were meant to educate but instead "worked, in effect, to immobilize" women's responses ("Hermeneutics" 74). "I have a brother and sister," she writes, and "my mother does not care for thought, and father, too busy with his briefs to notice what we do. He buys me many books, but begs me not to read them, because he fears they joggle the mind. They are religious, except me, and address an eclipse, every morning, whom they call their 'Father'" (L268).

4. Ellen Moers credits George Eliot and George Sand with enriching the novel form

"by extending its terrain into the mind of the girl-child," but this assessment should also include Brontë and Browning (52).

5. References to *Aurora Leigh* are cited by book and line number.

6. When David is beaten by the vicious Mr. Murdstone and locked in his room for five days, he never mentions reading despite his lengthy retrospective description of how he spent the time. In the first of the innovative "Retrospects" chapters (chap. 18), in which grown-up David suddenly turns to the present tense to remember and retell his schooldays as vividly as possible, he describes his fights with the butcher boy, crushes on girls, and academic success, all without needing to mention his direct interaction with any particular books. Throughout the novel, compared to the girls', his passion for reading seems flat and unpersuasive: "All this time I was so conscious of the waste of any promise I had given, and of my being utterly neglected, that I should have been perfectly miserable, I have no doubt, but for the old books. They were my only comfort; and I was as true to them as they were to me, and read them over and over I don't know how many times more" (147).

7. In her 1850 "Biographical Notice" introducing her sister's *Wuthering Heights* (1847), Charlotte Brontë describes a solitary, studious community of sisters. "About five years ago, my two sisters and myself, after a somewhat prolonged period of separation, found ourselves reunited, and at home. Resident in a remote district where education had made little progress, and where, consequently, there was no inducement to seek social intercourse beyond our own domestic circle, we were wholly dependent on ourselves and each other, on books and study, for the enjoyments and occupations of life" (319). Loeffelholz suggests that "the Brontës' writing may have served as a kind of collective female muse to Dickinson's poetry" (*Boundaries* 85).

8. This is not to say that boys faced no pressures of their own as readers. While some exercised the option of ignoring books—"Luke, like Tom, doesn't like reading," says Eliot (27)—the more studious or intellectually curious ones, like Demi from Louisa May Alcott's *Little Men*, "who knows lots and reads like anything," often felt the pressure of becoming practical, physically strong, successful, and worldly: "Very fond of books, and full of lively fancies, born of a strong imagination and a spiritual nature, these traits made his parents anxious to balance them with useful knowledge and healthful society, lest they should make him one of those pale precocious children who amaze and delight a family sometimes, and fade away like hot-house flowers, because the young soul blooms too soon, and has not a hearty body to root it firmly in the wholesome soil of this world" (21).

9. Little David Copperfield easily finds productive uses for the narratives he has learned. At Salem House he plays the (female) role of "Sultana Scheherazade" to Steerforth for many months, telling the plots of the stories he had learned in his father's books (94). Occasionally it becomes an onerous duty, but mostly the narrating role inspires him with "great pride and satisfaction" (93). He recalls, "Whatever I had within me that was romantic and dreamy, was encouraged by so much story-telling in the dark" (95). And he blooms when he tells stories to little Em'ly: "The best times were when she sat quietly at work in the doorway, and I sat on the wooden step at her feet, reading to her" (141).

10. These female authors are sometimes criticized for their depictions of weakness and starvation. F. R. Leavis complains that a "disastrous weakness" dominates *The Mill on the Floss*: "The emotional quality represents something, a need or hunger in George Eliot, that shows itself to be insidious company for her intelligence—apt to supplant it and take command" (39).

11. Margaret Homans writes: "It may be that Eliot is articulating through Maggie the stages of her own education in feminine readership, in how to be a docile or self-suppressing reader. To submit to others' words in Maggie's case is to submit to the law of cause and effect and therefore to reach the unhappy end predicted for all dark heroines. Eliot thematizes both docility and disobedience to instruction through the relation between Maggie's reading and the pattern of her life: disobedient reading is incompatible with Victorian femininity, yet complete feminine docility leads to the self's silence and ultimately to death" (581).

12. Writing in the October 1848 *North American Review*, E. P. Whipple described the controversy created by *Jane Eyre*: "Not many months ago, the New England States were visited by a distressing mental epidemic, passing under the name of the 'Jane Eyre fever,' which defied all the usual nostrums of the established doctors of criticism. Its effects varied with different constitutions, in some producing a soft ethical sentimentality, which relaxed all the fibres of conscience, and in others exciting a general fever of moral and religious indignation" (355). The question of the author's sex was noisily debated by many reviewers, Whipple among them. Dickinson certainly read the June 1848 issue of the Amherst College student publication *The Indicator*, and probably knew the anonymous author of the review of *Jane Eyre*. Their pompous self-certainty makes for good reading: "We doubt not that it will soon cease to be a secret; but on one assertion we are willing to risk our critical reputation—and that is, that no woman wrote it. This was our decided conviction at the first perusal, and a somewhat careful study of the work has strengthened it. No woman in all the annals of feminine celebrity ever wrote such a style, terse yet eloquent, and filled with energy bordering sometimes almost on rudeness: no woman ever conceived such masculine characters as those portrayed here: and to use a test which, trifling as it seems, has weighed not a little with us, no woman ever made such blunders in discussing millinery, and the various articles of feminine [*sic*] apparel! For the truth of this last criticism we appeal to all our fair readers" ("Jane Eyre" 31). There is no record of how Dickinson reacted when it was revealed, in 1851, that the book *was* written by a woman, but it would have been one more reason to identify with the writer that Elizabeth Gaskell later described, in an 1857 volume Dickinson owned, as "the plain, short-sighted, oddly-dressed, studious little girl they called Charlotte Brontë" (109).

13. Habegger, Margaret Homans, and Judith Farr have all drawn attention to the parallel between Jane's relationship with Rochester and Dickinson's with her lover, down to the use of words like "Master" and "Sir" (Homans 205–6). Arguing in this vein that the book was "full of explosive material that looks like a twisted or idealized account of Dickinson's own experience," Habegger asks biographical questions that have never been answered: "Having herself resisted indoctrination at freezing Mount Holyoke, what did she think of Lowood, the Calvinist school

for girls (but run by a man)? How did she feel about lordly, romantic Rochester, or dictatorial St. John Rivers, who insists that Jane become his missionary wife, or the diminutive heroine herself, repeatedly defying authoritative men after first obeying them" (226)?

14. Here is one place where Dickinson defines this: "We noticed smallest things - / Things overlooked before / By this great light upon our minds / Italicized - as 'twere" (Fr1100).

15. And along with moving the book's plot into Jane's mind, the long, accurate quotation has the effect of opening up a complex intertextual situation. This time we can hardly attribute such long quotations to Jane's memory, so we become aware that *Bewick's*—as well as the quotations in *Bewick's*—are simultaneously present and visible to both Janes and the author Brontë. But the different levels are not explicitly thematized, and the narrator does not remark on how she has changed since childhood "at the distance of—I will not say how many years." The quotation from James Thomson's *The Seasons* would have been easily recognized by Dickinson, for she had studied the poem in school: "Where the Northern Ocean, in vast whirls / Boils round the naked, melancholy isles / Of farthest Thule; and the Atlantic surge / Pours in among the stormy Hebrides."

16. Rousseau writes: "Sophie has a mind pleasing without being brilliant, and solid without being profound—a mind of which people say nothing, because they never observe in it either more or less than in their own. She always has a mind which pleases the people who speak to her, although it is not copiously adorned according to the notion which we have of the intellectual culture of women; for hers has not been formed by reading, but only by the conversations of her father and mother, by her own reflections, and by the observations which she has made in the little of the world which she has seen" (*Émile* 291–92).

17. John Evangelist Walsh argues that Dickinson plagiarized *Aurora Leigh*. Mary Janice Rainwater suggests more persuasively that she was inspired by the way Browning used certain images, such as "bells, planks, and flies," to depict psychological states (142).

18. Reading mediates Aurora's relationship with every important character in the book. When Romney comes home from college with a book in hand, Aurora cannot help peeking inside; she finds "mere statistics" (1.525). Marian Erle, who is modeled on Margaret Fuller as Aurora is on Browning herself, reads the way Habegger says Dickinson does: aggressively and sporadically. Despite the fact that "she had grown, this Marian Erle of ours / To no book-learning" and was "ignorant / Of authors,—not in earshot of the things / Out-spoken o'er the heads of common men," she found a way to read Burns, Bunyan, Selkirk, Thomson, Milton, Gray, and others (3.998–1002). She "weeded out / Her book-leaves" and rejected the ones that hurt, making a nosegay of the "sweet and good / To fold within her breast, and pore upon / At broken moments of the noontide glare" (3.990–92). Altogether it is a less deconstructive version of Aurora's own strategy. We also receive detailed reports on the reading of Aunt Leigh and cousin Romney, both of whom pressure Aurora to read traditional books in traditional ways. Lady Waldemar reads social theory only in order to attract Romney.

19. Along with a list of the subjects and books she was forced to read, Aurora de-

scribes the ones she was forced *not* to, which of course suggests that she learned them independently:

> I learnt the collects and the catechism,
> The creeds, from Athanasius back to Nice,
> The Articles, the Tracts *against* the times,
> (By no means Buonaventure's "Prick of Love,")
> And various popular synopses of
> Inhuman doctrines never taught by John,
> Because she liked instructed piety.
> I learnt my complement of classic French
> (Kept pure of Balzac and neologism)
> And German also, since she liked a range
> Of liberal education,—tongues, not books.
> *(1.392–406)*

The list continues with "a little" algebra, royal genealogies, Burmese history, and geographical names (including two mountains that Dickinson used in her poetry: Chimborazo and Teneriffe). Thinking back on these "years of education" with her aunt, Aurora wonders if "Brinvilliers suffered more / In the water-torture" than she did (1.466–67). The high-water mark of her bitterness is reached when she excoriates the "books on womanhood" (1.427) she was forced to read in order to "prove, if women do not think at all, / They may teach thinking, (to a maiden-aunt / Or else the author)—books that boldly assert / Their right of comprehending husband's talk / When not too deep" (1.428–32).

20. De Staël writes: "Leibnitz . . . prononça cet axiome sublime: 'Il n'y a rien dans l'intelligence qui ne vienne par les sens, si ce n'est l'intelligence elle-même" (418).

21. In section 2.1.2, titled "All ideas come from sensation or reflection," Locke writes: "Let us then suppose the mind to be, as we say, white paper, void of all characters, without any ideas:—How comes it to be furnished? Whence comes it by that vast store which the busy and boundless fancy of man has painted on it with an almost endless variety? Whence has it all the materials of reason and knowledge? To this I answer, in one word, from EXPERIENCE."

22. Rainwater recalls that in book 2, Romney refuses to read any of Aurora's poetry: "I saw at once the thing had witchcraft in it, / Whereof the reading calls up dangerous spirits: / I rather bring it to the witch" (2.78–80; Rainwater 100–101).

6. With Bolder Playmates Straying

1. Starting in her youth, Dickinson privileged the tumultuous danger and vastness of the sea over the safety and smallness of the shore. "The shore is safer, Abiah," wrote Dickinson at the age of fourteen, "but I love to buffet the sea – I can count the bitter wrecks here in these pleasant waters, and hear the murmuring winds, but oh, I love the danger! You are learning control and firmness. Christ Jesus will love you more. I'm afraid he don't love me *any*!" (L39). A similar gesture

of thought brought Dickinson to compose "The Sea said 'Come' to the Brook -" (Fr1275) and to write to Judge Lord in 1878, "The Creek turns Sea – at thought of thee" (Leyda 2:305).

2. In many poems Dickinson affirms the worth, figured sometimes in economic terms, of phase two experiences, and taken together they tend to give more "value" to this world than to the "next" or to any other. "Dare you see a Soul at the 'White Heat'?" (Fr401) is a famous example, and another links "Our Best Moment" to real self-risk: "Did Our Best Moment last - / 'Twould supersede the Heaven - / A few - and they by Risk - procure - / So this Sort - are not given -" (Fr560).

3. In 1882, the year "Of Death" was written, Dickinson thanked Mabel Loomis Todd for her painting of Indian pipes: "That without suspecting it you should send me the preferred flower of life, seems almost supernatural, and the sweet glee that I felt at meeting it, I could confide to none. I still cherish the clutch with which I bore it from the ground when a wondering Child, an unearthly booty, and maturity only enhances mystery, never decreases it" (L769).

4. The critic who has commented at greatest length on "Of Death I try to think like this" is Rebecca Patterson, and her reading could not be more different from mine. She uses the poem as an example in a much larger discussion of symbols: "The erotic symbol becomes the death symbol it has all along threatened to become. This development is more complicated than can be easily explained. The Well of Death, she tries to persuade herself, may be like a 'Brook'. . . and she remembers straying in childhood beside a 'Brook that seemed a Sea,' then bravely leaping it to clutch the alluring 'Purple Flower' beyond. Now purple is her death color . . . and is appropriately associated with the West, the region of death, but it is also love's color: 'Purple' is the 'Color of a Queen.' . . . A number of poems suggest that her love-death symbol was further complicated and intensified by the fact that the beloved actually lived westward from Massachusetts." For Patterson, the allure of linking color symbolism to Dickinson's life is so much more zestful than the poem's narrative that she does not need to notice that in the poem Dickinson (or the speaker) is not the one who bravely leaps to clutch the flower. Just the opposite: the poem highlights the contrast between Dickinson's lack of physical courage as a child and her bold "thinking of death" as an adult. See also Wolfgang Rudat, "Dickinson and Immortality," who finds resonances of Milton and Virgil in the poem.

5. For another powerful meditation on the paradox of italicizing the now instead of concentrating on the future, see "Did life's penurious length" (Fr1751).

6. The introduction to the Schiller section includes a suggestive source for Dickinson's interest in the peaks of Teneriffe and Chimborazo: "Schiller can seem higher than Goethe only because he is narrower. Thus to unpracticed eyes, a Peak of Teneriffe, nay, a Strassburg Minster, when we stand on it, may seem higher than a Chimborazo; because the former rise abruptly, without abutment or environment; the latter rises gradually, carrying half a world aloft with it; and only the deeper azure of the heavens, the widened horizon, the 'eternal sunshine' disclose to the geographer that the 'Region of Change' lies far below him" (Hedge 373).

7. In the introduction to his 1845 translation of Schiller's writings, John Weiss ar-

gues that Dickinson's New England culture suffers from an underdeveloped play impulse: "So far as the sports of a people are indicative of its aesthetic culture and the development of its Play-impulse, the sons of the Puritans may be judged to be still in a state of nature. With us it is most emphatically 'all work and no play.' Our life is hard, austere, thoroughly empirical; the oscillation to the subjective extreme has just commenced. . . . [I]n short, tried by Schiller's aesthetic rules, we are not so enormously removed from the savages whom we have just dispossessed, and whose arrow-heads the New England plough still turns up in numbers" (Schiller, *Aesthetic* xxvi). Weiss also supplied the translations of Schiller in Frederic Henry Hedge's 1848 *Prose Writers of Germany*.

8. Dickinson wrote "Of Death I try to think like this" in 1882, the same year that Nietzsche's *The Gay Science* first announced and elaborated the idea that "God is dead." While Roger Lundin is right to distinguish between the joy Nietzsche felt at the death of God and Dickinson's conflictedness, this poem may nonetheless be taken as a private, deeply felt experience of what Nietzsche analyzed on the broader level of European culture. "Of Death" exemplifies the tenacious rationality of an advanced Calvinist puritan tradition, but it also defines a crucial question and a range of possible answers for every Christian who had lost or was questioning faith.

9. Dickinson often exalts play in the Bataillean sense. In one poem she cannot decide whether to say that bliss is the "Plaything," "sceptre," or "trinket" of the child" (Fr1583). And in other poems she uses children as a means of expressing social bonds or human experiences that are too primal or existential to be intelligible in civilized, religious, or political terms. The boy in "The nearest Dream recedes - unrealized -" (Fr304) and the child in "These are the days when the Birds come back -" (Fr122) are archetypal children in very Schillerian senses.

Works Cited

The following abbreviations refer to the writings of Emily Dickinson:

Fr   *The Poems of Emily Dickinson.* Ed. R. W. Franklin. 3 vols. Cambridge: Harvard University Press, 1998. Citation by poem number; variant is A unless otherwise indicated.

L   *The Letters of Emily Dickinson.* Ed. Thomas H. Johnson and Theodora Ward. 3 vols. Cambridge: Harvard University Press, 1958. Citation by letter number.

Abercrombie, John. *The Philosophy of the Moral Feelings.* Ed. Jacob Abbot. Boston: Otis, Broaders, and Company, 1844.

Abel, Elizabeth, Marianne Hirsch, and Elizabeth Langland, eds. *The Voyage In: Fictions of Female Development.* Hanover, N.H.: University Press of New England, 1983.

Alcott, Louisa May. *Little Men: Life at Plumfield with Jo's Boys.* Boston: Little, Brown, and Co., 1917.

Altieri, Charles. "Taking Lyrics Literally: Teaching Poetry in a Prose Culture." *New Literary History* 32 (2001): 259–81.

Anderson, Charles R. "The Conscious Self in Emily Dickinson's Poetry." In *On Dickinson: The Best from American Literature.* Ed. Edwin H. Cady and Louis J. Budd. Durham: Duke University Press, 1990. 33–51.

———. *Emily Dickinson's Poetry: Stairway of Surprise.* New York: Holt, Rinehart, and Winston, 1960.

"The Assault on Locke." In *The Cambridge History of American Literature.* Vol. 2: *Prose Writing, 1820–1865.* Ed. Sacvan Bercovitch. New York: Cambridge University Press, 1994. 350–61.

Bain, Alexander. *The Senses and the Intellect.* 1855. 3rd ed. New York: D. Appleton & Co, 1868.

Barnes, Daniel R. "Emily Dickinson and the Proverb." In *Wise Words: Essays on the Proverb.* Ed. Wolfgang Mieder. New York: Garland, 1994. 439–65.

Barth, John. "The Literature of Exhaustion." In *Narrative Theory.* Ed. David H. Richter. White Plains, N.Y.: Longman, 1996. 77–86.

Barthes, Roland. "From Work to Text." In *Textual Strategies: Perspectives in Post-Structuralist Criticism*. Trans. Josué V. Harari. Ithaca: Cornell University Press. 1979. 73–81.

Bataille, Georges. *Oeuvres complètes*. Vol. 8. Paris: Gallimard, 1976.

———. *Le Procès de Gilles de Rais*. Paris: Pauvert, 1965.

———. *L'Expérience intérieure*. Paris: Gallimard, 1954.

Baym, Nina. *American Women of Letters and the Nineteenth-Century Sciences: Styles of Affiliation*. New Brunswick, N.J.: Rutgers University Press, 2002.

———. "Emily Dickinson and Scientific Skepticism." In *American Women of Letters and the Nineteenth-Century Sciences: Styles of Affiliation*. New Brunswick, N.J.: Rutgers University Press, 2002. 133–51.

Beaty, Jerome. *Misreading "Jane Eyre": A Postformalist Paradigm*. Columbus: Ohio State University Press, 1996.

Beecher, Catharine. *The Elements of Mental and Moral Philosophy, Founded upon Experience, Reason, and the Bible*. Hartford: Peter B. Gleason & Co., 1831.

Béjoint, Henri. *Tradition and Innovation in Modern English Dictionaries*. Oxford: Oxford University Press, 1994.

Bentley, Rensselaer. *The Pictorial Reader: Containing a Variety of Useful and Instructive Lessons upon Familiar Subjects; With Illustrations to Render them Interesting and Attractive*. New York: George F. Cooledge & Bros., 1847.

Benvenuto, Richard. "Words within Words: Dickinson's Use of the Dictionary." *ESQ: A Journal of the American Renaissance* 29, no. 1 (1983): 46–55.

Bergson, Henri. *Matter and Memory*. New York: Zone Books, 1988.

———. *Time and Free Will: An Essay on the Immediate Data of Consciousness*. Trans. R. L. Pogson. New York: Macmillan, 1912.

Bianchi, Martha Dickinson. *The Life and Letters of Emily Dickinson*. Boston: Houghton Mifflin, 1924.

Bingham, Millicent Todd. *Emily Dickinson's Home: Letters of Edward Dickinson and His Family*. New York: Harper & Brothers, 1955.

Blackmur, R. P. "Emily Dickinson's Notation." In Sewall, *Emily Dickinson: A Collection of Critical Essays*. 78–87.

Blake, Caesar R., and Carlton F. Wells. *The Recognition of Emily Dickinson: Selected Criticism since 1890*. Ann Arbor: University of Michigan Press, 1968.

Blanchot, Maurice. *The Infinite Conversation*. Trans. Susan Hanson. Minneapolis: University of Minnesota Press, 1992.

Blau, Joseph. "Kant in America I: Brownson's Critique of the *Critique of Pure Reason*." *Journal of Philosophy* 51, no. 26 (1954): 874–80.

Bloom, Harold. "Emily Dickinson: Blanks, Transports, the Dark." In *The Western Canon: The Books and School of the Ages*. New York: Harcourt Brace, 1994. 291–309.

Bogus, Diane. "Not So Disparate: An Investigation of the Influence of Elizabeth Barrett Browning on the Work of Emily Dickinson." *Dickinson Studies* 49 (1984): 38–46.

Bozeman, Theodore. *Protestants in an Age of Science: The Baconian Ideal and Antebellum American Religious Thought*. Chapel Hill: University of North Carolina Press, 1977.

Brantley, Richard. *Experience and Faith: The Late-Romantic Imagination of Emily Dickinson.* New York: Palgrave Macmillan, 2004.

Breazeale, Daniel. Review of *The Early American Reception of German Idealism. Journal of the History of Philosophy* 42, no. 2 (2004): 229–31.

Brontë, Charlotte. "Biographical Notice." In Emily Brontë, *Wuthering Heights.* Oxford: Oxford University Press, 1998. 319–28.

———. *Jane Eyre.* Ed. Richard J. Dunn. New York: W. W. Norton & Co., 2001.

Brown, Richard. *Knowledge Is Power: The Diffusion of Information in Early America, 1700–1865.* New York: Oxford University Press, 1989.

Brown, Thomas. *Lectures on the Philosophy of the Human Mind.* 2 vols. Hallowell: Masters, Smith & Co., 1848.

Browning, Elizabeth Barrett. *Aurora Leigh.* Ed. Margaret Reynolds. New York: W. W. Norton & Co., 1996.

Buckingham, Willis J. "Emily Dickinson and the Reading Life." In Orzeck and Weisbuch. 233–54.

———. "Emily Dickinson's Dictionary." *Harvard Library Bulletin* 25 (October 1977). 489–92.

Buell, Lawrence. *Emerson.* Cambridge: Harvard University Press, 2003.

Burke, Edmund. *A Philosophical Enquiry into the Origin of Our Ideas of the Sublime and Beautiful.* Ed. Adam Phillips. New York: Oxford University Press, 1998.

Bushnell, Horace. *God in Christ.* Hartford: Brown and Parsons, 1849.

The Cambridge History of American Literature. 8 vols. Ed. Sacvan Bercovitch. New York: Cambridge University Press, 1994.

Cameron, Sharon. *Choosing Not Choosing: Dickinson's Fascicles.* Chicago: University of Chicago Press, 1992.

———. *Lyric Time: Dickinson and the Limits of Genre.* Baltimore: Johns Hopkins University Press, 1979.

Capps, Jack L. *Emily Dickinson's Reading, 1836–1886.* Cambridge: Harvard University Press, 1966.

Carlyle, Thomas. *The Life of Friedrich Schiller, Comprehending an Examination of His Works.* London: Taylor & Hessey, 1825.

———. *Sartor Resartus.* Ed. Peter Sabor. New York: Oxford University Press, 1999.

Cary, Cecile W. "*The Mill on the Floss* as an Influence on Emily Dickinson." *Dickinson Studies* 36 (1979): 26–39.

Cazeaux, Clive. *The Continental Aesthetics Reader.* London: Routledge, 2000.

Charvat, William. *The Origins of American Critical Thought, 1810–1835.* Philadelphia: University of Pennsylvania Press, 1936.

Cmiel, Kenneth. *Democratic Eloquence: The Fight over Popular Speech in Nineteenth-Century America.* New York: William Morrow, 1990.

Coleridge, Samuel Taylor. *Aids to Reflection in the Formation of a Manly Character, on the Several Grounds of Morality, Prudence, and Religion.* Burlington, Vt.: C. Goodrich, 1829.

Conser, Walter. *God and the Natural World: Religion and Science in Antebellum America.* Columbia: University of South Carolina Press, 1993.

Crabb, George. *English Synonymes Explained in Alphabetical Order; with Copi-*

ous Illustrations and Examples Drawn from the Best Writers. New York: J. & J. Harper, 1826.

Crumbley, Paul. "Dickinson's Dialogic Voice." In Grabher, Hagenbüchle, and Miller. 93–109.

———. *Inflections of the Pen: Dash and Voice in Emily Dickinson*. Lexington: University of Kentucky Press, 1996.

Csengei, Ildikó. "The Unreadability of the Bildungsroman: Reading Jane Eyre Reading." *The AnaChronist* (2000): 102–38.

Cummings, Preston. *A Dictionary of Congregational Usages*. Boston, 1855.

Cutter, Calvin. *A Treatise on Anatomy, Physiology, and Hygiene Designed for Colleges, Academies, and Families*. New York: Clark and Maynard, 1852.

Day, Jeremiah. *An Introduction to Algebra: Being the First Part of a Course of Mathematics, Adapted to the Method of Instruction in the American Colleges*. 28th ed. New Haven: Hezekiah Howe, 1837.

De Man, Paul. *Allegories of Reading: Figural Language in Rousseau, Nietzsche, Rilke, and Proust*. New Haven: Yale University Press, 1982.

———. *Blindness and Insight: Essays in the Rhetoric of Contemporary Criticism*. Minneapolis: University of Minnesota Press, 1983.

———. *Critical Writings, 1953–1978*. Ed. Lindsay Waters. Minneapolis: University of Minnesota Press, 1989.

———. "Criticism and Crisis." In *Blindness and Insight*. 3–19.

Derrida, Jacques. *Acts of Literature*. Ed. Derek Attridge. New York: Routledge, 1992.

———. "Structure, Sign, and Play in the Discourse of the Human Sciences." In *Writing and Difference*. 278–93.

———. *Writing and Difference*. Trans. Alan Bass. Chicago: University of Chicago Press, 1978.

De Staël, Madame de (Anne-Louis-Germaine). *De l'Allemagne*. Paris: Garnier Frères, 1815.

Dickens, Charles. *David Copperfield*. Ed. Jeremy Tambling. London: Penguin, 1996

Dickie, Margaret. "Dickinson in Context." *American Literary History* 7, no. 2 (1995): 318–33.

———. "Dickinson's Discontinuous Lyric Self." *American Literature* 60, no. 4 (December 1988): 537–53.

Diehl, Joanne Feit. "Emerson, Dickinson, and the Abyss." *ELH* 44, no. 4 (Winter 1977): 683–700.

———. *Dickinson and the Romantic Imagination*. Princeton: Princeton University Press, 1981.

Dobson, Joanne. *Dickinson and the Strategies of Reticence: The Woman Writer in Nineteenth-Century America*. Bloomington: Indiana University Press, 1989.

Doriani, Beth Maclay. "Emily Dickinson and the Calvinist Sacramental Tradition." *ESQ: A Journal of the American Renaissance* 34 (1987): 67–81.

———. *Emily Dickinson, Daughter of Prophecy*. Amherst: University of Massachusetts Press, 1996.

Dwight, Timothy. "The Life of Dr. Henry Boynton Smith." *The New Englander* 4, no. 6 (November 1881): 792–810.

Eberty, Felix. *The Stars and the Earth; or, Thoughts upon Space, Time, and Eternity.* 4th ed. London: H. Bailliere. 1850.

Eberwein, Jane. *Dickinson: Strategies of Limitation.* Amherst: University of Massachusetts Press, 1985.

———, ed. *An Emily Dickinson Encyclopedia.* Westport, Conn.: Greenwood Press, 1998.

———. "'Is Immortality True?' Salvaging Faith in an Age of Upheavals." In Pollak, *A Historical Guide to Emily Dickinson.* 67–102.

———. "Dickinson's Local, Global, and Cosmic Perspectives." In Grabher, Hagenbüchle, and Miller. 27–43.

Eco, Umberto. *The Open Work.* Trans. Anna Cancogni. Cambridge: Harvard University Press, 1989.

———. *The Role of the Reader: Explorations in the Semiotics of Texts.* Bloomington: Indiana University Press, 1984.

Eliot, George. *The Mill on the Floss.* Ed. Carol Christ. New York: W. W. Norton & Co., 1994.

———. *Scenes of Clerical Life.* Vol. 2. Leipzig: Bernhard Tauchnitz, 1859.

———. *The Wit and Wisdom of George Eliot.* Boston: Roberts Brothers, 1878.

Emerson, Ralph Waldo. *Essays and Lectures.* New York: Library of America, 1983.

———. *The Letters of Ralph Waldo Emerson.* Vol. 6: *1868–1881.* Ed. Ralph L. Rusk. New York: Columbia University Press, 1939.

———. *Poems.* Boston: James Munroe, 1847.

Erkkila, Betsy. "Dickinson and the Art of Politics." In Pollak, *A Historical Guide to Emily Dickinson.* 133–74.

Evans, Rand B. "The Origins of American Academic Psychology." In *Explorations in the History of Psychology in the United States.* Ed. Joseph M. Brozek. Lewisburg, Pa.: Bucknell University Press, 1984. 17–60.

Farr, Judith. "Dickinson and the Visual Arts." In Grabher, Hagenbüchle, and Miller. 61–92.

Ferlazzo Paul, ed. *Critical Essays on Emily Dickinson.* Boston: G. K. Hall & Co., 1984.

Fiske, Nathan Welby. *Outlines of Mental Philosophy or Psychology: In a System of Questions.* Amherst: J. S. & C. Adams, 1842.

Folsom, Ed. "Whitman and Dictionaries." In *Walt Whitman's Native Representations.* Cambridge: Cambridge University Press, 1994. 12–26.

Fraiman, Susan. "*The Mill on the Floss,* the Critics, and the *Bildungsroman.*" In Yousaf and Maunder. 1–30.

Franklin, Benjamin. *Poor Richard's Almanac.* New York: David McKay Company, 1973.

Friday, Jonathan, ed. *Art and Enlightenment: Scottish Aesthetics in the Eighteenth Century.* Exeter: Imprint Academic, 2004.

Fried, Debra. "In Daisy's Lane: Variants and Personification in Emily Dickinson." In *Tradition and the Poetics of Self in Nineteenth-Century Women's Poetry.* Ed. Barbara Garlick. New York: Rodopi, 2002. 57–76.

Friend, Joseph Harold. *The Development of American Lexicography, 1798–1864.* The Hague: Mouton, 1967.

Gall, François Joseph [Franz]. *On the Organ of the Moral Qualities and Intellectual*

Faculties and The Plurality of the Cerebral Organs. 6 vols. Trans. Winslow Lewis. Boston: Marsh, Capen & Lyon, 1835.

Garbowsky, Maryanne M. *The House without the Door.* Cranbury, N.J.: Associated University Presses, 1989.

Garlick, Barbara, ed. *Tradition and the Poetics of Self in Nineteenth-Century Women's Poetry.* New York: Rodopi, 2002.

Gaskell, E. C. *The Life of Charlotte Brontë.* New York: D. Appleton and Company, 1858.

Gelpi, Albert. *Emily Dickinson: The Mind of the Poet.* Cambridge: Harvard University Press, 1965.

———. "Emily Dickinson's Word: Presence as Absence, Absence as Presence." *American Poetry* 4, no. 2 (1987): 41–50.

———. *The Tenth Muse: The Psyche of the American Poet.* Cambridge: Harvard University Press, 1975.

Gilbert, Sandra M., and Susan Gubar. *The Madwoman in the Attic: The Woman Writer and the Nineteenth-Century Literary Imagination.* New Haven: Yale University Press, 1979.

Goethe, Johann Wolfgang von. *The Sorrows of Young Werther.* Trans. Elizabeth Mayer and Louise Bogan. New York: Random House, 1990.

Good, James A., ed. *The Early American Reception of German Idealism.* 5 vols. Bristol: Thoemmes Press, 2002.

Gooder, R. D. "Language as a Plastic Medium: The Progress of Emily Dickinson Studies." *Cambridge Quarterly* 16, no. 1 (1987): 60–81.

Gorman, Herbert S. *The Procession of Masks.* Boston: B.J. Brimmer Company, 1923. 43–54.

Grabher, Gudrun. *Emily Dickinson: Das Tranzcendentale Ich.* Heidelberg: Carl Winter Universitätsverlag, 1981.

Grabher, Gudrun, Roland Hagenbüchle, and Cristanne Miller, eds. *The Emily Dickinson Handbook.* Amherst: University of Massachusetts Press, 1998.

Green, Jonathon. *Chasing the Sun: Dictionary Makers and the Dictionaries They Made.* New York: Henry Holt & Co., 1996.

Greenleaf, Benjamin. *The National Arithmetic, on the Inductive System, Combining the Analytic and Synthetic Methods; Forming a Complete Course of Higher Arithmetic.* Boston: Robert S. Davis & Co., 1857.

Griffith, Clark. *The Long Shadow: Emily Dickinson's Tragic Poetry.* Princeton: Princeton University Press, 1964.

Guthrie, James. *Emily Dickinson's Vision: Illness and Identity in Her Poetry.* Gainesville: University of Florida Press, 1998.

Habegger, Alfred. *My Wars Are Laid Away in Books: The Life of Emily Dickinson.* New York: Random House, 2001.

Habermas, Jürgen. *The Structural Transformation of the Public Sphere: An Inquiry into a Category of Bourgeois Society.* Trans. Thomas Burger with the assistance of Frederick Lawrence. Cambridge: MIT Press, 1989.

Hagenbüchle, Roland. "Dickinson and Literary Theory." In Grabher, Hagenbüchle, and Miller. 356–84.

———. "Emily Dickinson's Aesthetics of Process." In *Poetry and Epistemology:*

Turning Points in the History of Poetic Knowledge. Ed. Roland Hagenbüchle and Laura Skandera. Regensburg: Pustet, 1986. 135–47.

———. "Precision and Indeterminacy in the Poetry of Emily Dickinson." *ESQ: A Journal of the American Renaissance* 20 (1974): 33–56.

———. "Sign and Process: The Concept of Language in Emerson and Dickinson." *ESQ: A Journal of the American Renaissance* 25 (1979): 137–55.

Hale, Sarah Josepha, ed., *Flora's Interpreter; or, The American Book of Flowers and Sentiments,* 7th ed. Boston: Marsh, Capen & Lyon, 1839.

Hallen, Cynthia Leah. "Cognitive Circuits: The Circumference of Dickinson's Lexicon." *Emily Dickinson Journal* 6, no. 2 (1997): 76–83.

———. *Philology as Rhetoric in Emily Dickinson's Poems.* PhD diss., University of Arizona, 1991.

Haraway, Donna Jeanne "From *A Manifesto for Cyborgs: Science, Technology, and Socialist Feminism in the 1980s.*" In *From Modernism to Postmodernism: An Anthology.* Ed. Lawrence Cahoone. London: Blackwell, 2003. 464–81.

Harris, James A. *The Dictionary of Nineteenth-Century British Philosophers.* 2 vols. Bristol: Thoemmes Press, 2002.

Harris, Samuel. "Prof. N. W. Fiske." *The New Englander* 8, no. 29 (February 1850): 67–80.

Harris, Susan. *Nineteenth-Century American Women's Novels: Interpretive Strategies.* Cambridge: Cambridge University Press, 1990.

———. "Responding to the Text(s): Women Readers and the Quest for Higher Education." In *Readers in History: Nineteenth-Century American Literature and the Contexts of Response.* Ed. James Machor. Baltimore: Johns Hopkins University Press, 1993. 259–82.

Hart, Ellen Louise, and Martha Nell Smith, eds. *Open Me Carefully: Emily Dickinson's Intimate Letters to Susan Huntington Dickinson.* Ashfield, Mass.: Paris Press, 1998.

Haven, Joseph. *Mental Philosophy: Including the Intellect, Sensibilities, and Will.* 1857. Boston: Gould & Lincoln, 1865.

Hedge, Frederic Henry. *Prose Writers of Germany.* Philadelphia: Carey and Hart, 1848.

Hedge, Levi. *Elements of Logick; or, A Summary of The General Principles and Different Modes of Reasoning.* Boston: Hilliard, Gray & Co., 1837.

Heidegger, Martin. *Being and Time.* Trans. John Macquarie and Edward Robinson. San Francisco: Harper & Row, 1962.

———. *Poetry, Language, Thought.* Trans. Albert Hofstadter. New York: Perennial Library, 1975.

Henneberg, Sylvia. "Neither Lesbian nor Straight: Multiple Eroticisms in Emily Dickinson's Love Poetry." *Emily Dickinson Journal* 4, no. 2 (1995): 1–19.

Hickock, Kathleen. "'Not Yet Orthodox'—The Female Characters in *Aurora Leigh.* In *Critical Essays on Elizabeth Barrett Browning.* Ed. Sandra Donaldson. New York: G. K. Hall & Co., 1999. 129–40.

Hickock, Laurens Perseus. *Empirical Psychology; or, The Human Mind as Given in Consciousness. For the Use of Colleges and Academies.* New York: S. C. Griggs & Co., 1854.

———. *Rational Psychology; or the Subjective Idea and the Objective Law of All Intelligence.* New York: Derby, Miller, & Co., 1849.

Higgins, David J. M. "Emily Dickinson's Prose." In Sewall, *Emily Dickinson: A Collection of Critical Essays.* 162–77.

Higginson, Thomas Wentworth. "Letter to a Young Contributor." *The Atlantic Monthly: A Magazine of Literature, Art, and Politics* 9, no. 14 (April 1862): 26–36, 401–11.

———. *Out-of-Door Papers.* Boston: Ticknor and Fields, 1863.

———. *Short Studies of American Authors.* Boston: Lee and Shepard; New York: Charles T. Dillingham, 1880.

Hirsch, Marianne. "Spiritual *Bildung*: The Beautiful Soul as Paradigm." In *The Voyage In: Fictions of Female Development.* Ed. Elizabeth Abel, Marianne Hirsch, and Elizabeth Langland. Hanover, N.H.: University Press of New England, 1983. 23–48.

Hitchcock, Edward. *Elementary Geology.* Amherst: J. S. & C. Adams, 1841.

———. *The Power of Christian Benevolence Illustrated in the Life and Labors of Mary Lyon.* Northampton, Mass.: Hopkins, Bridgman, and Company, 1852.

———. *Reminiscences of Amherst College: Historical, Scientific, Biographical, and Autobiographical.* Northampton, Mass.: Bridgman and Childs, 1863.

Hoeveler, J. David Jr. *James McCosh and the Scottish Intellectual Tradition.* Princeton: Princeton University Press, 1981.

Hoffman, Tyler B. "Emily Dickinson and the Art of War." *Emily Dickinson Journal* 3 (1994): 1–18.

Homans, Margaret. *Women Writers and Poetic Identity: Dorothy Wordsworth, Emily Brontë, and Emily Dickinson.* Princeton: Princeton University Press, 1980.

Householder, Fred W., and Sol Saporta, eds. *Problems in Lexicography.* Bloomington: Indiana University Press; The Hague: Mouton. 1967.

Howe, Susan. *My Emily Dickinson.* Berkeley: North Atlantic Books, 1985.

Hume, David. *A Treatise of Human Nature.* Ed. David Fate Norton and Mary J. Norton. New York: Oxford University Press, 2000.

Humphrey, Heman. *Memoir of Rev. Nathan W. Fiske, Professor of Intellectual and Moral Philosophy in Amherst College; Together with Selections from His Sermons and Other Writings.* Amherst: J. S. & C. Adams, 1850.

———. *A Tribute to the Memory of Rev. Nathan W. Fiske: Late Professor of Intellectual and Moral Philosophy in Amherst College.* Amherst: J. S. & C. Adams, 1848.

Huntington, Frederic D. *Christian Believing and Living: Sermons.* Boston: Crosby, Nichols, 1860.

Hutchinson, Allan. "The Three R's: Reading/Rorty/Radically." Review of Richard Rorty, *Contingency, Irony, and Solidarity. Harvard Law Review* 103 (1989): 555–85.

Iser, Wolfgang. *The Act of Reading: A Theory of Aesthetic Response.* Baltimore: Johns Hopkins University Press, 1980.

Jackson, Virginia. *Dickinson's Misery: A Theory of Lyric Reading.* Princeton: Princeton University Press, 2005.

Jacobus, Mary. "Men of Maxims and *The Mill on the Floss.*" In Yousaf and Maunder. 83–100.

Jameson, Fredric. "Postmodernism and Consumer Society." In *The Continental Aesthetics Reader.* Ed. Clive Cazeaux. London: Routledge, 2000. 282–94.

———. *Postmodernism, or, The Cultural Logic of Late Capitalism.* Durham: Duke University Press, 1991.

"Jane Eyre." *The Indicator: A Literary Periodical conducted by Students of Amherst College* 1, no. 1 (1848): 27–31.

Jenkins, MacGregor. *Emily Dickinson: Friend and Neighbor.* Boston: Little, Brown, & Co. 1930.

Johnstone, Peggy R. F. "Narcissistic Rage in *The Mill on the Floss.*" In Yousaf and Maunder. 122–42.

Juhasz, Suzanne. "The Irresistible Lure of Repetition and Dickinson's Poetics of Analogy." *Emily Dickinson Journal* 9, no. 2 (2000): 23–31.

———. *The Undiscovered Continent: Emily Dickinson and the Space of the Mind.* Bloomington: Indiana University Press, 1983.

Kafka, Franz. *The Castle.* Trans. Mark Harman. New York: Schocken Books, 1998.

Kames, Henry Home, Lord. *Elements of Criticism.* New York: F. J. Huntington, 1846.

Kant, Immanuel. *Critique of Judgement.* Trans. James Creed Meredith. Oxford: Clarendon Press, 1989.

Kaplan, Cora. Introduction. [From *Elizabeth Barrett Browning: "Aurora Leigh" and Other Poems.*] In *Critical Essays on Elizabeth Barrett Browning.* Ed. Sandra Donaldson. New York: G. K. Hall & Co., 1999. 71–101.

Keller, Karl. *The Only Kangaroo among the Beauty: Emily Dickinson and America.* Baltimore: Johns Hopkins University Press, 1979.

Kelley, Donald R. *The Descent of Ideas: The History of Intellectual History.* Burlington, Vt.: Ashgate, 2002.

Kierkegaard, Søren. *"Fear and Trembling" and "The Sickness unto Death."* Trans. Walter Lowrie. New York: Doubleday, 1954.

Kimpel, Ben. *Emily Dickinson as Philosopher.* New York: Edwin Mellen Press, 1981.

Kinnell, Galway. "The Deconstruction of Emily Dickinson." In *Visiting Emily: Poems Inspired by the Life and Work of Emily Dickinson.* Ed. Sheila Coghill and Thom Tammaro. Iowa City: University of Iowa Press, 2005. 51–52.

Kirkby, Joan. "Dickinson Reading." *Emily Dickinson Journal* 5, no. 2 (1996): 247–54.

Kuklick, Bruce. *Churchmen and Philosophers: From Jonathan Edwards to John Dewey.* New Haven: Yale University Press, 1985.

———. *A History of Philosophy in America, 1720–2000.* Oxford: Clarendon Press, 2001.

———. *The Rise of American Philosophy: Cambridge, Massachusetts, 1860–1930.* New Haven: Yale University Press, 1979.

Lacoue-Labarthe, Philippe, and Jean-Luc Nancy. *The Literary Absolute: The Theory of Literature in German Romanticism.* Trans. Philip Barnard and Cheryl Lester. Albany: State University of New York Press, 1988.

Ladin, Jay. "'Goblin with a Gauge': Teaching Emily Dickinson." *Emily Dickinson Journal* 9, no. 2 (2000): 32–41.

———. "'So Anthracite: To Live': Emily Dickinson and American Literary History." *Emily Dickinson Journal* 13, no. 1 (2004): 19–50.

Landau, Sidney. *Dictionaries: The Art and Craft of Lexicography.* 2nd ed. Cambridge: Cambridge University Press, 2001.

Landes, Margaret W. "Thomas Brown: Associationist (?)" *Philosophical Review* 35, no. 5. (September 1926): 447–64.

Lanman, Charles. *Dictionary of the United States Congress: Containing biographical sketches of its members from the foundation of the government. . . .* Philadelphia: J. B. Lippincott & Co., 1859.

Leavis, Frank Raymond. *The Great Tradition: George Eliot, Henry James, Joseph Conrad.* London: Chatto & Windus, 1948.

Leavitt, Robert Keith. *Noah's Ark: New England Yankees and the Endless Quest.* Springfield, Mass.: G. & C. Merriam Co., 1947.

Leonard, James S. "Dickinson's Poems of Definition." *Dickinson Studies* 41 (December 1981): 18–25.

Leverett, F. P., ed. *A New and Copious Lexicon of the Latin Language.* Boston: J. H. Wilkins and R. B. Carter, 1839.

Leyda, Jay. *The Years and Hours of Emily Dickinson.* 2 vols. New Haven: Yale University Press, 1960.

Lindberg-Seyersted, Brita. *The Voice of the Poet: Aspects of Style in the Poetry of Emily Dickinson.* Uppsala: Almqvist & Wiksells, 1968.

Locke, John. *An Essay Concerning Human Understanding.* Ed. Peter H. Nidditch. Oxford: Clarendon Press, 1975.

Loeffelholz, Mary. "The Compound Frame: Scenes of Emily Dickinson's Reading." PhD diss., Yale University, 1986.

———. *Dickinson and the Boundaries of Feminist Theory.* Urbana: University of Illinois Press, 1991.

———. "'Question of Monuments': Emerson, Dickinson, and American Renaissance Portraiture." *Modern Language Quarterly: A Journal of Literary History* 59, no. 4 (1998): 445–69.

Lokke, Kari. "Sybilline Leaves: Mary Shelley's *Valperga* and the Legacy of *Corinne.*" In *Cultural Interactions in the Romantic Age: Critical Essays in Comparative Literature.* Ed. Gregory Maertz. Albany: State University of New York Press, 1998. 157–73.

Lowenberg, Carlton. *Emily Dickinson's Textbooks.* Lafayette, Calif.: Carlton Lowenberg, 1986.

Lundin, Roger. *Emily Dickinson and the Art of Belief.* Grand Rapids, Mich.: Wm. B. Eerdmans, 2004.

The Lyman Letters: New Light on Emily Dickinson and Her Family. Ed. Richard B. Sewall. Amherst: University of Massachusetts Press, 1965.

Lyotard, Jean-François. *Lessons on the Analytic of the Sublime.* Trans. Elizabeth Rottenberg. Palo Alto: Stanford University Press, 1994.

———. *The Postmodern Condition.* Trans. Geoff Bennington and Brian Massumi. Minneapolis: University of Minnesota Press, 1984.

Machor, James L. "Historical Hermeneutics and Antebellum Fiction: Gender, Response Theory, and Interpretive Contexts." In *Readers in History: Nineteenth-Century American Literature and the Contexts of Response*. Ed. James Machor. Baltimore: Johns Hopkins University Press, 1993. 54–84.

MacKenzie, Cynthia, ed. *Concordance to the Letters of Emily Dickinson*. Boulder: University Press of Colorado, 2000.

Mahan, Asa. *A System of Intellectual Philosophy*. New York: Harper & Brothers. 1847.

Malachowski, Alan, ed. *Reading Rorty: Critical Responses to "Philosophy and the Mirror of Nature" (and Beyond)*. Oxford: Basil Blackwell, 1990.

Martin, Terence. *The Instructed Vision: Scottish Common Sense Philosophy and the Origins of American Fiction*. Bloomington: Indiana University Press, 1961.

McCumber, John. "Reconnecting Rorty: The Situation of Discourse in Richard Rorty's Contingency, Irony, and Solidarity." *Diacritics* 20, no. 2 (Summer 1990): 2–19.

McGann, Jerome. *Black Riders: The Visual Language of Modernism*. Princeton: Princeton University Press, 1993.

Mcintosh, James. *Nimble Believing: Dickinson and the Unknown*. Ann Arbor: University of Michigan Press, 2000.

Menand, Louis. *The Metaphysical Club: A Story of Ideas in America*. New York: Farrar, Straus and Giroux, 2001.

Micklethwait, David. *Noah Webster and the American Dictionary*. London: McFarland & Co., 2000.

Miller, Cristanne. *Emily Dickinson: A Poet's Grammar*. Cambridge: Harvard University Press, 1987.

Miller, Perry. *The Life of the Mind in America: From the Revolution to the Civil War: Books One through Three*. New York: Harcourt, Brace & World, 1965.

Moers, Ellen. *Literary Women: The Great Writers*. New York: Doubleday & Co., 1977.

Montgomery, Benilde. *Emily Dickinson and the Meditative Tradition*. Stony Brook, N.Y.: SUNY Press, 1981.

Moretti, Franco. *The Way of the World: The Bildungsroman in European Culture*. Trans. Albert Sbragia. New York: Verso, 2000.

Morey, Frederick L. "Dickinson-Kant: The First Critique." *Dickinson Studies* 60 (December 1986): 1–70.

———. "Dickinson-Kant: Part II." *Dickinson Studies* 64 (December 1987): 3–30.

———. "Dickinson-Kant: Part III." *Dickinson Studies* 67 (December 1988): 3–60.

———. "Dickinson-Kant: Part IV." *Dickinson Studies* 74 (December 1990): 1–61.

Morris, Tim. "The Free-Rhyming Poetry of Emerson and Dickinson." *Essays in Literature* 12, no. 2 (1985): 225–40.

———. Review of *A Historical Guide to Emily Dickinson*, ed. Vivian Pollak. *Emily Dickinson Journal* 13, no. 2 (2004): 116–18.

Mueller-Vollmer, Kurt. "Staël's *Germany* and the Beginnings of an American National Literature." In *Germaine de Staël: Crossing the Borders*. Ed. Madelyn Gutwirth, Avriel Goldberger, and Karyna Szmurlo. New Brunswick, N.J.: Rutgers University Press, 1991. 141–58.

Muldoon, Paul. "Polar Expeditions: 'I tried to think a lonelier Thing' by Emily Dickinson. *New England Review* 24, no. 2 (2003): 6–24.

Nancy, Jean-Luc. *A Finite Thinking.* Ed. Simon Sparks. Palo Alto: Stanford University Press, 2003.

———. "Sharing Voices." In Ormiston and Schrift. 211–59.

———. *The Inoperative Community.* Minneapolis: University of Minnesota Press, 1991.

———. "The Sublime Offering." Trans. Jeffrey Libbrett. In *A Finite Thinking.* 211–44.

Nehamas, Alexander. *Nietzsche: Life as Literature.* Cambridge: Harvard University Press, 1985.

Nietzsche, Friedrich. *Beyond Good and Evil.* Trans. Helen Zimmern. New York: Prometheus, 1989.

———. *The Gay Science.* Trans. Walter Kaufmann. New York: Vintage, 1974.

———. "On the Uses and Disadvantages of History for Life." In *Untimely Meditations.* Trans. R. J. Hollingdale. Cambridge: Cambridge University Press, 1983. 57–124.

———. *Thus Spake Zarathustra.* Trans. Walter Kaufmann. New York: Modern Library, 1995.

Noble, Marianne. *The Masochistic Pleasures of Sentimental Literature.* Princeton: Princeton University Press, 2000.

Noll, Mark A. "Common Sense Traditions and American Evangelical Thought." *American Quarterly* 37, no. 2. (Summer 1985): 216–38.

Nuland, Sherwin. *How We Die: Reflections on Life's Final Chapter.* New York: Vintage, 1995.

Oakes, Karen. "Welcome and Beware: The Reader and Emily Dickinson's Figurative Language." *ESQ: A Journal of the American Renaissance* 34, no. 3 (1988): 181–206.

Olmsted, Denison. *A Compendium of Natural Philosophy: Adapted to the Use of the General Reader, and of Schools and Academies. To Which is now Added a Supplement Containing Instructions to Young Experimenters, Accompanied by Minute Directions for Performing Them.* New Haven: S. Babcock, 1844.

Ormiston, Gayle L., and Alan D. Schrift, eds. *Transforming the Hermeneutic Context: From Nietzsche to Nancy.* Albany: State University of New York Press, 1990.

Orzeck, Martin, and Robert Weisbuch, eds. *Dickinson and Audience.* Ann Arbor: University of Michigan Press, 1996.

Paglia, Camille. *Sexual Personae: Art and Decadence from Nefertiti to Emily Dickinson.* New York: Random House, 1991.

Patterson, Rebecca. *Emily Dickinson's Imagery.* Amherst: University of Massachusetts Press, 1979.

Pawley, Christine. "Seeking 'Significance': Actual Readers, Specific Reading Communities." *Book History* 5 (2002): 143–60.

Perlmutter, Elizabeth F. "Hide and Seek: Emily Dickinson's Use of the Existential Sentence." *Language and Style: An International Journal* 10 (1977): 109–19.

Perloff, Marjorie. "Emily Dickinson and the Theory Canon." http://epc.buffalo.edu/authors/perloff/articles/dickinson.html. Accessed April 15, 2005.

Peschel, Richard E., and Enid Rhodes Peschel. "'Am I in Heaven Now?': Case History, Literary Histories." *Soundings: An Interdisciplinary Journal* 66, no. 4 (Winter 1983): 469–80.

Peterson, Margaret. *American Women Writers: A Critical Reference Guide from Colonial Times to the Present.* Vol. 1: *A to E.* Ed. Lina Mainiero. New York: Frederick Ungar Publishing Co., 1979.

Petrino, Elizabeth. *Emily Dickinson and Her Contemporaries: Women's Verse in America, 1820–1885.* Hanover, N.H.: University Press of New England, 1998.

Phillips, Elizabeth. *Emily Dickinson: Personae and Performance.* University Park: Pennsylvania State University Press, 1988.

Phillips, Kate. *Helen Hunt Jackson: A Literary Life.* Berkeley: University of California Press, 2003.

Pillow, Kirk. *Sublime Understanding: Aesthetic Reflection in Kant and Hegel.* Cambridge: MIT Press, 2000.

Plato. *Apology.* Trans. F. J. Church. New York: Bobbs-Merrill, 1956.

Pochmann, Henry A. *German Culture in America: Philosophical and Literary Influences, 1600–1900.* Madison: University of Wisconsin Press, 1957.

Pollak, Vivian. *The Anxiety of Gender.* Ithaca: Cornell University Press, 1984.

———. "Emily Dickinson's Literary Allusions." *Essays in Literature* 1 (1974): 54–68.

———, ed. *A Historical Guide to Emily Dickinson.* Oxford: Oxford University Press, 2003.

———. "Thirst and Starvation in Emily Dickinson's Poetry." *American Literature* 51, no. 1 (March 1979): 33–49.

Porter, David. "Dickinson's Unrevised Poems." In Orzeck and Weisbuch. 11–29.

———. *The Modern Idiom.* Cambridge: Harvard University Press, 1981.

Rainwater, Mary Janice. "Emily Dickinson and Six Contemporary Writers: Her Poetry in Relation to Her Reading." PhD diss., Northwestern University, 1975.

Ransom, John Crowe. "Emily Dickinson: A Poet Restored." In Sewall, *Emily Dickinson: A Collection of Critical Essays.* 88–100.

Reid, Thomas. *An Inquiry into the Human Mind: On the Principles of Common Sense.* Ed. Derek R. Brookes. University Park: Pennsylvania State University Press, 2000.

Rollins, Richard W. *The Long Journey of Noah Webster.* Philadelphia: University of Pennsylvania Press, 1980.

Rorty, Amélie. "Cartesian Passions and the Union of Mind and Body." In *Essays on Descartes' Meditations.* Ed. Amélie Oksenberg Rorty. Berkeley: University of California Press, 1986. 513–34.

Rorty, Richard. *Contingency, Irony, and Solidarity.* Cambridge: Cambridge University Press, 1989.

———. Foreword. In Vattimo, *Nihilism and Emancipation.* ix–xx.

———. *Philosophy and the Mirror of Nature.* Princeton: Princeton University Press, 1979.

———. *Philosophy and Social Hope.* New York: Penguin, 1999.

———. *Take Care of Freedom and Truth Will Take Care of Itself: Interviews with Richard Rorty.* Ed. Eduardo Mendieta. Stanford: Stanford University Press, 2006.

————. *Truth and Progress: Philosophical Papers*. Vol. 3. Cambridge: Cambridge University Press, 1999.

Rosenbaum, S. P., ed. *A Concordance to the Poems of Emily Dickinson*. Ithaca: Cornell University Press, 1964.

Rothleder, Dianne. *The Work of Friendship: Rorty, His Critics, and the Project of Solidarity*. Albany: State University of New York Press, 1999.

Rousseau, Jean-Jacques. *Rousseau's Émile; or, Treatise on Education*. Trans. William H. Payne. New York: D. Appleton and Co., 1895.

Rudat, Wolfgang E. H. "Dickinson and Immortality: Virgilian and Miltonic Allusions in 'Of death I try to think like this.'" *American Notes and Queries* 16, no. 6 (February 1978): 85–87.

St. Armand, Barton Levi. *Emily Dickinson and Her Culture: The Soul's Society*. Cambridge: Cambridge University Press, 1984.

Saintine, M. D. (Xavier Joseph Boniface). *Picciola: The Prisoner of Fenestrella; or, Captivity Captive*. Philadelphia: Lea and Blanchard, 1839.

Schiller, Friedrich. *The Aesthetic Letters, Essays, and the Philosophical Letters of Schiller*. Trans. John Weiss. Boston: Charles C. Little and James Brown, 1845.

————. "Upon Naïve and Sentimental Poetry." Trans. John Weiss. In Hedge, *Prose Writers of Germany*. 372–82.

Schmidt, George Paul. *The Old-Time College President*. New York: Columbia University Press, 1930.

Schneider, Herbert. *A History of American Philosophy*. New York: Columbia University Press, 1963.

Sewall, Richard. *The Life of Emily Dickinson*. 2 vols. Cambridge: Harvard University Press, 1974.

————, ed. *Emily Dickinson: A Collection of Critical Essays*. Englewood Cliffs, N.J.: Prentice-Hall, 1963.

Smith, Elizabeth L., ed. *Henry Boynton Smith: His Life and Work*. New York: A. C. Armstrong & Son, 1881.

Smith, Martha Nell. "Dickinson's Manuscripts." In Grabher, Hagenbüchle, and Miller. 113–37.

Snyder, Kim Allen. *Defining Noah Webster: A Spiritual Biography*. Washington, D.C.: Allegiance Press, 2002.

Spiro, Lisa. "Reading with a Tender Rapture: *Reveries of a Bachelor* and the Rhetoric of Detached Intimacy." *Book History* 6 (2003): 57–93.

Stewart, Dugald. *Elements of the Philosophy of the Human Mind*. Albany: E. and E. Hosford, 1822.

————. *Elements of the Philosophy of the Human Mind*. Boston and Cambridge: James Munroe & Company, 1855.

Stonum, Gary Lee. *The Dickinson Sublime*. Madison: University of Wisconsin Press, 1990.

————. "Dickinson's Literary Background." In Grabher, Hagenbüchle, and Miller. 44–60.

Strickland, Georgiana. "Emily Dickinson's Philadelphia." *Emily Dickinson Journal* 13, no. 2 (2004): 79–115.

The Student and Schoolmate and Forrester's Boys & Girls Magazine: A Reader for

Schools and Families 14, no. 2. Ed. William T. Adams (Oliver Optic). Boston: Joseph H. Allen, 1864.

Tate, Allen. "New England Culture and Emily Dickinson." 1932. Reprinted in *The Recognition of Emily Dickinson: Selected Criticism since 1890*. Ed. Caesar R. Blake and Carlton F. Wells. Ann Arbor: University of Michigan Press, 1968. 153–67.

Taylor, Charles. *A Secular Age*. Cambridge: Harvard University Press, 2007.

Taylor, Jane. *Wouldst Know Thyself; or, The Outlines of Human Physiology: Designed for the Youth of Both Sexes*. New York: George F. Cooledge & Brothers, 1858.

Thackeray, William Makepeace. *Vanity Fair: A Novel without a Hero*. New York: Garland, 1989.

Todd, Mabel Loomis, and Millicent Todd Bingham. *Bolts of Melody: New Poems of Emily Dickinson*. New York: Harper and Brothers, 1945.

Tompkins, Jane. *Sensational Designs: The Cultural Work of American Fiction, 1790–1860*. New York: Oxford University Press, 1985.

Toulmin, Stephen. *Cosmopolis: The Hidden Agenda of Modernity*. New York: Free Press, 1990.

Townsend, Harvey Gates. *Philosophical Ideas in the United States*. New York: Octagon Books, 1968.

Trench, Richard Chenevix. *The Study of Words*. New York: Redfield, 1855.

Tuckerman, Frederick. *Amherst Academy: A New England School of the Past, 1814–1861*. Amherst, Mass.: Printed for the Trustees, 1929.

Tupper, Martin Farquhar. *Proverbial Philosophy: A Book of Thoughts and Arguments, Originally Treated*. London: J. Hatchard and Son, 1847.

Tyler, William Seymour. *History of Amherst College during Its First Half Century, 1821–1871*. Springfield, Mass.: Clark W. Bryan, 1873.

Unger, Harlow. *Noah Webster: The Life and Times of an American Patriot*. New York: John Wiley and Sons, 1998.

Upham, Thomas C. *Elements of Mental Philosophy*. New York: Harper and Brothers, 1842.

Vattimo, Gianni. *After Christianity*. Trans. Luca D'Isanto. New York: Columbia University Press, 2002.

———. *Beyond Interpretation: The Meaning of Hermeneutics for Philosophy*. Trans. David Webb. Stanford: Stanford University Press, 1997.

———. *The End of Modernity: Nihilism and Hermeneutics in Postmodern Culture*. Trans. Jon R. Snyder. Baltimore: Johns Hopkins University Press, 1991.

———. *Nihilism and Emancipation: Ethics, Politics, and Law*. Ed. Santiago Zabala; trans. William McCuaig. New York: Columbia University Press, 2004.

———. *The Transparent Society*. Trans. David Webb. Baltimore: Johns Hopkins University Press, 1992.

Vattimo, Gianni, and Richard Rorty. *The Future of Religion*. Ed. and trans. Santiago Zabala. New York: Columbia University Press, 2005.

Vattimo, Gianni, and Santiago Zabala. "'Weak Thought' and the Reduction of Violence: A Dialogue with Gianni Vattimo." Trans. Yaakov Mascetti. *Common Knowledge* 8, no. 3 (2002): 452–63.

Vendler, Helen. "Emily Dickinson Thinking." *Parnassus* 26, no. 1 (2001): 34–56.

———. *Poets Thinking: Pope, Whitman, Dickinson, Yeats.* Cambridge: Harvard University Press, 2004.

Walsh, John Evangelist. *The Hidden Life of Emily Dickinson.* New York: Simon & Schuster, 1971.

Wardop, Daneen. *Emily Dickinson's Gothic: Goblin with a Gauge.* Iowa City: University of Iowa Press, 1996.

Watts, Isaac. *Horae Lyricae and Divine Songs by Isaac Watts.* Boston: Little, Brown & Co., 1854.

———. *On the Improvement of the Mind.* Ed. Joseph Emerson. New York: A. S. Barnes & Co., 1849.

Weber, Max. *The Protestant Ethic and the Spirit of Capitalism.* Trans. Talcott Parsons. New York: Routledge, 2001.

Webster, Noah. *An American Dictionary of the English Language.* 2 vols. Amherst: J. S. & C. Adams. 1844.

———. *An American Dictionary of the English Language.* Springfield, Mass.: G. & C. Merriam, 1856.

———. *A Manual of Useful Studies; For the Instruction of Young Persons of Both Sexes in Families and Schools.* New Haven: published by the author, 1842.

Weisbuch, Robert. *Emily Dickinson's Poetry.* Chicago: University of Chicago Press, 1972.

Weiskel, Thomas. *The Romantic Sublime: Studies in the Structure and Psychology of Transcendence.* Baltimore: Johns Hopkins University Press, 1976.

Wells, Anna Mary. "Early Criticism of Emily Dickinson." *American Literature* 1, no. 3 (November 1929): 243–59.

Whicher, Stephen. *This Was a Poet: Emily Dickinson.* 1938. Ann Arbor: University of Michigan Press, 1957.

Whipple, Edwin P. *Lectures on Subjects Connected with Literature and Life.* Boston: Ticknor and Fields, 1859.

Whitman, Walt. *Daybooks and Notebooks of Walt Whitman.* Ed. William White. 3 vols. New York: New York University Press, 1978.

Wilbur, Richard. "Sumptuous Destitution." In *Emily Dickinson: A Collection of Critical Essays.* Ed. Judith Farr. Upper Saddle River, N.J.: Prentice Hall, 1996. 53–61.

Williams, Bernard. "Auto-da-Fé: Consequences of Pragmatism." In *Reading Rorty: Critical Responses to "Philosophy and the Mirror of Nature" (and Beyond).* Ed. Alan Malachowski. Oxford: Basil Blackwell, 1990. 26–37.

Wilson, Suzanne M. "Structural Patterns in the Poetry of Emily Dickinson." *American Literature* 35 (1963): 53–59.

Winters, Yvor. "Emily Dickinson and the Limits of Judgment." 1938. In Sewall, *Emily Dickinson: A Collection of Critical Essays.* 28–40.

Wittgenstein, Ludwig. *Philosophical Investigations.* Trans. G. E. M. Anscombe. Oxford: Blackwell, 1958.

Wolff, Cynthia Griffin. *Emily Dickinson.* New York: Knopf, 1986.

Wolosky, Shira. "Dickinson's Emerson: A Critique of American Identity." *Emily Dickinson Journal* 9, no. 2 (2000): 134–41.

———. *Emily Dickinson: A Voice of War.* New Haven: Yale University Press, 1984.

———. "Public and Private in Dickinson's War Poetry." In Pollak, *A Historical Guide to Emily Dickinson.* 103–31.

Wortman, Marc. "The Place Translation Makes: Celan's Translation of Dickinson's 'Four Trees-Upon a Solitary Acre-.'" In *Translating Tradition: Paul Celan in France.* Ed. Benjamin Hollander. *Acts: A Journal of New Writing* 8–9 (1988): 130–43.

Yousaf, Nahem, and Andrew Maunder, eds. *The Mill on the Floss and Silas Marner.* New York: Palgrave, 2002.

Zabala, Santiago, ed. *Weakening Philosophy: Essays in Honour of Gianni Vattimo.* Montreal: McGill–Queen's University Press, 2007.

Zaleski, Philip, and Carol Zaleski. *Prayer: A History.* Boston: Houghton Mifflin, 2005.

Index of Poems and Letters

Letters

General Index

Abercrombie, John, 89, 91, 219n20
Abbott, Jacob, 89, 219n20
Academy of American Poets, 1
accomplished nihilism, 8, 21, 40–41, 127, 150, 154, 162, 166, 184
Adonis, 198
agency, philosophical theme of, 7, 13, 35, 38–40, 73, 105, 107, 130, 154, 156, 168, 170, 182. *See also* self-creation; subjectivity
aesthetic idea, Kantian theory of, 52, 62, 122, 134, 136, 211n1, 231n36
aesthetics, philosophy of, 26, 52. *See also* aesthetic idea; beautiful; sublime
Albert, Prince of England, 115
Alcott, Louisa May, 234n8
Aldrich, Henry *(Logic)*, 162
Altieri, Charles, 209n5
Amherst Academy, 54, 85, 88–90, 93, 106, 218n18, 223n39
Anderson, Charles, 23–24, 206n6
Andrews, Jesse, 223n39
Anthon, Catherine Scott (Turner), 221n19
anthropologist persona: in Dickinson's poems and letters, 11, 14, 33; in *Jane Eyre*, 171

anti-foundationalism, 8, 17, 21, 36–38, 41, 154–55, 223n36; and lexicography, 118, 154. *See also* post-metaphysical thought; weak thought
Arabian Nights: David Copperfield's reading of, 157; Austin Dickinson's reading of, 88. *See also* Arabian tales
Arabian tales, Jane Eyre's reading of, 174
Aristotle, 14, 36, 75, 92, 110, 229n24, 230n28
Arminianism, 82
articles, in Dickinson's poems, 46, 66, 144, 187. *See also* syntax
associations, in Dickinson's poems, 45, 47, 106–8, 126–27, 215n29, 220n24; and Kantian sublime, 52, 136–37, 231n36. *See also* associationism
associationism, philosophy of, 77, 91–108, 126, 211n2, 218n17, 219n22, 220nn24–26, 221nn27–30, 222n34, 223n35, 232n42
astronomy, 54–57
Atlas, 188
Aurora Leigh, 18, 75, 154, 156–62, 175–83, 236n17. *See also* Barrett Browning, Elizabeth

Emerson, Joseph, 56, 218–19n20
Emerson, Ralph Waldo, 1, 5, 17,
21–22, 27, 43, 61, 77–78, 82, 85,
104–6, 108, 114, 146, 148, 151,
165, 204, 207n15; "The American
Scholar," 1, 77, 85; as bad influence
on Dickinson's religious beliefs,
207–8n15; "Circles," 9; and
Cousin, 224n45; and dictionaries,
114; "English Traits," 146;
"Experience," 21; and Helen Hunt
Jackson, 221–22n32; letter to
Merriam brothers, 114; *Letters
and Social Aims*, 213n15; "Ode
Inscribed to W. H. Channing," 43;
"The Oversoul," 108; "The Poet,"
213n11; *Representative Men*,
206n10; "The Transcendentalist,"
146, 206n11, 232n43
Emily Dickinson Lexicon, 225n1
empiricism, philosophy of, 53–55,
76–79, 82, 86, 88, 103, 105–7, 149
Emmons, Henry, 217n12
Erasmus, Desiderius, 206n10
Eschenburg, *Manual of Classical
Literature*, 217n10
Euclid, 125, 162
Eurystheus, 188
Evans, Marian. *See* Eliot, George
Evans, Rand, 77, 93, 105, 219–20n23
Everett, Alex, 105
Everett, Edward, 105
existential thought, 8, 12, 19, 58,
67, 122, 125, 144, 158, 184–85,
196–97, 203–4, 206n7, 239n9
experience: Bacon on, 53; Common
Sense philosophy on, 88; of
Dickinson's readers, 8, 12, 70,
147–48; Dickinson's writings
on, 25–26, 59, 146–49; Emerson
on, 21, 232n43; inner, 90, 108;
Locke on, 92, 237n21; nineteenth-
century aphorisms, 145–46; pre-
conversational, 45; Vattimo on, 23,
26. *See also* beautiful; open work;
sublime

experimental, Dickinson's poetry as,
25, 53, 56, 63, 69–70, 76, 95, 136,
145, 184–85, 219n22
experiments, mental and philosophical,
53–56
Eyre, Jane. *See* Brontë, Charlotte

Farr, Judith, 233n1, 235–36n13
feminism, 2, 19, 31, 111, 155,
205nn1–2, 233n1, 233n3,
234nn7–8, 235n11
Fichte, Johann Gottlieb, 78, 106, 108
figural language: Dickinson's comment
on, 132; in Dickinson's writings, 2,
12–13, 16, 37–39, 52, 57–58, 66–
67, 96–97, 100–101, 108, 112, 135,
137, 141, 143–45, 149, 158, 181,
185–204, 228–29n20, 229–30n25,
232n38, 232n40, 238n2; in *Jane
Eyre*, 174; in Stewart, 95–96; in
Watts, 55–56
Fillmore, Millard, 113–14
final vocabulary, 32, 165, 209n11
finite thinker, 9, 57
Fiske, Ann, 82
Fiske, Deborah, 82
Fiske, Helen. *See* Jackson, Helen Hunt
Fiske, Nathan Welby, 79–82, 86–87,
90, 97, 217nn9–10, 220n24,
224–25n46
Fiske, Samuel, 217n12
Follen, Carl, 103
Foucault, Michel, 17, 38
foundationalism, 21, 24, 26, 38, 43,
208–9n3, 223n36. *See also* anti-
foundationalism
Fowler, Emily, 227n10
Fowler, Lorenzo and Niles, 87, 96
Fox's Book of Martyrs, 169
Franklin, Benjamin, 125, 145–46, 148
Franklin, Sir and Lady John, 214n23
Friend, Joseph, 115, 225n1
Freud, Sigmund, 24, 36
Fuller, Margaret, 104, 223n37,
236n18
Fullerton, Georgiana, 6